HENRY VAUGHAN
The Achievement of *Silex Scintillans*

Thomas O. Calhoun

Newark
University of Delaware Press
London and Toronto: Associated University Presses

© 1981 by Associated University Presses, Inc.

Associated University Presses, Inc.
4 Cornwall Drive
East Brunswick, New Jersey 08816

Associated University Presses
69 Fleet Street
London EC4Y 1EU, England

Associated University Presses
Toronto M5E 1A7, Canada

Library of Congress Cataloging in Publication Data

Calhoun, Thomas O
   Henry Vaughan, the achievement of Silex scintillans.

   Bibliography: p.
   Includes index.
   1. Vaughan, Henry, 1622-1695. Silex scintillans.
I. Title.
PR3742.S43C3   821'.4   79-51851
ISBN 0-87413-165-0

Printed in the United States of America

HENRY VAUGHAN
The Achievement of *Silex Scintillans*

Also by Thomas O. Calhoun:

Andrew Marvell: The Garden

What fix'd Affections, and lov'd *Laws*
(Which are the hid, magnetic *Cause;*)
Wise *Nature* governs with, and by
What fast, inviolable *tye*
The whole Creation to her ends
For ever provident she bends:
All this I propose to rehearse
In the sweet *Airs* of solemn Verse.

> —Boethius, *De Consolatione,* Metrum 2, Lib. 3, 11. 1–8, trans. Henry Vaughan

Contents

Preface	9
Acknowledgments	13
1. The Lyric Sequence: *Poems* (1646)	17
2. Crises in Breconshire, 1645–55: *Olor Iscanus*	35
3. An Interregnum Poetics	54
4. Natural Music	77
5. Natural Magic	97
6. *Silex Scintillans* 1650: "The Resurrection of the Dead"	127
7. *Silex Scintillans* 1655: "The Life of the World to Come"	182
Appendix	216
Notes	223
Bibliography	247
Index	256

Preface

People read according to ideas of what they are reading. Words on a page excite preconceptions, expectations. The shapes of sentences are nearly familiar patterns which readers trace and complete by understanding. We read what we already know, or suspect we know, in order to place ourselves in forms more successfully arranged and revealing than ordinary experience may provide. But literary forms control the warp of the reflection and should determine the way a reading proceeds, guiding us toward its comprehension, its values, and ourselves. If the pace, the pauses, the emphases, tone, interconnections, continuity, and closure of a literary work become our critical concerns, we will be led to an awareness of conventions and finally of genre.

Contemporary students of poetry, those schooled in or affected by postwar, new-critical America, are likely to consider literary form in terms of the whole poem. A closed and self-sufficient unit becomes the context for verbal developments occurring within its serial structure and contributing to its closedness and self-sufficiency. Generic terms from epigram to epic, paradigms confirmed or created by Renaissance poetics but not inseparable from the examples they describe, support a finite view of poems just as periods close sentences. They establish necessary limits. No one, a young reader of Ariosto once told me, can read (or be) forever.

Henry Vaughan's *Silex Scintillans* presents a problem both to readers thus predisposed and to critics seeking a descriptive language to define its composition and meaning, for Vaughan's poems exist in series. These extend, creating an inner architecture, and finally compose a structure—comprehensive but de-limiting as well—for the two discrete but interrelated "books" published as *Silex Scintillans*. As a number of critics have advised, Vaughan is best read several poems at a time, so that one can begin to observe the way his figures and themes fragment into variations, accumulate, and then reform as analogues interplay and serial patterns emerge. But the scheme and meaning of Vaughan's volatile and curiously interrelating parts will not be clear until an adequate preconcept of the poet's total form is achieved, and until a way is found to talk about his poems in terms of the continuities among them.

One could say, of course, that any poem is placed in juxtaposition to others, that all may be placed in a collection, that the collection exists as part of a poet's overall production, that the complete works are a repository for much preceding literature, and that all of this will be seen in the context of contemporary or subsequent literature. But the problem with Vaughan is not simply a matter of widening contexts. It rests, instead, upon the distinction between a collection, or miscellany, and a book deliberately designed from the start. Vaughan is writing, I shall maintain, in the tradition of the lyric sequence. His book is the last great Renaissance example of that form.

Silex Scintillans begins as surly winds blast the "infant buds" of a young novice. Just so, or nearly so, a winter's rage blasted the "timely buds" of a love-struck Colin Clout, ushering the unquiet thought of Spenser's amorist. At the end of *Silex Scintillans*, a mild "art of love" is the acknowledged and praised conqueror. Far earlier, Petrarch's anguished version of love's conquest has been crowned with such a vision fair, serene, and mild. Throughout Vaughan's book the shaping forces of Renaissance love poetry are very much in evidence. The evidence, however, will not be useful or informing unless the sequence of literary realities it points to is accessible. Readers need an abstract of the sonnet cycle, or lyric sequence, and the "meta-genre" is elusive.

Though the existence of a form for containing and arranging individual lyrics is today generally acknowledged, partly because the practice of Elizabethan and earlier seventeenth-century poets confirms *their* acceptance of such a form, the sequence itself is still best known by particular examples. The examples vary widely in detail, but many share a common dramaturgical design and, arguably, a common model: Petrarch's *Rime*. This seminal text, along with others of its kind, will be considered as secular precedents for Vaughan's *Poems* (1646) in chapter 1. The lyric sequence, seen in the particular example of Vaughan's first book, then can be used as a structural preconception for *Silex Scintillans*. It will serve as a guide to the retelling of Vaughan's complex, intimate story in chapters 6 and 7.

An awareness of genre, like knowing the foundation plan for a building, helps to shape appropriate expectations for the work to come. But blueprints do not predict detail, and though a reliable generic structure will suggest the approximate scope, dramaturgy, and theme of *Silex Scintillans*, it does not account for the selection and serial patterning of specific content within the sequence. Nor are the poet's self-projection (persona) and choices of subject for the earlier *Poems* very helpful. The poems in *Silex Scintillans* are significantly affected by Vaughan's reassessment of the poet's nature and function, of the Nature to be imitated, and of the way a poem imitates its subject. So chapters 2, 3, 4, and 5 will examine, following a rough chronology, the activities, researches, and publications that fall between Vaughan's initial work and his completion of *Silex Scintillans* in 1655. The intent of this survey of context and text is to discover causes for the poet's revisions and to study their effects. Focal topics, chapter by chapter, are: biographical circumstance as it affects the poet's self-image and craft; historical circumstance as it affects the exercise and articulation of poetic theory; stylistic revisions; and the cumulative effect of former concerns on a conceptual model for shaping whole poems. Collectively, these chapters attempt to define the medium in which and by which *Silex Scintillans* was achieved.

Each of these chapters is limited in area and selection of evidence, and my conclusions in any one of them are applicable to some but not all of the developments in *Silex Scintillans*. The multiform approach follows an early recognition that my schooled assumptions of artistic wholeness—assumptions perhaps your own—were at odds with the kind of continuity represented by lyric sequences. Sequences are not, as one might expect, "organic." That is, each part is not integral to a single conception or desired response. Sequences are not uniform. Rather, within the framework of a motivating cause or crisis and its resolution, they contain a wide range of ideas, figures, voices, moods, and in Vaughan's case a remarkable variety of lyric and meditational verse forms.

Vaughan's work is varied. It changes because this poet, like earlier authors of lyric sequences, seeks to recreate and lay claim to a series of changes in his life. His final claim, however, is for the effectiveness of them all. The series of shocks, disjunctions, momentary victory, and extended disappointment results in his perception of complete personality as reflected in the final coherence of the literary work. This cumulative unity, though it conforms to and is confirmed by generic formulae and framework, develops from within. Its specific patterns derive from the poet's consent to experience, to an empirical measure of philosophical as well as literary orders.

This is not to say that Vaughan denies the validity of prior order but to suggest that he comes to see "order" in the plural. Vaughan accepts a prelegislated subject matter. He believes, that is, as he translates from Boethius, in "lov'd *Laws* . . . wise *Nature* governs with." Yet he comes to regard these laws, as he would regard a text for translation, not as "givens" that are reproduced or rigorously imitated, but as motives for a series of contemplations, tests, and transformations. Like some scientists (even physicists) of our own day, Vaughan views the workings of one natural grouping as perhaps similar to but not necessarily the same as the workings of another. What can be said of stars, plants, or animals, for example, may not apply equally to people. And what is characteristic of a person in one time, place, or status may not adequately represent him in another. So the world of *Silex Scintillans*, in this respect a prevision of ours, is fragmented, parceled out. In it coherences depend upon constructive analogies, not homologies. The poet's task, incredibly, is to render that world (as it once seemed to him and as he imagines it will be) concordant, healed, and whole. To accomplish this, Vaughan must demonstrate the efficacy of analogous bonds, mysterious and invisible—bonds, like love, manifest in relationships between self and other, and in temporal transitions, verse to verse, from one form to another ultimately unlike it. Such is the transition from sickness to health, from old to new life, that Vaughan knew as the great mystery of his own experience and that confirmed the Christian and medical themes he found expressed elsewhere: the sequence is redeeming; its process is therapeutic.

Acknowledgments

Today, some three centuries after its composition and initial release, *Silex Scintillans* has achieved a wide readership and popularity. The book has appeared in three new editions and one facsimile reprint within the past few decades, Vaughan's poems have been included in many recent anthologies, and considerable scholarly attention has been paid to the "prowd and humerous" Welsh doctor who wrote so little yet so well. I, like any contemporary student of Henry Vaughan, owe an incalculable debt to Gwenllian Morgan, Louise Guiney, F. E. Hutchinson and L. C. Martin for the *Life* and edited *Works* of the poet. I have used Vaughan's complete works as both a guide and a rein in finding commentary on *Silex Scintillans*, and have added but few details to what is now gratefully known about the poet's life. The critical books of Messrs. Durr, Garner, Pettet and Simmonds have been a help as well. I hope I will be able to open as many doors for others as they have for me.

I would like to thank Professors L. B. Holland, T. P. Roche, Jr., Alan Gaylord, the late Alan Markman and A. W. Allison, Austin Warren, Frank Newman, Jay Halio, and especially Frank Huntley and Gale Carrithers for the instruction, advice, and encouragement they have given in various stages of my apprenticeship and this book's growth.

HENRY VAUGHAN
The Achievement of
Silex Scintillans

[1]
The Lyric Sequence: *Poems* (1646)

Imagine a young man, struggling with the turns and returns of Boethius's prose and verse. He is working, as Henry Vaughan once did, with songs from the first book of the *Consolation*. Words are disjoined and regrouped; an idea is caught and elaborated in English. A passage is written down. The young translator at last stands back to read what he has done: "You who would see the truth of things now must look within. To mend the troubles of your times, retreat from them. In solitude, look to the stars." For any active and practical modern man, the discovery of such sentences would likely end the Latin lesson forever. Were there time for disagreement, he might argue that the solitary man leads a life of no value. There is no visible—not to mention useful—connection between one's inner world and all that really happens. Truth is empirical, relative, projectable in statistics, measurements, and models. To be fanciful one moment longer, let us imagine Henry Vaughan, seventeenth-century poet and doctor, alive to our hypothetical student and replying, "Your science is no good if you are not good."

Vaughan may not have been born in modern times, but he knew the conditions and effects of alienation that characterize the term "modern." The crises of his youthful life taught him as no existential author ever could that personal existence lies detached from all conceivable substantial or transubstantial orders. To reflect on things, the mind must be apart from them. But through the experience of solitude, Vaughan came to maintain, in the face of ever-growing dissent, that contemplation, self-knowledge, and reform could effect a general well-being. He argued a case for the bond between mind and matter—the soul and body of the world—at a time when such magical axioms were suffering their severest challenge: the toll of an eventual but not irrevocable defeat. His aims, worthy or impractical as they may appear, need not be judged antique. For the mechanical and mathematical universe that displaced Vaughan's more mysterious world has not held our allegiance, and our knowledge of the mind, of the way it reflects and reconstructs the "outer" world, is scarcely more advanced than the old wisdom and newer discoveries to be found in a book like *Silex Scintillans*. Here, in hymns and songs and longer lyric verse, Vaughan represents moments in a realization of himself. Part by part, one straining often to reject another, some only loosely bound in place—yet in their place—an individual emerges from obscure fragments of his past through pathways of a search for love, knowledge, and peace. At the end the man stands whole and comprehended.

For the success of such a self-discovery, let alone a success as stunning as Vaughan's, there must be a great desire, a means of expression, and a sense—conscious or otherwise—of the final form to be attained. The immediate nature of Vaughan's need and purpose, the historical and personal crises that bring on his quest, are documented in chapter 2. Vaughan's poetics, his expressive craft and way of thinking, then will be examined in order. But his task demands a broader formal cause—a sense of where to go, of scope and architecture. The moments of enlightenment or acknowledgment, the intuitive awareness that meditation may encourage and a lyric poem capture, must somehow be bound within a wide scheme of time and conscious thought, so that such recognitions can become known and useful elements for the necessary continuance of living.

As a poet who learned his craft from other poets, Vaughan knew a discipline, a prior form, that he could recreate both as he wrote and as he developed an order for the poems in his book. He knew the outline of other poets' trials, wherein separate lyrics, detached, hostile to expansive movement, fulfilling no order greater than their own, could be cast in a

The Lyric Sequence

continuously mobile yet enduring design. *Silex Scintillans* evolves in a pattern forged by the (so-called) secular lovers of the past who arranged their songs, sonnets, and longer lyric poems to form complete and coherent books. Vaughan's understanding of the sonnet-sequence, its shape, its scope, and its intent, is the first point to acknowledge about the nature of his art as well as the last to recognize, in chapters 6 and 7, about the form that art achieves in *Silex Scintillans.*

For proof of Vaughan's practical knowledge of sequence, look no further than his first published book—the *Poems* of 1646.[1] But to understand how a form designed to dispose the affairs of the heart—the love of man and woman—can possibly assist or shape Vaughan's anticipations of self-knowledge and fulfillment through the love of a man and God, we need to survey its historical development and major examples. The history will display an evolution of overt concern, from secular to sacred love. But it also reveals that evolution is very much a matter of shifting emphases and developing potentials that the sequence, from the beginning, provides. Dante knew that all love is ultimately one. Vaughan sees this point too, but from a far different perspective. The love and truth Dante at last conceived as a transcendent, final cause becomes a god incarnate, effecting the dynamic operations of Nature and human nature for Vaughan. And access to the "one," the pathway linking mortal eros and eternal love, is for the later poet largely an earthbound course. Despite his will and efforts to do so, Vaughan does not sustain the purifying steps and celestial heights of saintly men he so admired. But the avenues of the human heart are open to him, and he can pursue a living deity as earlier lovers found their ways through the body of the world, through sensation and experience less clear but no less captivating than those of Paradise, toward whatever vision, distress, or comforts lie in store.

Only for the young, perhaps, is passion less awesome than the language that makes it known. But, by Petrarch's testimony, great love, like great sorrow, seldom ages. So, careless of generation and with an eye for the commonplaces of love, let us survey the verbal territory where Vaughan nourished his hopes sufficiently to utter these impassioned words:

> To Amoret.
> The Sigh.
>
> Nimble Sigh on thy warme wings,
>   Take this message, and depart,
> Tell *Amoret*, that smiles, and sings,
>   At what thy airie voyage brings,
>   That thou cam'st lately from my heart.
>   (*Works*, p. 5)

Vaughan had heard "To Cupid, Upon a dimple in Castara's cheeke":

> Nimble boy in thy warme flight,
> What cold tyrant dimm'd thy sight?
> Hadst thou eyes to see my faire,
> Thou wouldst sigh thy selfe to ayre. . . .²

If centuries of preceding imitations are bypassed, Petrarch's

> *Quando io movo i sospiri a chiamar voi*
> *E 'l nome che nel cor mi scrisse Amore*
> [When I call upon my sighs, to beckon you,
> With the name inscribed by Love within my heart]³

still must yield precedence to Dante's more deliberate sonnet 32:⁴

> *Venite a intender li sospiri miei,*
>   *oi cor gentili, chè pietà 'l disia:*
>   *li quai disconsolati vanno via.* . . .
> [Come and listen to the sighs of mine,
> oh gentle hearts, for pity desires it:
> those sighs arising from my misery].

Dante will forever sigh for his lady who is gone, and he rightly proclaims that his sighs will be forever heard. Vaughan listened, through intermediary voices, to the love story Dante was first to fashion: *La Vita Nuova*. The story is told in retrospect, but its form is withheld until the end.

A child sees his loved one for the first time. All his senses tremble and come to life. He becomes Love's novitiate. Years pass, and he dreams the woman. He writes sonnets in which his love is hidden, and sometimes intentionally obscured. Poems

The Lyric Sequence 21

are written to other ladies, as a defense against Love. His lady denies him, but finally yields a sign of greeting. At this, a flame of charity burns within him, consuming all past offenses. He anticipates a glorious union but his body, like a lifeless stone, will not respond. He falls into a state of grief, and wanders in a maze of doubt and fear. He begs for pity. The lady is idealized, and the idea praised above substance. He dreams that she will die, but Love, an accident in substance, will not die. She appears and he approaches her, but others are present. In the end, the poet's love is unrequited. The unattainable loved one dies, but the image of her beauty remains to inspire him with a vision of their meeting in Paradise.

> *Oltre la spera che più larga gira*
> *passa 'l sospiro ch'esce del mio core. . . .*
> [The sigh which breaks from my heart
> moves above the highest sphere of the cosmos.][5]

This narrative of love's birth, growth, deceit, despair, bright revelation, literal failure, and final transcendence would scarcely be perceivable had Dante not considered the plight of the reader confronted with his lyrics alone. Scattered songs are arranged in a chronology that is in turn framed and explained by a prose narration. Dante recognized that songs and sonnets in the "sweet new style" were forms best suited to the expression of a single feeling, a single moment of subjective experience, an unevolving state of being. Truth is revealed by their tightly unified structure, but not developed. If one agrees that truth is omnipresent and that in moments of heightened emotion or insight this reality can be comprehended and somehow expressed, then a systematic, serial development, a life story from beginning to end, is an unnecessary literary consequence of the way things are. But memory, reason, and centuries of scholastics insist that larger sequential patterns are necessary for any kind of understanding. Memory conceives of time and structures events within its conception; reason perceives causal relationships and distinguishes validity by its formal structuring; and the schools maintain that awareness of truth must be approached systematically. By the application of method to experience, and by crowning method with doctrine, enlightenment is not momentarily attained but progressively achieved. Dante incorporates both of these views, the first essentially Platonic and the second Aristotelian, because neither is singularly sufficient. Intuitively, emotionally, one arrives at truth all the time or at any time; but intellectually no one gets there without a scheme, a pathway, and a reliable guide.

The lyric sequence is born of a need to make moments of heightened emotion and insight both intelligible and cumulatively enlightening. The mind leads the heart from its lyric seclusion into a "story" that can aim at final felicity. But as Dante says, *"Che 'ntender no la può chi no la prova"*: who has not felt this will never understand.

La Vita Nuova is a curious prototype, for it has no direct literary descendants. Petrarch's *Rime* follows Dante's model in most ways, but not in one: the prose narration, spoken by the poet as he reviews and structures his past emotions, is missing. Sonnets comprise 317 of the 366 poems in Petrarch's collection. The ballade and the canzone, a longer lyric form with greater narrative potential, are incorporated—again according to Dante's precedent—along with madrigals and sestinas. But without the explicit architecture offered by Dante's "reader's guide," Petrarch's book is often regarded as a personal anthology of "scattered rhymes." The opening sonnet can be seen as introducing a volume of *"rime sparse."*

There are major difficulties with this approach. First of all, a sense of narrative context arises from individual poems. Petrarch may be writing about discrete, fragmentary moments in his life, but such moments suggest the scope and pattern of the whole. Here in sonnet 46, for example:

> L'oro e le perle, e i fior vermigli e i bianchi
>   Che 'l verno devria far languidi e secchi,
>   Son per me acerbi e velenosi stecchi,
>   Ch'io provo per lo petto e per li fianchi:
> Però i dì miei fien lagrimosi e manchi;
>   Ché gran duol rade volte aven che 'nvecchi.
>   Ma più ne colpo i micidiali specchi,
>   Che'n vagheggiar voi stessa aveste stanchi.
> Questi poser silenzio al signor mio,
>   Che per me vi pregava; ond'ei si tacque
>   Veggendo in voi finir vostro desio.

The Lyric Sequence

> Questi fuor fabbricati sopra l'acque
> D'abisso, e tinti ne l'eterno oblio;
> Onde 'l principio di mia morte nacque.[6]

[The golden and pearl, vermillion and pale, / Flowers that winter would wither and dry, / Stay for me the bitter, poison thorns / I feel in my heart and my side. / My days must be piteous, and wrong, / For a great sorrow seldom ages. / But I blame the deadly mirrors, / The ones you have wearied by fond glances. / They taught silence to my Lord, my Master / Who begged you for me, and then went speechless, / Seeing you turning upon yourself, alone. / Mirrors, fashioned on the deep waters, / Colored in endless oblivion; / In them, see how I began to die.]

This abrasive, powerful, and subtle portrayal of the lover whose passion is thrown back upon him by a self-loving woman relates a momentary encounter, brief as a gasp of painful recognition. But the sonnet projects a future that will follow, surely as a moment's silence will be broken or held breath exhaled in sighs. The terms of the lyric establish anticipations that are met in succeeding sonnets. Likewise, preceding sonnets prepare the reader for this one. Sonnet 45 identifies the figures of the mirror and the flower and calls our attention to the story of Narcissus. Without such preparation, some of the terms of sonnet 46 may appear obscure. Of course, with the preparation, one's interpretive freedoms are restricted to some extent—confined, but not altogether determined by place.

The second problem, then, with the "scattered rhymes" of Petrarch's collection develops from a sequential reading of the poems. The sonnets relate to one another analogically or like clauses rendered asyndetically. A fabric of relationships necessarily will occur to any reader of the book, though the particular weave of connections may be perceived variously and sustained for varying intervals. Furthermore, a successive reading of the poems will engage them in a chronology created in part by the reader's own time scheme and pace. Interrelationships among separate poems suggest at the least a kind of progressive development resulting from the reader's own predisposition and active ability to create analogues. At best, a sequential structure may be regarded as the order imposed by the author upon his fugitive pieces.

We are frequently advised of the effort Petrarch made to revise and refine his lyrics, but we are less frequently reminded that he disposed the poems of the final collection in an "authorized" order. Theodor Mommsen introduces a notation from Vatican Manuscript No. 3196, Petrarch's "working-copy" of the *Rime*, by saying:

> That Petrarch gave a great deal of thought to determining which of his earlier poems were worthy of inclusion in his final collection is well demonstrated by the following note at the end of the sonnet "*Voglia mi sprona*" (*Rime* No. 211): "Amazing. This poem was once crossed out by me and condemned. Now, by chance reading it again after a lapse of many years, I have acquitted it and copied it in the right place."[7]

The remark indeed suggests that Petrarch was discriminating in the choice of materials for his final edition. But, like Minos, he also assigned his choices to their proper place. This consideration is difficult to comprehend. Since nothing is explained, the final form to which all parts contribute and which determines their rightful place must be reconstructed imaginatively. Petrarch is as silent on this matter as Dante is vocal and explicit.

The only structural division marked in Petrarch's manuscripts is an interruption of seven blank pages separating sonnet 263 from canzone 264. From this it has been determined that the book is in two parts, the first containing poems written about Laura's lifetime and the second containing poems written about times after her death. Such a distinction, generally supported by the content of the poems, invites an initial awareness of the book's design. If the lyrics are read within this two-part frame, it can be determined that a story is told; but it is not based on concrete event and chronology, as is Dante's. Petrarch, more courtly, more discrete, and far less yielding to tenets of scholastic method than his predecessor, creates a disjunctive chronology of inner experience beginning with the critical, near-mystical first meeting of the lovers and following with efforts to deny love as it becomes more insistent. The paradoxical repulsion and attraction of love, Petrarch's dominant concern, is reevaluated upon the death of the loved one. Unrequited bodily love is transformed to an uncertain spiritual love. Themes of forgiveness and intercession develop. In the end a prayer is offered to the "Vergine bella," a conversion of will is fully acknowledged, and celestial union is anticipated. Although the *Rime* is far more expansive and various than *La Vita Nuova*, the labyrinthine trials of love are here deployed in a pattern anticipated by Dante in all its parts and in its restrospective form: initiation; trial; deception; momentary acceptance and joy; pathos; death; a metamorphosis and retrial of love; and anticipations of transcendence.

To see the *Rime* as a whole, Dante's model is helpful, if not necessary. Petrarch surely knew the design, from *La Vita Nuova* directly, from comprehensive themes that Dante inspired in other Italian and Provençal poets or that they had earlier inspired in him, from Ovid's far earlier tales of love's pathos and metamorphosis, and simply from the experience of love that, for all the variations time can conceive, happens to proceed in a particular way. The problem is how to recognize the design. If Petrarch indeed composed a sonnet sequence, is it reasonable to expect that readers will put to test their capacity for analogical thought, sustain the progress of an elliptically evolving pattern, and stand finally, beyond the concluding canzone, with an awareness of narrative and thematic continuity and final form? Without such problems, literary history would have no reason for being.

Petrarch's first English readers chose not to acknowledge a continuity for the *Rime*. Wyatt and Surrey translated single poems, imitated conceits and themes, and wrote original poems in sonnet form. Sir Philip Sidney, however, composed a partial "Petrarchan" sonnet sequence. Vaughan documents the commonplace relationship between *Astrophil and Stella* and the *Rime*,[8] and though one cannot say that Vaughan read Petrarch, Sidney's sequence undoubtedly served him as a model.

Like his precessors, and quite aware of them, Sidney's Astrophil is by no means gracefully entered into Love's domain. Any talk remotely transubstantial he considers dangerous and dishonest. As the sequence begins, he is heard raging and railing about his study, among his books, denouncing orators, pastoralists, and other contrivers of lofty, artificial splendor, "enam'ling with pied flowers their thoughts of gold." Particularly disdained are those who write in the manner of Petrarch:

> Some Lovers speake when they their Muses entertaine,
> Of hopes begot by feare, of wot not what desires:
> Of forces of heav'nly beames infusing hellish paine:
> Of living deaths, deare wounds, faire stormes
>   and freesing fires:
> ....
> I can speake what I feele, and feele as much as they. . . .

With Astrophil we are fixed in a world of feelings, impressions, attitudes, postures—a veritable chaos of sensation and opinion. Astrophil's world is variousness itself; the master of it changes his views on Love as often as views humanly can be had and changed. He protests Petrarchan language as feigned paradox, and Love's philosophical content—beauty, virtue, harmony—is not accepted a priori but tested against physical and sensuous reality. This spirit will be permitted no autonomous existence.

Astrophil's protests amount in one important sense to a desire for a non-conceited, unparadoxical, simple, rewarding, and ultimately self-redeeming love. Why should love not be a natural part of things? Why cannot I speak of love, simply, in the way I speak? Who wants to be torn apart by wounds that cannot, in the world and time, be healed? Thus Astrophil, master egoist, wills to be himself—or that part of himself he can consciously control. But can an absolute be tried or tied by the tenets of an apparent and phenomenal world? Or should it be? And is this man as self-contained as he would like us to think? What unacknowledged forces are being silenced by his loud, long, self-assertion? In another sense Astrophil's initial position, as he will in the end regret, amounts to a running away from a truth that is not the same as the one he consciously designs. His denunciations of "living deaths" and "freezing fires" will come back to haunt him when, as his story unfolds, not only the language of "poore Petrarch's long deceased woes" but the experience of the woes themselves descend upon him. For Sidney's Astrophil, for good or ill, old conceits and measures of expression become intensely real:

> Oh voice, ô face, mauger my speeche's might,
> Which wooed wo, most ravishing delight
> Even those sad words even in sad me did breed.
>   (*Astrophil and Stella,* sonnet 58)

The Lyric Sequence

Sidney achieves a most distinctive kind of unity through the speaking voice, the breathtaking inner maneuvers, and the variety of tensions dramatized by his persona. This remarkable part is acted upon the stage of an evolving pattern less easily perceived than the discords and reversals it contains, but given the tradition of the amorist's sequence the architecture of Astrophil's experience generally is predictable, even though this protagonist struggles desperately against its successive demands.

The story is to begin with the lovers' initial encounter—love at first sight. "Not at the first sight, nor with a dribbed shot / Love gave the wound, which while I breath will bleed," announces Astrophil. The first twenty-eight sonnets initiate the reluctant persona, and by sonnet 29 he is Love's full-fledged slave. Sonnets 30–40 comprise a set of nighttime meditations that reveal a pure vision of Stella—a vision by no means earthbound, nor necessarily capable of involvement in a wakened world. Sonnets 41–68, including the first song in the sequence, are generally ceremonious and controlled steps, an ascent, working toward a moment of resolution or engagement. Virtue and desire contest. The dreamed and real images of Stella collide. But in a ceremony of "joy too high for my low stile to show," Stella grants Astrophil the conditional monarchy of her heart. Virtue subordinates his desire. Sonnets 69–72 celebrate the union. But the body cries its protest almost immediately. Desires resume their call just moments after they had been silenced. Song 2 and sonnets 73–82 mingle jealousies and fantastic kisses. From this point on, the romance is in decline. The narrative, now strongly reinforced by a greater frequency of longer lyrics, courses through a period of absence, a return, insults, "mazeful solitariness," sickness, and final disillusioned sorrow.

Rather than permitting Astrophil some final residence in a pastoral, a visionary, or the starry world he sought, Sidney maintains fidelity to love's psychology. The course of the sequence turns away from a harmony or even an acceptable tension between the affairs of soul and body, beauty and desire, and the reader returns with Astrophil from the heights of expectation to the earthbound state departed from at first but rendered sorrowful, at last, by the memory of an ideal that seemed attained but indeed was not. This pattern reappears in the first book, or 1650 edition, of *Silex Scintillans* where not the woman but the god of stars, who once walked on the earth, is sensed and sought. The pursuit takes the form of nighttime meditations and soul's ascents. A union is prepared for by self-denials and rigorous resolutions. In sacramental ceremony the god is met—the seeker seems fulfilled, complete. But the moment, the wholeness, vanishes from time and conscious touch. The god is gone, from the heart and from the tombs of earth. But is there not something left behind, within? Is there nowhere to go from here?

Sidney does not complete a full Petrarch sequence in *Astrophil and Stella,* so he offers no real answers to these questions—though he surely incites them. He offers us no transfiguration of the loved one, no thematic resolution, no final "one." As in the case of Spenser's *Amoretti,* it is implied that such conclusions lie beyond the scope of the courtly lover and his trials. But one might turn to the *Certaine Sonnets* appended to *The Countess of Pembroke's Arcadia* to find, in two sonnets that Sidney's sister thought should follow Astrophil's torment, the preeminence of virtue restored and eternal love invoked. And to the final agonies of the *Amoretti* Spenser adds his "epithalamion," where marriage brings an end to courtly love altogether.

After the first decade of the seventeenth century, the sonnet sequence suffers an apparent decline in popularity. Actually, it is undergoing a metamorphosis, for the Elizabethan sonneteers offer both a model and a challenge to succeeding lyric poets. The influential model, as far as Vaughan is concerned, is the series as a whole, rather than the shape of its component parts. By its distinctive structure, the sequence allows that the experience of the soul, the heart, the psyche, has an extended and comprehensive form—an inner architecture—that the poet can recreate. Here is a most significant permission. One's inner life is individually, not institutionally shaped. But is that shape sufficient, or complete? How can the experience of love honestly be composed, Sidney seems to be asking, in imitation of the way lives are actually, inwardly lived, and at the same time engage rewards or consolations relegated to conventions of times past, to fictions, soul's ascents, or heavenly spheres? What will it take to conjure the pure harmony and wholeness that at imaginative heights or psychic depths the heart and mind can sense, into the atmosphere of a life inescapably committed to consciousness, to time, and to the sustaining of sequences? How can Stella, heavenly star, rejoin our earthly lives as an actual influence, companion, lover, guide? Such a challenge, worthy of the greatest magus, inaugurates the "metaphysical" era of English poetry.

John Donne and George Herbert, the great voices of the earlier seventeenth century, stand in relation to the sequence somewhat as Wyatt and Surrey had earlier. Both are masters of the discrete lyric, both write distinctive sonnets, and both are vastly influential in parodying love sonnets, turning them into sacred poems. But neither attempts a traditional sequence. Though it may be tempting to consider Donne's *Poems* of 1633 as a sequence, the poems were collected and published after his death. Who knows how he may have seen their interrelationships, serial order, and cumulative form? And though it is even more tempting to consider his holy sonnets as a sequence, as a possible model for Vaughan, the order of these poems is not beyond doubt. Prose is really Donne's "extended" form. The possibility of *The Temple* standing as a historical bridge between the Elizabethan sequences and *Silex Scintillans* is most tempting of all, but on examination of George Herbert's book, this conceivable link dissolves. No single man offered Vaughan more than Herbert did as far as phrases, lines, and even ideas for poems are concerned, but no one could offer him less in terms of an overall pattern for the experience of love. For Herbert, love is ultimately and each moment mastered, structured, and sustained by the Church. Though his heart may rebel, though he may wish and will himself without, ecclesiastical walls are always, maternally, there to hold him in. Vaughan's situation is precisely the inverse. Though he wishes for boundaries, the Church is in ruin and he is on his own. The medium and thus the shape of Vaughan's experience, then, is far from Herbert's, but not so far from those who kept more closely to the old pattern of love-poem sequences.

William Drummond's *Poems* (1616) appears at the onset to be a perfect Petrarchan imitation. The first part of the book, beginning "in my first yeeres," traces in sonnets, songs, madrigals, and sestinas the birth and progress of love. A blissful climax, near but not at the end of the sequence, leads to absence, solitude, and despair. Instead of ending here, as Sidney had, a second part ensues. The first sonnet is about death and ascension:

> Loe, in a flash that Light is gone away,
> Which dazell did each Eye. Delight each Minde,
> And with that *Sunne* (from whence it came) combinde,
> Now makes more radiant Heavens eternall Day.[10]

Thirteen sonnets, five madrigals and two lengthy songs follow, relating the poet's responses to his loved one's death. In the last song the poet lies asleep, as if dead. A virgin appears in a dream vision and speaks to him of eternal life. This brief sequence is a miniature version of the *Rime,* poems 264–366. Having completed the Petrarchan pattern and moving to fulfill its promise explicitly, Drummond adds an elegy upon the death of Prince Henry and then concludes his second part with *Urania,* a sequence of nine sacred sonnets, three madrigals, and a final song on the transcendent life following Judgment Day.

In an early sonnet George Herbert anticipates his later work by asking:

> My God, where is that ancient heat towards thee,
>   Wherewith whole showls of *Martyrs* once did burn,
>   Besides their other flames? Doth Poetry
>   Wear Venus Livery? only serve her turn?
>   Why are not *Sonnets* made of thee?[11]

With the "conversion" of the sonnet, formerly exclusive distinctions such as *cupiditas* and *caritas* are brought into an immediate and initially tense juxtaposition. The metaphysical conceit, child of Petrarchan parents, is born. In William Drummond's hands, such a conversion is accomplished linearly. By writing of experiences that follow the first and apparently ruinous encounter with love, by adding this material to his first book of poems, Drummond recovers and recreates Petrarch's solution to the courtier's dilemma. The unredeeming tensions of mortal love are seen from a new perspective and redefined. And the sequence as a whole engages not only the recognition of a new relationship or order of things, caught and momentarily held by a figure of speech, but also the serial development toward that recognition and the consequences it brings about. An overall therapy, then, may be seen and understood retrospectively. No Orphic power resummons the woman. But her image, verbally embodied and sanctified, stands as the promise of reform. The agent of that vision is time, a redeeming continuance between death and the Word.

A similar transformation occurs as William Habington adds material to his original "two-book" edition of *Castara* (1634). For the second edition Habington prepares prose characters to epitomize the concerns of Books I and II. The first is "A Mistris," the second, "A Wife." Book I proceeds in traditional ways. Castara's discretion and virtue are causes for both praise and complaint. Hopes for a meeting succumb to absence and sorrow. Finally, Castara is set apart from her lover, in "retirement" with her parents. She is sinless and pure;

> All her vowes religious be
> And her love she vowes to me.[12]

In Book II Castara recovers from a serious illness and becomes the poet's wife. Habington here follows Spenser's lead, but his book continues according to the model of Drummond's *Poems*. Thoughts of age and death intrude upon Book II. Elegies are interspersed among poems to Castara. Finally, poems on married love cease altogether. The character "A Friend" introduces eight elegies upon the death of Habington's best friend and kinsman, George Talbot. A third book, introduced by the character "A Holy Man," contains twenty-two poems with biblical mottoes—primarily from Job and the Psalms—wherein the sufferings and joys of God's lover are set forth. In the end, the paradoxical state of the Petrarchan lover is "translated." Sidney had concluded: "So strangely, alas, thy works in me prevail, / That in my woes for thee thou art my joy, / And in my joys for thee my only annoy." Habington would have us meditate on Paul's Epistle to the Philippians, 1:23. In context, the verse reads:

> 21. For to me to live *is* Christ, and to die *is* gain.

> 22. But if I live in the flesh, this *is* the
>   fruit of my labour: yet what I shall choose
>   I wot not.
> 23. For I am in a strait betwixt two,
>   having a desire to depart, and to be with
>   Christ, which is far better:
> 24. Nevertheless to abide in the flesh
>   *is* more needful for you.

As the sequence expands to accept the burden of a new theme, additional lyric forms begin to threaten the autonomy of the fourteen-line sonnet. Though Petrarch's precedent is partly responsible for this, especially in Drummond's case, Habington's holy poems are written in stanzas of four, five, and six lines, or in undesignated monostrophic forms. A number of his poems to Castara, including "Upon a Dimple in Castara's Cheeke," are written in lyric forms other than the sonnet. A number of causes might be cited for the decline of the Italianate structure, not the least of which would be the powerful influence of Ben Jonson's varied verse forms. Jonson abandons both the god of love and the "numbers" he inhabits in the first poem of *The Forrest* (1616). And he compiles a short, parodic sequence of love poems to Charis where she is celebrated in ten "Lyrick Peeces" of varying length. The sonnet sequence becomes simply the lyric sequence, as it will be in the case of Vaughan's *Poems*.

The cumulative resources of a literary tradition, spanning over three centuries to reach Henry Vaughan, offer a blueprint for *Silex Scintillans*. The architecture of his two-book collection is traceable to Petrarch and Dante, but it contains modifications anticipated by English versions of the lyric sequence and interior variations of Vaughan's own making. This matter will be rejoined in chapter 6. To conclude this introductory survey, however, Vaughan's song-cycle to Amoret stands in waiting.

Six of the thirteen poems in this miniature sequence are addressed to Amoret herself. Two others are epistolary verses and the rest are versions of longer lyric forms including an elegy and a "Rhapsodie." The text of *Poems* is very short, and since a translation of Juvenal's tenth satire is appended to it, the volume may appear at a distance as simply an assortment of juvenilia—imitations and translations. But close readings have consistently revealed a thematic and narrative continuity[13]—similar to the scheme of Habington's *Castara*—containing the love poems and placing the book firmly within the tradition of the lyric sequence. The evidence of Vaughan's later publications suggests that by 1646 he had written quite a number of love lyrics.[14] Poems addressed to Fida and Etesia, mistresses more luxurious and more prone to Petrarchan perversities than Amoret, were probably set aside so that a "marriage sequence" could be composed.

The central character of Vaughan's book vacillates between two personalities and voices. On one hand there is a conventional though unnamed persona who is, at first, love's victim and then the more contented repository of Platonic affections. On the other hand Vaughan writes in an "ingenuous" voice, pretending to be no persona at all but, authentically, himself. The latter approach, however, tends toward satire and self-parody. It yields the Donne-like hyperboles of "An Elegy," the fashionably drunken toasts at the Globe Tavern of "A Rhapsodie," the more humorous ironies of a reformed Cavalier now gratefully penniless in "To Amoret Weeping," and leaves the impression of a far more artificial, convention-seeking young man than the more overtly traditional voice. By assuming the literary role of the lover, Vaughan finds a form to contain his most characteristic language and observation.

At first this liberating tendency is scarcely noticeable. The poet, addressing his "Ingenuous Friend R.W.," bids urban foolishness farewell and urges his fellow wit to imagine, beyond the grave, an "Elesium" of poets and lovers. The shades of Jonson and his "son" Thomas Randolph are encountered, but the journey ends in the drowsy fields of Lethe where miserable lovers' souls, "murther'd by some perjur'd face," lament Petrarchan agonies. With this preface, and from this traditional territory, "Les Amours" recalls

> ... all those teares,
> And sighs I spent 'twixt hopes, and feares;
> By thy owne glories, and that houre
> Which first inslav'd me to thy power.
>
> (*Works*, p. 4)

The expected sequence follows. Sighs are sent as petitions of love; pale and silent suffering is humorously invoked in the image of a friend and chastized; Love's artifices, feigned tears, delays, and rebukes, are portrayed in a song of complaint; the poet and Amoret join in a moment of "predestin'd sympathie" gauged by the stars; next, Amoret is absent; jealousies ensue; hyperbolic protests lead to the poet's own retreat into artificial worlds of urban night-life and *ignes fatui;* Amoret yields, weeping; the lovers unite and retire to a country life. At last, upon death and resurrection to a genuine Elesium, the man and wife are seen in their eternal union.

This mandatory framework, concluded by Habington's modification, contains an interior story of the birth, growth, and flourishing of love rendered in a language more characteristically Vaughan's. Sidney's Astrophil wished for a new love language; Vaughan employs one. In the initiation poem "Les Amours," the poet is "slain" by Love's first glance. With his presumed last breath he prays:

> Let not your hate in death appeare,
> But blesse my ashes with a teare:
> This influxe from that quickning eye,
> By secret pow'r which none can spie,
> The cold dust shall informe, and make
> Those flames (though dead) new life partake.
>
> (*Works,* p. 5)

Though the poem turns back immediately to conventional figures of speech, Vaughan has created a distinctive version of the lover's plea for pity. The onslaught of love, traditionally murderous, must be appeased by an "influxe" that will "informe" dust and raise the dead. This is a "secret pow'r," hidden to the world at large. Vaughan calls for induction to a process extended by analogy from courtly love, through alchemy, to divine mystery. Thus is love born and nourished.

In "To Amoret, Walking in a Starry Evening," lovers' attraction becomes the analogue of astral magnetism. A star sends down its rays of "sympathie," and thus do lovers come together. Vaughan next documents the entire realm of creatures, flowers, and streams, bound in love of the life-giving sun by a "loose tye of influence." Nature's process parallels and includes the poet and Amoret in love. As the sun sets, the streams hush, the flowers lean westward in lament, and the poet languishes for "Amoret gone from him." The mind's ascendancy over passion follows as the false fires of evening, "spurious flames suckt up from slime, and earth," are discerned as transient and misleading. "Just so base, Sublunarie Lovers hearts/Fed on loose prophane desires."

The lovers finally unite in a grove where natural, human, and celestial processes work in harmony. The cycle of nature and of married life, guided by the "Amorous Sunne" and stars, works to fulfill a divine cycle. Upon the last day, the grove will be "transplanted," and the lovers translated to a place like Eden:

> So there againe, thou 'lt see us move
> In our first Innocence, and Love:
> And in thy shades, as now, so then,
> Wee'le kisse, and smile, and walke agen.
>
> (*Works*, p. 16)

The conventional process of love's birth and growth, which had implicated the resurrection of the dead by Vaughan's terminology, now reveals its "secret" plan. Love's operation, at first *like* a resurrection, is now fulfilled by the force of its divine analogy.

For Vaughan, courtship and married love are part of a system of corresponding processes. So he tells the story on various interrelated levels, aiming at a version that is ultimately redeeming. The framework of his *Poems* is traditional, but interior conventions are adapted to serve the development of organic parallels to the courtier's ancient trials. The analogical but integrated patterns both give new life and a final justice to the form of the lyric sequence.

A pattern for the disposition and understanding of emotional experience is set, for Vaughan, by 1646. His further experience, far more complex, more introspective, far more demanding on personal and poetic resources, nevertheless will be comprehended and disposed along the same basic lines. The form of the lyric sequence, achieved in the *Poems,* works with the power of an assumption, a principle of explanation, to contain and display the intricate tracery of *Silex Scintillans.* The two books share as well Vaughan's fundamental respect for a kind of spontaneous intercommunication between organic, cosmic, and human affairs. Lovers are redeemed by a sanctified natural magic. The world at large, likewise, will be redeemed.

The *Poems* of 1646 and *Silex Scintillans* have little else in common. The most significant difference is style and voice. For the persona of the *Poems,* Vaughan is content to equate "ingenuous" speech with the candor of satire. Lyric and philosophic pronouncements, conceivably more intimate and honest, issue from postures of the traditional lover in rhythms, lines, and rhymes common to the "sons of Ben." These forms dominate, by necessity, a man who is not yet capable nor really anxious to say much about himself. To attempt the divine love story of *Silex Scintillans,* Vaughan will have to turn his capacity for ingenuous talk away from cavalier pursuits and toward the kinds of subject he has begun to entertain while rapt in the guises of love. From certain crises, temporal and personal, a new voice and style will emerge.

[2]
Crises in Breconshire, 1645–55: *Olor Iscanus*

I heard last *May* (and *May* is still high Spring,)
The pleasant *Philomel* her Vespers sing.
The green wood glitter'd with the golden Sun
And all the West like Silver shin'd; not one
Black cloud, no rags, nor spots did stain
The Welkins beauty: nothing frown'd like rain;
But e're night came, that Scene of fine sights turn'd
To fierce dark showrs; the Air with lightnings burn'd;
The woods sweet Syren rudely thus opprest,
Gave to the Storm her weak and weary Breast.
I saw her next day on her last cold bed;
And *Daphnis* so, just so is *Daphnis* dead!
. . . .
  A fatal sadness, such as still foregoes,
Then runs along with publick plagues and woes,
Lies heavy on us. . . .
—Henry Vaughan, "An Elegiac *Eclogue*"

In modeling this figure upon myself, I
have had to fashion and compose myself
so often to bring myself out, that the
model itself has to some extent grown
firm and taken shape. Painting myself
for others, I have painted my inward
self with colors clearer than my original
ones. I have no more made my book than
my book has made me—a book consubstantial
with its author, conceived with my own
self, an integral part of my life.
—Montaigne, *Essays* 2. 18,
  "Of Giving the Lie"

Readers of Renaissance sonnet sequences have always valued the form as a mode of autobiography. The authentic life of the mind, the heart, and the daily experience of lovers seem just on the verge of breaking through clouds of courtly discretion and conceited talk. Who was Laura? Who was the Dark Lady? Such questions are asked again and again, for the form that incites them also conceals the answers.

The lyric sequence of Vaughan's *Poems* tells something of the way the poet's mind works but reveals little about his character or his youthful life other than the way he may have wanted these to be. And this is by design. Vaughan is aiming at and recreating a cavalier persona—a style of life that he can put on like a suit of clothes. He knows the model well and can shape his amorous experience by its forms and within its bounds. Likewise, his ideas about the nature of love, the vital world of plants and creatures, and the reigning powers of the stars become meaningful expressions within the traditional pattern of the sequence. A literary form permits Vaughan knowledge of himself, but it is a kind of knowledge largely dictated by that form.

At the end of the *Poems* the world of ingenuous cavaliers and languishing lovers merges with the hills of Breconshire and vanishes, at last, into the beautiful, orderly Priory Grove where the cathedral, like a fortress, stands to protect married lovers against all harm. The beauty, the order, the pastoral calm will not last long. The persona and career projected by Vaughan's early poems were brought to ruin at the onset of one brief decade during which the storied fame of British royalty and Anglican supremacy was battered as well beyond any but symbolic repair. At the beginning of his second book, *Olor Iscanus* (signed 1647, though not published until 1651), Vaughan attempts a brief sketch of his life. "Ad Posteros" is spoken by no conventional lover. Here is another man who identifies himself by a particular time and place and whose voice is ominous, cryptic, veiled in Latin. Translated, the poem reads:

> I was born in Wales, where father Usk meanders through wide valleys beneath cloud-capped mountains. Then that very great scholar Mr. [Matthew] Herbert, the pride of Latin scholarship, took me into his gentle care. With him as my master I made good progress for six years.... In order that you may be well informed

about the times in which I lived, let me tell you that they were cruel. I lived among the furious conflicts of Church and state. At the outset, while the wretched inhabitants raged through their pleasant fields, the base weed laid low the holy rose. They disturbed the fountains, and peace perished beneath the flood, and a gloomy shadow overspread the light of heaven. But . . . let me tell you that I took no part in that great slaughter. . . . I schooled myself to endure suffering like a chaste mother, and to make my fate easier to bear by watering it with my tears. So you see, I have never done violence to sacred things by stirring up fearful tumults, and neither my mind nor my hand has been malevolent. If you fear God, seek to know no more. Let the wise man go from here having heard enough: as for fools, I do not write for them.[1]

The eulogistic and then defensive rhetoric of this piece conceals more than it explains. And in the midst of these postures another language—base weed; holy rose; the fountains; the flood—turns plain detail into apocalyptic metaphor. Here the critical, cruel times dwarf and dictate to the speaker, imposing a mixed language, a shifting voice, and then silence upon him. These are responses to a new era that appears to be, initially, completely disjoined from the comprehendable past and the future it so promisingly held.

When King Charles I formally declared civil war on August 22, 1642 and moved his forces from Nottingham toward the Marches of Wales, Henry Vaughan was twenty-one years old and prepared for little beyond the fashionable life he was living in London. He had studied "Logicals" for several years at Wales's contribution to Oxford, Jesus College. He and his older brother Thomas, who was to stay on for a fellowship and master of arts degree, may have spent some time at Oxford's famous Physic-Garden where the German Jacob Bobart was preparing his *Catalogus Plantarum Horti medici* and teaching how the stars and the "signatures" of plants determine medical applications. But since Vaughan's family thought that law would be a more promising career for him, they urged him on to London and he went, with no apparent complaint. What matters the course of study, after all, to a young poet who, gazing at the court, could see himself a part of its style and ceremony?

Vaughan followed the king back to Wales, maintaining perhaps the ambitions of a court-poet but falling back upon his limited legal training to serve as secretary to Judge Marmaduke Lloyd, a royalist appointee for the Brecon circuit and a man of moderate means and authority until he was imprisoned, fined, and discharged from office in 1645.[2] After this, Vaughan had nowhere to go but home. At Newton, on the river Usk, in the parish of Llansantffraed, he became the "Silurist" whom we have heard speaking *ad posteros.* This is a literary nom de guerre honoring an ancient warrior tribe of Breconshire as well as an early name for the district including Monmouthshire, Glamorgan, Carmarthenshire, and parts of Gloucestershire, Herefordshire, and Breconshire. The name "Silurian" also designates one of the earliest Freemasons' lodges in South Wales.[3]

Military aspects of the civil war seem not to have affected Breconshire directly, for even though its citizens were recruited and impressed to fight as early as 1643, no actual battles were fought there. Vaughan defensively denies any hand in the violence, but Herbert Price of Brecon Priory, borough representative to Parliament before the war and among the first Commissioners of Array to raise troops for the king, seems to have had the young man in his regiment. One "Vaughan, Hen. L[ieutenant] to Capt. [Her]bart Price"[4] claims payment in 1663 for military services that probably included a part in the royalist defeat at Rowton Heath in 1645. Whether Vaughan was there or not, he wrote about the battle. In "An Elegy on the death of Mr. R. W. slain ... at *Routon* Heath," Vaughan conceives the disconcerting immediacy and lack of perspective imposed by war upon its participants. For the warrior, word must become deed as the ordinarily distant issues of life and death are confronted in one single moment of a scheme no longer recognizable as time.

> O that day
> When like the *Fathers* in the *Fire* and *Cloud*
> I mist thy face! I might in ev'ry *Crowd*
> See Armes like thine, and men advance, but none
> So neer to lightning mov'd, nor so fell on.
> Have you observ'd how soon the nimble *Eye*
> Brings th' *Object* to *Conceit,* and doth so vie
> Performance with the *Soul,* that you would swear
> The *Act* and *apprehension* both lodg'd there,
> Just so mov'd he: like *shott* his active hand
> Drew bloud, e'r well the foe could understand.
> But here I lost him. . . .[5]

The equation of word and deed, apprehension and act, is regarded in the light of classical virtue here, and Vaughan's powers of eulogy and analysis straighten out a sequence of events in the lines above. But the comment on perception belies its rhetorical disposition. In the context Vaughan is attempting to define, and in the behavior of his poem's hero, levels of reality are all reduced to one. Past and future collapse into the present. Cause does not lead comfortably to effect, for apprehension and the act are simultaneous. The flickering images of war cannot be mused upon (though they are in the poem, since Vaughan's idea is not permitted to forge a form like itself), so things must be what they seem. The "conceit" must be contained by the object seen.

The elegy to R. W. is no more conclusive about Vaughan's activities on the Chester Plains than are later documents claiming payment for his service there. But he is alert to the experience of battle, the coincidence of perception and action indeed affects him, and the poems of *Silex Scintillans* frequently recreate in style as well as statement the condition Vaughan attributes to the friend he lost in fight. The speaker of his sacred poems is seen initially in the posture of a man trapped by the immediacy of the present, lacking the guidance of a useful past and thus the facility to see what is in store for him. Vaughan often clings to the reality of a visible presence, probing the object for its innate conceit, seeing the world as a mysterious, impenetrable emblem concealing an incarnate truth. And the poems of *Silex Scintillans* often depend upon dislocations of time structure that effect disruptions of logic and sometimes yield momentary sightings of a visionary reality.

To say more about Vaughan's connection with military affairs requires inference beyond assuring evidence, yet Hutchinson maintains that Henry's younger brother William was a probable victim of the war (*Life,* p. 97). William's death, from whatever cause, is most likely the event prompting a series of untitled elegies in *Silex Scintillans,* and Vaughan's growing interest in martyrology could be attributed to a cause so immediate as this family tragedy. By taking liberties with his text to translate "because Christ is gone thither before, and hath provided a place for us, the greatest blessing, and highest reward of holynesse is short life, and an unseasonable, or violent death" (*Works,* p. 289), the poet hints at a literal death, sanctified by its untimeliness, and turns the clue into a charge worthy of any Silurian Celt. Vaughan continues from the text of Johannes Eusebius Nierembergius: "Hee that suffers an immature death for the good of his Country, for the sacred lawes or the vindication of the truth of God . . . to a man that dies thus, all men are indebted" (*Works*, p. 306). Vaughan held thoughts like these; no one knows what he was doing during the later 1640s, and the silence of "Ad Posteros" will be respected. But once he began to write *Silex Scintillans*, such thoughts became prayers for spiritual regeneration:

> Lord, then said I, *On me one breath,*
> *And let me dye before my death!*
> ("Regeneration," *Works*, p. 399)

Although Breconshire was never a literal battleground, its residents still recall the war fought over edicts of the Puritan parliament. For even a nominal Anglican and royalist, the anger and despair at seeing churchmen ejected from their livings during the late 1640s ("the base weed laid low the holy rose") must have been unendurable.[6] These ejections were carried out for the most part under the euphemistically titled "Act for the Propagation of the Gospel in Wales" that Parliament passed in 1650. But even before this legalization, the Parliamentary Committee for Scandalous Ministers and the Committee of Plundered Ministers had managed to replace seven "inefficient" clergymen of Breconshire with promising Puritan preachers. Among those to go were Vaughan's dear friend Thomas Powell of Cantref, the gentle "pride of Latin scholarship" Matthew Herbert of Llangattock, and Vaughan's fellow physician-poet Rowland Watkyns of Llanfrynach.[7] These parishes are all within two or three miles of Vaughan's residence at Newton.

Nearly all of the clergy from the vale of Usk directly southeast of Brecon were to be removed. Even Matthew Herbert's replacement, Matthew Williams, was ejected by the Propagators, possibly because he had become influenced by the "delinquent and scandalous" sympathies of his parishioners. Henry Vaughan's brother Thomas, sent to preach at Llansantffraed after his stay at Oxford, Richard Williams of Llandetty, and John Griffith of Llanfihangel Tal-y-llyn were all marked for "retirement" by Committee sequestrators in 1649. They won an appeal of this decision, but were ejected under the Propagation Act months later.

Terms of dismissal under the Propagation Act added slander to the earlier and obvious rationale of Anglican and therefore anti-parliamentary activity. Thomas Vaughan was denounced as a common drunkard, a common swearer, no preacher, and in arms against the Parliament. John Perrott, rector of nearby Cathedine, swore, drank, and helped the king. The parish of Llanhamlach was sequestered because its rector, Samuel Prytherch, was a drunkard, a liar, a fornicator, and quarrelsome. These men were Vaughan's relatives, friends, and close neighbors. Even the poet's father, "very decrepit, and about 70 years old," was arrested, jailed, and fined for refusing to cooperate with authorities in a matter involving taxes on parish land in Llansantffraed.[8] By 1651 the parochial system that provided both religious services and schooling was essentially closed down. Only David Williams of Tretower (the Vaughan family home inherited by the poet's uncle) and John Griffiths of Tal-y-bont, across the river from Newton, remained to keep school for the children Vaughan must have seen from day to day.

The traditional economy was pillaged, and with clerical livings gone, modes of living violently altered. The psychological pressures of times like these could be just as deadly in their way as the sword and gun at Rowton Heath. Thomas Powell, whose "Unpardonable Crimes, as assigned by the *Propagators themselves*, were Adhering to the King, and Reading *Common-Prayer*," showed much promise and some achievement as a scholar. But he became immersed in petitions and legal quarrels. "I do not know," Powell states in the preface to his *Quadriga Salutis,* "whither I may live to finish a better Piece than this, being long since taken away from the book, by secular cares and encumbrances, to make up breaches of a ruinous fortune, seldom retiring within my self, and that by snatches and *broken* intervals."[9] Powell survived the war and interregnum, but on December 31, 1660, year of the Restoration and the year his Brecon living was returned, his appointment as canon of St. Davids confirmed and a nomination as Bishop of Bristol offered, he died. Matthew Herbert, who had built up considerable clerical and financial expectations as rector of Llangattock (Breconshire), Cefnllys in Radnor, and possibly several other parishes as well, tried to sue some of his old parishoners for "non-payment of tithes to him as rector" and ended up in Brecon jail for seventeen weeks, "not suffered to go at liberty till he had given a guarantee in writing 'not to molest the tenants,' under penalty of £200."[10] The gentle scholar, treated none too gently, required the considerable efforts of a friend and Parliamentarian, Henry Herbert of Coldbrook, Monmouthshire, to escape banishment. These men, upon whom Vaughan most relied for instruction, guidance, and companionship, lost more than their money and position. An entire way of life that made sense to them was gone, and they found themselves acting and being acted upon in what must have seemed a barbarous and truly surreal world.

During the 1650s Parliament took revenues from the parishes but did little to fill the clerical positions it had seized. Churches were frequently out of use, and people began to hold religious services in private homes. Itinerant ministries were arranged by Puritan authorities or were self-arranged as voluntary preachers toured and took up temporary residence in abandoned parishes. An evangelical movement, always latent in particularly rural counties like Breconshire, emerged under the auspices of various denominations. Independents such as Walter Cradock and his converts Vavasor Powell and the poet Morgan Llwyd possibly had some effect on the religious temper of Breconshire during the war and interregnum. At least they were present in the area. Local tradition maintains that Powell preached a notorious midnight sermon on Matthew 10:28—"Fear him not that can kill the body"—after suffering a citizens' arrest near Llanafan Fawr.[11] Cradock, "the chiefest Priest in South-Wales," was suggested as a temporary minister for Brecon, where the people were "growing into a carelesse content of being without a preacher."[12] George Fox, whose Society of Friends would assimilate many of the earlier reform movements, records his astonished arrival at Brecon where "all ye tounde was uppe in an uproare: & when I came Into ye Inn ye chamber was full of people & they were speakinge in

Welch."[13] Such dissension could not have been caused by a united anti-Quaker front. The voices of non-conformity were being heard and vigorously debated. Perhaps as a result, Thomas Vaughan was ejected from his parish at Llansantffraed a second time in 1662—having just been restored to it—for non-compliance with the new Anglican Act of Uniformity that demanded full assent to the contents of the Book of Common Prayer. Giles Nichols held the parish at Llangynidr, across the Usk from Tretower, from 1638 through the early Restoration years, and apparently never submitted to anyone's authority but his own. He too refused alliance with Restoration Anglicans, got away with it, and was last heard from in 1665, loathing and battling against visitation fees for arch-deacons.

The very existence of *Silex Scintillans* and *The Mount of Olives, or Solitary Devotions,* attests the seriousness with which Vaughan viewed the problems attending the churchman, of any faith, during this period. Both are books of private worship, and they complement one another as demonstration complements expository instruction. *The Mount of Olives* is a manual of prayers and religious exercises offered to churchmen without a church. The following "Prayer in time of persecution and Heresie" is typical of its contents:

> Consider, O Lord, the teares of thy Spouse which are daily upon her cheeks. . . . The Wayes of *Zion* do mourne, our beautiful gates are shut up, and the Comforter that should relieve our souls is gone far from us. Thy Service and thy Sabbaths, thy own sacred Institutions and the pledges of thy love are denied unto us; Thy Ministers are trodden down, and the basest of the people are set up in thy holy place. . . . *Behold, the robbers are come into thy Sanctuary, and the persecuters are within thy walls. We drink our own waters for money, and our wood is sold unto us. Our necks are under persecution, we labour and have no rest.* (*Works,* p. 166)

We know what Vaughan is talking about here. Let us consider the way he is talking. His lines are both devoutly grieved and aggressive, with only bitter awe. What begins as a prayer, resembling the Anglican "Prayer in the time of War," becomes very nearly a diatribe as the language of Common Prayer yields to a more concrete argument drawn from actual events, glossed by language from the Lamentations of Jeremy, and held in check by the action of this kind of paraphrase. Vaughan is both grieved and outraged. His feelings are complex and demand that fixed patterns of prayer be expanded, that various ecclesiastical voices be combined. What often results, in prose and poetry as well, is an expression of mixed, unresolved, and in this sense immediate experience.

Vaughan diverges from the authority of the Anglican Prayer Book in a most interesting way. His tendency toward new combinations and distillations of biblical phrase and voice is typical of the volatile rhetoric, the headlong, seemingly endless glosses upon urgent passions uttered by Independents like Cradock and Vavasor Powell, or found in journals of men like Fox. Their inner conflicts and convictions, or the experience they are recording, determines which verse or voice is to be drawn upon, and when. Compare this method with that of a sermon by Lancelot Andrewes, or even John Donne, where a passage from the Bible is presented first, and all reasonable truth follows from it. In the case of Vaughan's prose prayers, the Bible becomes less a source of truth in itself than a means for expressing and revealing the truth possessed within and so possessing the speaker. The Bible is a vocabulary for the inner man. Experience determines the form its language will take.

The temporal order of the church—"Thy Service and thy Sabbaths, thy own sacred Institutions" that had provided a coherent framework for Common Prayer—was lost through a series of Parliamentary injunctions. Two days before Christmas of 1644, Parliament acted to abolish the observance of Christmas and Good Friday.[14] Vaughan records the fact as an outright sacrilege. As Hadrian once set an idol of Jupiter on Calvary and built a mosque in Bethlehem, so "some men amongst us have done the like: Two *Seasons* in the year were consecrated by the *Church* to the memory of our *Saviour*: the *Feast* of his *Nativity* and *Circumcision*, and the *Feast* of his *Passion* and *Resurrection*. These two they have utterly taken away: endeavouring (in my opinion) to extinguish the *memory* of his *Incarnation* and *Passion*, and to race his blessed name out of those *bright columns of light*, which the *Scripture* calls *daies*" (*Works*, p. 379). This abolition of holy days was followed on January 4, 1645, by Parliament's outlawing of the episcopacy and use of the Book of Common Prayer. Then, when the Anglican clergy were ejected and so many churches closed, the remaining services of morning and evening prayer, observance of the Sabbath, the sacraments of baptism and communion, and the rites of burial ceased to be offered.

An ecclesiastical structure for days, weeks, and the year could have been in some way restored, had the plan of Parliament been fully realized. But a sudden outgrowth of presbyteries was not forthcoming, and ordinary parishioners, especially those in rural districts, lost their way of telling time. For many people the ritual order of the Church had provided a continuous and progressive time scheme with its bells, music, and the symbolic rewards of the Sabbath and the sacraments,[15] which offered relief from repetitious daily labor. But now, as Vaughan relates in *The Mount of Olives* and its companion essay, "Man in Darkness," the rhythms of country life are terrifyingly uneven and unsure. "A day, an hour, a minute . . . is sufficient to overturn and extirpate the most settled governments. . . . And what comfort then, or what security can poor man promise to himself? whose breath is in the hand of another, and whose few dayes are most commonly outlived by every creature, and sometimes by a *flower* of his own *setting*" (*Works*, p. 171). A common sense of time and continuity is shattered; the events and trials of daily life impose themselves on the mind with new and frightening immediacy. The chance for some perspective on events, or as Vaughan would say, the means of spiritual ascent to "the *Courts* of the *Lord*," could be recovered or improvised by those who still cared to do so. But, the poet states, "the *land* of *darkness* lies in our way. . . . We run all after the present world, and the Primitive Angelical life is quite lost" (*Works*, p. 169).

The interregnum major general for Wales, James Berry, was probably right in his assessment that many residents of Brecon were content without any religious authority or regimen,[16] but Henry Vaughan could not have been counted among the careless. As the pattern of his reading and writing takes shape, it is clear how his efforts focus on a kind of self-schooling and self-healing that leads to the schooling and healing of others. His interest in the lives of exiled writers, men whose circumstances were at least in one way like his own, appears in poetic translations printed in *Olor Iscanus*. It has been argued that Vaughan arranged these translations in such a way as to suggest stages in a single, evolving life—literally the life of a reader selecting books as guides—which is marked by a growth of seriousness and spiritual aspiration.[17] The first selections are from Ovid's *Tristia* and *Pontic Epistles*. In these both author and translator explore the workings of fate and the working out of bitterness, anger, grief, and defeat. Through the sophisticated, oblique turns of Ovid's argument and tone, Vaughan renders some simple truths:

> ... And now I must forget
> Those pleas'd *Idoea's* I did frame and set
> Unto my selfe, with many fancyed *Springs*
> And *Groves,* whose only losse new sorrow brings.
> (*Works*, pp. 67–68)

    These translations are followed by thirteen poems from Boethius's *Consolation of Philosophy*. The sequence seems not inadvertent. The wit, outrage, and grief found in Ovid's lines and voice are muted and transformed by Boethius. Mere exile becomes imprisonment, and sorrow becomes a reflective prelibation of death. Next is a series of odes from the books of the Polish Jesuit Casimire Sarbiewski. These appear in Vaughan's context as responses to the ancient argument favoring a life of rural retirement over active, worldly pursuits.

    The way of life that Casimirus advocates is presented most explicitly in a poem titled "In Answer to that Ode of *Horace*, Beatus Ille qui procul negotiis, &c." Vaughan's translation of this poem deserves attention since it displays the poet's first attempt at charting the kind of spiritual ascent he will later write about in *Silex Scintillans*. The poem begins and ends with references to the "happy man" of Horace's second epode, an ironic pastoral spoken by Alfius the usurer, who continues collecting and investing money despite his dreams of rural retirement. Casimirus's answer to this is an argument that turns the naive or cynical pastoral fancy into a viable and redeeming way of life. First of all, retirement can be understood as spiritual solitude, and Horace should describe his "blessed man" as saintly.

> That title only fits a *Saint,*
> Whose free thoughts far above restraint

> And weighty Cares, can gladly part
> With *house* and *lands,* and leave the smart
> Litigious troubles, and lowd strife
> Of this world for a better life.
>
> (*Works,* p. 89 lines 5–10)

The solitary man weeps for the sins of his past years, or as Vaughan interpolates, "having tasted those *rich Joyes* / Of a Conscience without *noyse,*" he sits down "and doth give / To his *wild thoughts* rules how to live" (lines 17–20). What is it that makes the difference between an isolated, lonely life of unredeemed despair and the harmony, the understanding, and the happiness such solitude dreamingly might be said to offer? Vaughan adds lines to suggest that self-examination and confession yield a joyful "taste" of the rewards of a pure conscience. This anticipates Casimirus's answer—a spiritual awakening that is described in lines 21–62. The event has been called a "garden ecstasy."[18] It opens with an evening reprise from daily trials. The stars begin, silently, to shine, and through the night the solitary man watches them:

> Beholds th'*eternall flames* with mirth,
> And *globes* of *light* more large then *Earth,*
> Then weeps for *Joy,* and through his tears
> Looks on the *fire-enamel'd* Spheres,
> Where with his *Saviour* he would be
> Lifted above mortalitie.
>
> (*Works,* p. 90, lines 23–28)

The man undergoes a sense of penitence, and a redirection of feeling follows, away from himself and toward the God of the stars. As the sun then begins to rise, amazingly, "he turns *anger* into *love*": contempt of the world, which predicates his desire to be "lifted above mortalitie," becomes the love of a new world.

In the light of day, the eyes of the saint, "accustom'd to the skyes," see things differently. The world has become, for him, new and imminently divine. He sees all nature as part of himself, as flowers and creatures reenact his vigilant desires.

> ". . . O how
> "These flowres With hasty, stretch'd heads grow
> "And strive for heav'n, but rooted here

> "Lament the distance with a teare!
> "The Honey-suckles Clad in white,
> "The Rose in Red point to the light,
> "And the Lillies hollow and bleak
> "Look, as if they would something speak,
> "They sigh at night to each soft gale,
> "And at the day-spring weep it all.
>
> (*Works*, pp. 90–91, lines 47–56)

The change in perception undergone by Casimirus's saintly man is like that of Plato's cave-dweller in reverse. There, a novitiate-philosopher moves from an enclosed world of shadows to the intense brightness of true, natural light, and is temporarily blinded. Here, the saintly man, following a visionary prospectus set forth originally in books attributed to Hermes Trismegistus, returns from a night of astral meditation to the natural world of "*Veyles,* and *shades*" and sees that world anew. The effect is an inverted telesthesia. To eyes grown used to celestial lights gazed upon through a film of tears, objects close at hand now reveal more than ordinary senses could detect. Nature becomes hieroglyphic as the philosopher-saint returns to see, and thus to make it so.

In the poems of *Silex Scintillans*, patterns of enlightenment like the one described here—visions of life's sanctity that can transform the cold and brutal surface of the earth—become more than a recreational rationale for Vaughan's staying out of Oxford, London, and out of the war. But his readings from the Jesuit Sarbiewski and his casual composition of *Olor Iscanus* occur at a time when he sought just such an argument. The motto for the book, adapted from Vergil *Georgics* 2, says as much:

> ———*O quis me gelidis in vallibus ISCAE*
> *Sistat, & Ingenti Ramorum protegat umbra!*
> [O who will set me in the cool valleys of the Usk
> and shield me with the generous shade of the branches!]
>
> (*Works*, p. 34)

Who will grant me solace? Who will convince me that the failure of ambition, career, and this return to the isolation of rural origins—now ravaged and desolate—can lead to some good? "To make thee what man should be," Vaughan's brother writes, "is not in another's power, but it is much in thy own."[19] There is no institution now, nor living man nor oracle to consult. But the beginnings of self-recognition are reflections from the outer world, from the expressions of others, and Casimirus offers at least the concept of a profitable search extending outward as far as the fixed stars and inward toward a reformed and true peace of mind. Vaughan pursues the idea. He expands his interest in the lives of saintly men by reading, excerpting and translating from Dionysius the Areopagite, St. Anselm, Johannes Nierembergius, Bishops Eucherius and Guevara, and Paulinus, among others; and he seeks a way to follow such wholesome examples, to become like these men, by studying the literal way to health, or the art of medicine.

Vaughan had a copy of *D. Johannis Rainoldi . . . Orations 5. cum aliis quibusdam opusculis* from which he "Englished" three Latin translations from the Greek of Plutarch and Maximus of Tyre. The first is a paradoxical discourse, "Of the Benefit Wee may get by our Enemies," from Plutarch. But the latter two selections are brief, generalized medical treatises, both titled "Of the Diseases of the Mind and the Body." Both works argue a reciprocal harmony of soul and body, denying dualist distinctions which maintain that the soul is free of disease and only bodies can fall sick. The soul, nevertheless, is regent to the body, and its illnesses are far more serious than physical ones. Spiritual health, it is argued, precedes the effectiveness of those healing arts that can restore the body. Later, in Vaughan's 1655 translation of Heinrich Nolle's *Systema Medicinae Hermeticae generale,* the basic principle voiced by Plutarch and Maximus is expanded to become a working theory of homeopathy—"that famous principle of the *Hermetists: Every like is cured by its like."* But Vaughan's earlier translations—done prior to 1651 and published at the end of *Olor Iscanus*—are not much concerned with specifics of the healing arts.

Vaughan too, prior to 1653 or 1654, is clearly more concerned with spiritual than physical remedies. But in his preface to the 1655 edition of *Silex Scintillans,* he describes his recovery from an illness that nearly killed him.

> By the last *Poems* in the book (were not that *mistake* here prevented) you would judge all to be *fatherless,* and the *Edition* posthume; for

> (indeed) *I was nigh unto death,* and am still at no great distance from it; which was the necessary reason for that solemn and accomplished *dress*, you will now finde this *impression* in.
>
> But *the God of the spirits of all flesh,* hath granted me a further use of *mine,* then I did look for in the *body;* and when I expected, and had (by his assistance) prepared for a *message* of *death,* then did he *answer* me with *life.* (*Works,* p. 392)

Vaughan's illness is physical, and the death he refers to here is meant literally. His falling sick and recovering are comprehended, however, interiorly. Recovery is an internal process guided by the "spirits of all flesh" and ultimately by God. For this chain of influences to work, the spirit itself must be in health, in touch with God. Only then can it transmit a condition like itself to the flesh. Disease, furthermore, is not a natural condition—matter is not inherently sick or forever damned—but a state to which the body falls when the confident, ministering spirit is absent from it.

These considerations argue against Hutchinson's conclusion that Vaughan did not approach the concerns of medicine—the life and health of the body—with practical or professional interest until *Silex Scintillans* was completed.[20] The evidence of Vaughan's later life, or rather the lack of any significant publication from him after 1655, may perhaps support the notion that this man was prone to absolute conversions and abandoned a life of words for one of works. But the thrust of Vaughan's activities during the war and interregnum is a search for continuities, and these two modes of activity are integrally related. The work is made possible by the word; the motive of words is works. The sequential process of spiritual regeneration documented in *Silex Scintillans* is at once the pathway to actual health and at the end, as the poet's preface shows, the achievement of it. The aim of the inner life is redemption of the spirit. As we have heard, the redeemed spirit is an efficient cause of the body's health. And, as the last poems of Vaughan's book clearly show, this process portends the spirit's eternal life after death and the body's resurrection at the end of time. These interworkings, developed in greater detail, contribute to the conclusion that formal characteristics of Vaughan's poetry are influenced by patterns of observation and understanding directly traceable to texts on alchemy and hermetic or Paracelsian medicine. That conclusion, however, is extraneous to present concerns. Here, suffice it to establish that the poet had access to medical texts, and that they offered him a method for facing constructively the crisis of his life and of his times.

When Vaughan was at Oxford in the late 1630s, and in London later on, the intellectual atmosphere was beginning to take on the tincture of what medical historians have called a "Paracelsian revival."[21] This designation is attested by new works, excerpts, paraphrases, translations, and collections of older books dealing with Paracelsus's chemical remedies and with the hermetic background of his thought. The revival actually began in England during Elizabethan times and was guided by the researches of John Dee, exhibited in his practical work and magical experiments, and furthered by books in his library at Mortlake—a virtual Renaissance academy where interests, anticipating those of London's Royal Society, flourished nearly a century before their "official" charter.[22] The impact of Dee's books and works, submerged, diffused or discredited in England, was fully felt on the Continent during the earlier seventeenth century. As Frances Yates has shown,[23] Dee's combined interests and specifically his *Monas hieroglyphica* are foundations for the Rosicrucian movement, sounded by twin manifestoes, the *Fama* and *Confessio*, which Thomas Vaughan published in English as *The Fame and Confession of the Fraternity R.C., commonly, of the Rosie Cross* (1652).

The *Fama Fraternitatis* establishes, as the first agreement of R.C.'s "invisible fraternity," that none of its membership should "profess to any other thing than to cure the sick."[24] And the texts as a whole are concerned with remedies for illness—but not in any limited sense. The tenets of the brotherhood operate, ultimately, on the body of the world itself. The clinical cornerstone of Paracelsian medicine, the alchemical idea of the transmutation of matter, is expanded through a system of analogies to become the pattern of spiritual regeneration, ecclesiastical and political reform, the reform of the modes and aims of all learning, and the restoration of the world to an Eden-like utopia. Under the name of Paracelsian "Chymia," many books are promised—and many indeed appear from the pens of Robert Fludd, Michael Maier, Oswald Croll, Jacob Boehme, Francis Bacon, Joseph Duchesne and Vaughan's author, Heinrich Nolle, to name a few—which in one way or another advance the multiple formulae of alchemy, applied cures, spiritual health, new science, and a new world.

There is no evidence to suggest that Henry Vaughan, secluded in the vale of Usk, was connected directly with the Paracelsian medical circles, the London and Oxford "philosophicall clubs," or the early Freemasons' lodges[25] where so-called Rosicrucian ideas were being circulated. But Vaughan was on the fringes of the movement. It is likely that Thomas Vaughan's general interests were communicated to his brother during the 1640s, when both men were in Breconshire and while Thomas was preparing at least the first of his publications, *Anthroposophia Theomagica,* dedicated to the "regenerated Brethern R.C." and signed Oxford, 1648. There is reason to suspect that Matthew Herbert was in some way involved with the revival,[26] so Vaughan's beleaguered friend may have served as a source for ideas and books after his brother left Llansantffraed for Oxford and London. And there is proof that the poet was reading his brother's medical texts and beginning to collect his own library while the poems of *Silex Scintillans* were being composed.

Dates and inscriptions on a selection of books from Vaughan's medical library, texts recently discovered in the Library Company of Philadelphia, establish that Vaughan's practical study of medicine began no later than 1654.[27] He obtained Nicholaas Fonteyn's *Commentarius In Sebastianum Austrium: De Puerorum Morbis* (Amsterdam, 1642) in that year, and it is likely that he owned *Responsium & Curationum Medicinalium* (Amsterdam, 1639) by the same author, and had read and annotated his brother's copy of Jean Pecquet's *Experiments Nova Anatomica* (Paris, 1651) by 1654 or sometime prior to 1655.[28] At about this time, he translated Nolle's *Hermetic Medicine* and no doubt read the essay that follows in the same volume, *De Generatione Rerum naturalium*—an essay he later translated and gave to his brother for publication.[29] Further, Vaughan's notes to Nolle's text (*Works,* pp. 548, 558) establish his familiarity and active engagement with the ideas of Galen, Paracelsus, and with Scaliger's popular *Exercitationes,* written against the Galenist Jerome Cardan.

It can be reasonably suggested that the Paracelsian revival

and Rosicrucian prospectus sponsored or at least nourished Vaughan's interest in medicine and encouraged his later decision to profess himself a healer of the sick. But more to the point is the possibility that Vaughan discovered a way to gather together and direct the shattered aspects of his life in the broad design of the new movement. The various crises that he faced—the disintegration of church and state; the failure of ancient virtues to comprehend or survive the irrationality of war; the failure of economic and legal systems to provide security or justice; the closing of schools; a rampage of ignorance and brutality; the ruin of friends; the advancement of fools; a life's plan destroyed; a brother's death—are consolidated in the concerns and activities of the Rosicrucian "doctor" who works in virtual isolation, invisible to the world at large, to achieve a transmutation.

This single objective could be attempted in many ways. For the Scot Robert Moray, Thomas Vaughan's "patron" and possible source for the Rosicurcian manifestoes he published,[30] the attempt meant engagement in secret envoys to negotiate a treaty between France and Scotland for a settlement with Parliament and the restoration of Charles I. Though the treaty failed disastrously, Moray persevered and was a founding fellow of the Royal Society in the year his hopes were realized. For others like John Wilkins (later Bishop of Chester) and Robert Boyle, the attempt meant the reform of education through meetings of an "Invisible College" dedicated to the advancement of natural and experimental philosophy, open to scholars without regard to their politics or religion, and endeavouring "to put narrow-mindedness out of countenance, by the practice of so extensive a charity that it reaches unto everything called man, and nothing less than an universal goodwill can content it.[31] For Henry Vaughan, the attempt is to become "what man should be" himself. If one carries the Rosicrucian prospectus through, his songs of inner transmutation must be sent out in the form of books, under the name of "Chymia" ("Silex": the Philosopher's Stone), which will indicate to others the changes so desperately needed, show how one man's restoration is accomplished, and usher in the world resurrected to a new health that is willed by "the God of the spirits of all flesh."

A comment on the broad aims of Vaughan's writing appears

in a dedicatory poem written by Thomas Powell during the Civil War. "Fairly design'd!" Powell exclaims, "to charm our *Civil* Rage/With *Verse,* and plant *Bayes* in an *Iron* Age." But is the soul of fierce Mars so ductile that Love and Poetry may control it? "Yes," Powell answers, for "Such *Magick* is in *Vertue!*" In a poem preceding Powell's, the "matchless Orinda" (Katherine Philips) sees Vaughan, filled with joys, descending like Moses from the Mount with a sacred message that will restore the Golden Age. Orinda wittily wills to place her name in Vaughan's book, for "I have hopes, that standing so near thine / 'Twill loose its dross, and by degrees refine" (*Works,* pp. 617–18). The restorative aims and the magical or alchemical means of Vaughan's writing seem to have been recognized by his contemporaries. And for them, as for readers now, there is no mistaking a sacred paradigm underlying his hopeful scheme: by the resurrection of one, all will be resurrected. The medical mission that can be said to focus Vaughan's concerns and energies is fundamentally consistent with a life in imitation of Christ. The saintly man is thus a healer. His word is, simultaneously, his work.

When he composed "Ad Posteros," Vaughan really did not want anyone to know about his life. What little he says is veiled by the formalities of Latin language and rhetorical posture, and all is abruptly terminated when demanding questions about his own activities begin to surface. But by the time Vaughan decided to write *Silex Scintillans,* a compelling need to speak, not only to himself and to God but to all who would read and hear, must have been felt. Between these two times, or rather during transition from one recognizable attitude to another, it is certain that Vaughan carried out the business of reading and translating. His composition of *Olor Iscanus* is a crucial exercise, as are the translations and compositions of religious and medical prose that follow. To borrow a phrase from Montaigne, this kind of exercise creates the writer as he recreates the work. Vaughan is looking for approximations of himself, mirrors of language and voice in which aspects appear in colors clearer than mere experience could ever show. The ingenuous lover of the *Poems* now can merge with the words and manner of more candid, ranging, and contemplative personalities, to forge the dimensions of a spokesman more capable and in this way, too, more willing to confess himself.

But Vaughan has yet to display a poetic form—in the larger sense, the design of a whole poem—conceived and modeled upon himself, or upon the way he sees the outer world. In *Olor Iscanus* the poet remains a classicist, fitting new perceptions and new found expressions to old forms that he knows are collapsing in all external or empirical respects but without which he cannot do. But as Vaughan sets his sights on a new and most demanding task—a revised poetics—a natural style and music, and a distinctively new form drawn from the processes of "chymia," nature's inner magic, will be achieved.

[3]
An Interregnum Poetics

> How long, alas! has our mad nation been
>   Of epidemick war the tragick scene.
>   . . . .
>   But thou by heaven wert sent
>   This desolation to prevent,
> A medi'cine and a counter-poyson to the age.
>   . . . .
> By wondrous art, and by successful care
> The ruines of a civil war thou dost alone repair.
>   . . . .
>   Thou dost so temper, that we find
>   Like gold the body but refin'd,
>   No unhealthful dross behind.
>   —Abraham Cowley, "To Dr. Scarborough"

>   Thy richer *Verse*
> Creates all *Poets*, that can but *reherse*,
> And they, like *Tenants* better'd by their *land*,
> Should pay thee *Rent*.
>   —Thomas Vaughan, from "Upon the
>   following Poems," *Olor Iscanus*

> He that shall consider how many thousand several words have been . . . composed out of twenty-four Letters; withal, how many hundred lines there are to be drawn in the Fabrick of one Man, shall easily find that this variety is necessary.
>   —Sir Thomas Browne, *Religio
>   Medici*, pt. 2

Vaughan's response to the civil war, as detailed in "An Elegy on the death of Mr. R. W.," is the defiance of a recognition that the present is isolated from the past and deficient of constructive future consequences. Disorientation, loss, fear, immediate reactions to a fractured time scheme, barely conceal the awareness that human actions have been severed from the conscious mind that should determine them. Without temporal ordering and the priorities it can establish, without the possibility of a demonstrably overriding justice or the capacity of an individual to turn considered decisions into moral acts, what a person does can no longer be equated with what a person is, or who he is thought to be.

This condition, by analogy a submission to irrational senses and appetites, constitutes the world's "disease." By further analogy (one that Thomas Vaughan had made explicit, in *Anthroposophia Theomagica*, by 1648), this is the submission that brought about man's fall from Paradise and has constituted his nature ever since. So if the sickness at large is every man's sickness in particular, any cure must begin close to home. Before doing what might be considered worthwhile or good, one must be able to secure and confirm these qualities in himself.

Vaughan, at first, cares not to acknowledge such thoughts. As he considers the death of R. W., his mind and the form of the poem go one way, his subject and the war itself another. The poet, upholding remembered friendship and faith in character, claims what he never saw—that his man was a hero to the end. Formal elegy becomes a shield set against the momentary terror of the world out of time.

Similarly, Vaughan casts a cavalier's detached, disdainful eye upon spatial disruptions witnessed altogether too near his home. In "To his retired friend, an Invitation to *Brecknock*," he relates that the walls once erected to define and protect Brecon town—old walls, foul and decayed—have been thrown down to create an open city. This act prefigures the dissolution of fixed social roles and responsibilities, the societal leveling that Vaughan considers an unconfined, hellish confusion. A catalog of abuses, such as one finds in satires, offers appropriate form for Vaughan's ultimately disinterested perspective.

> Thou'ldst swear (like *Rome*) her foule, polluted walls
> Were sackt by *Brennus*, and the salvage *Gaules*.
> Abominable face of things! here's noise

> Of bang'd Mortars, blew Aprons, and Boyes,
> Pigs, Dogs, and Drums, with the hoarse hellish notes
> Of politickly-deafe Usurers throats,
> With new fine *Worships,* and the old cast *teame*
> Of Justices vext with the *Cough,* and *flegme.*
> Midst these the *Crosse* looks sad, and in the *Shire-*
> *-Hall furs* of an old *Saxon Fox* appear,
> With brotherly Ruffs and Beards, and a strange sight
> Of high Monumentall Hats ta'ne at the fight
> Of *Eighty eight;* while ev'ry *Burgesse* foots
> The mortall *Pavement* in eternall boots.[2]

The framing order of society has been torn away. As a consequence, and despite the fact that discrete types are still recognizable, conventional relationships among people have been shattered. Nothing is in its customary place. Living anachronisms and pretentious innovations only mask as orders of the day, for there is no order of the day. Everything is in strange flux, altered, modified—but one. "The *Crosse*" is still, though sadly, singular; a fixed truth still remains, without, to which firm inner convictions could attach. But rather than commanding a perspective on the general scene, rather than revealing the truth about anything other than itself, this fixed verity is merely one more aspect in the field of vision. The cross stands not above the crowd, but in its midst.

Unrestrained eccentrics, an awful variety, swarm across boundless exterior space. In the face of such abomination, Vaughan retires to a consciously confined interior:

> Come then! and while the slow Isicle hangs
> At the stiffe thatch, and Winters frosty pangs
> Benumme the year, blith (as of old) let us
> 'Midst noise of War, of Peace, and mirth discusse.

The imperative here is defensive. It is an act of will thrust against and screening out a new "society" where the savage seizure of liberties leave this witness not informed, hardly free, but overwhelmed and numb. It is, in another sense, a retreat to the past—an attempt to recover, preserve, and restore a friendship, peace, and poetry that had flourished in an earlier time. The act of restoration, as well, is proclaimed a way of improving the past. Friendship, having suffered absence, will be stronger and better. A new poetry will emerge as an old Muse, the inspiration of Renaissance lovers, is recovered, tested, and refined. As Vaughan puts it, he will offer his friend no ordinary wine. Instead,

> Here lives that *Chimick,* quick fire which betrayes
> Fresh Spirits to the bloud, and warms our layes,
> I have reserv'd 'gainst thy approach a Cup
> That were thy Muse stark dead, shall raise her up,
> And teach her yet more Charming words and skill
> Than ever *Cœlia, Chloris, Astrophil,*
> Or any of the Thredbare names Inspir'd
> Poor riming lovers with a *Mistris* fir'd.
>
> (*Works*, p. 47)

We are prepared to anticipate Vaughan's reliance on the scheme of the love-sonnet sequence as a substructure for *Silex Scintillans.* Now he is speaking directly, though in spirited humor, of a new language, "skill," and objective for the old lovers' Muse. These lines, furthermore, suggest a surprising reversal of traditional poetic ideals. For the Renaissance poet, purveyor of true forms, of things as they should be, the spirits of the blood are ordinarily refined by the ideas of the mind, not vice-versa. And *"Chimick"* fires belong to the world of natural change and transformation, not to the fixed, abstract world of ideas, pure forms, or ideal women. So, whatever this new poetry eventually may become, it scarcely can be achieved by the "occasional" poet of *Olor Iscanus,* who uses literary form essentially as a defense against the nature of things as they are and of himself. Nor is it achieved immediately, easily, or consistently by the poet of *Silex Scintillans,* who exercises will and conscious control against the "spirits of the blood" in an effort to transcend his own and nature's "chymick" body. As an earlier, cavalier ego had abandoned the city for a country home, so the spirit may condemn the body and the world to seek a country beyond the stars. The desire for spiritual elevation, for heightened perspective, indeed becomes a far more powerful defense against empirical nature and irrational inner nature than cavalier contempt of uncivil society had been against external circumstance. But the struggle for a disengaged vision is a preparation for the descent and diffusion of spirit into the body of the world—a return to its confines with the message of regeneration and health.

In an address to "The Most Illustrious and Truly Regenerated Brethren R. C., Elders of Election And Peaceable Apostles of the Church in this Storm-Driven Age," Thomas Vaughan explains the process in terms of the Creation. Originally, "God in love with His own beauty frames a glass, to view it by reflection. But the frailty of the matter excluding eternity was subject to dissolution." The war is just such dissolution, and in the face of it the mind seeks to flee to the past, to a former unity, to its first home or original state. In another sense, the soul seeks release to its heavenly or astral origin. But the secluded spirit discovers that

> Heaven hath in it a scene of earth, and had she been contented with ideas she had not travelled beyond the map. But excellent patterns commend their mimes: Nature that was so fair in the type could not be a slut in the anaglyph. This makes her ramble hither, to examine the medal by the flask; but while she scans their symmetry she forms it. Thus her descent speaks her original.[2]

Such is the magician's general theme: what is above is below; what is within is without. For the act of seeing form is the act of forming what one sees: "while she scans their symmetry she forms it." Idea and substance join, then, in this act of perception. Limited to a Cartesian or modern formula, the proposition is easy to grasp, for we are used to living in a world where strict divisions between spiritual and material realities are assumed. According to Descartes, these two completely different orders meet *only* in the human mind. By such fiat, essential quality or spiritual content is removed from the material or elemental world. Thus desanctified, it is manipulable, not by magicians, but by rational, natural philosophers or scientists. Thomas Vaughan, of course, maintains that the inner reality created by such a divinely sanctioned "perception" is a reflection of external reality as well. So, the whole of life is defined as the movement of spirit in matter. "I look on this life," he attests, "as the progress of an essence royal: the soul but quits her court to see the country."

While his brother was forcing fragments of a figurative language into new forms to accommodate his version of empiricism, the poet, whose efforts only appear far more conservative, was seeking to confront and represent the unaccommodated reality lying beyond and commonly shunned by prior Renaissance poetics. An empirical context for spiritual projection, desired transformation or reform, becomes the medium or format for the poems of *Silex Scintillans*. In a broad sense the associations of the lyric sequence, the sometimes tenuous, invisible correspondences among physically discrete and seemingly displaced parts, suggest the shattered mirror Vaughan held his world to be. Specifically, the poems have always been noted for their loose style, their immediacy, naturalness, and concrete descriptions. And Vaughan's now-pervasive use of the first person grants experiential, self-expressive authority to the poetry. He writes:

> I walkt the other day (to spend my hour)
> Into a field
> Where I sometimes had seen the soil to yield
> A gallant flowre,
> But Winter now had ruffled all the bowre
> And curious store
> I knew there heretofore.

The lines appear to be natural and descriptive. The rhythms are easy and colloquial, near to speech. Such authenticity is tested only slightly by the adjective "gallant," the verb "ruffled," and the mysterious phrase "curious store" that stands for a catalogue of presumably observed natural phenomena now gone from the winter field. But the action of this stanza is in the past. The experience described is recollected, though in a casual manner that does not call attention to the present act—a conscious restaging or restoring of the event. The past takes on an immediacy and vitality by appearing to be wholly absorbed by the present. Vaughan's narrative artifice, quite intentional, suggests a theme: that lost presence is alive; the past, the dead, live. As the poet's recollected tale proceeds, the root or bulb of the lost flower is discovered, fresh and green, beneath the earth.

> Then taking up what I could neerest spie
>   I digg'd about
> That place where I had seen him to grow out,
>   And by and by
> I saw the warm Recluse alone to lie
>   Where fresh and green
>   He lived of us unseen.

Vaughan's hypothetical experience goes through another transformation as the poem continues. By the fifth stanza, as the speaker decides to bury the vital root he has discovered, Vaughan's concerns are clearly seen to exceed the concrete details of his narrative.

> This past, I threw the Clothes quite o'r his head,
>   And stung with fear
> Of my own frailty dropt down many a tear
>   Upon his bed,
> Then sighing whisper'd, *Happy are the dead!*
>   What peace doth now
>   Rock him asleep below?

Here the earth becomes "Clothes," a hole dug in the ground becomes a bed, and the reburied "Recluse" is fully personified. The logic of these shifting terms is made apparent at the close of the poem. The poet has been, all along, meditating and mourning before the burial urn of a dead companion. But in the movement of the verse there is no clear transition from past to present, from field and flower to funeral urn. Two places, times, and objects merge. The poet elides whatever verbal directions are necessary for a sense of metaphor. The narrative action cannot be designated as an explanatory fiction or parable, since it is inseparable from the present, reflective experience.

The lines of this poem betray their allegiance to a present tense where phenomenal existence is transitory. One thing passes into another at this moment, and at every moment. But more than one level of consciousness is accessible to the meditating poet. As his current thoughts project upon the receptive content of memory, the visual images of a winter field and its hidden store become, momentarily, translucent embodiments, emblems, of an idea that comprehends and accommodates change. There *is* a primordial, regenerative, natural power. The perception, product of the reflective mind in contact with a mutable world, is drawn into or glossed upon the static image of the urn—the poet's immediate, personal awareness of the permanent loss of death. The merging yields a clouded understanding: *"Happy are the dead! What peace doth now / Rock him asleep below?"* Vaughan's exclamatory insight exists within a shroud of doubt and questioning. The past exists, assimilated and transformed by the protean framework of an empirical present that shows perhaps most prominently in the disturbing unevenness of the lines that shape these stanzas.

Vaughan's elegy concludes with a prayer that the transformations characteristic of the present extend to create a future.

> O thou! whose spirit did at first inflame
>   And warm the dead,
> And by a sacred Incubation fed
>   With life this frame
> Which once had neither being, forme, nor name,
>   Grant I may so
>   Thy steps track here below,
>
> That in these Masques and shadows I may see
>   Thy sacred way,
> And by those hid ascents climb to that day
>   Which breaks from thee
> Who art in all things, though invisibly;
>   Shew me thy peace,
>   Thy mercy, love, and ease,
>
> And from this Care, where dreams and sorrows raign
>   Lead me above
> Where Light, Joy, Leisure, and true Comforts move
>   Without all pain. . . .
>
>   (*Works*, pp. 478–79)

The speaker of this poem reflects upon one kind of reality and projects another, yet partakes fully of neither. He is not a part of the organic world, or the past, although he constructs an image of himself there. Nor can he participate in the world "above" where absolute ideas move, although he prays for new life there. He stands outside the contrary realities of matter and pure spirit to demonstrate only what he can—their simultaneity. At the beginning of time, spirit joins with substance. At the end, substance joins spirit. Now, in time, all is moving. There is no clear beginning or ending, no categorical partaking of mental or phenomenal existence, above or below, for what is above is below, invisibly changing, preserving, rendering comprehensible the transitory world through which the Word is realized. This simultaneity and the message it renders—associations between the mysterious winter-death of plants, human death, and the doctrine of resurrection—exists in a third reality that may be called perceptual. This is the reality of seeing form and forming what one sees. It is a conjoining of rational and sensational awareness to create a moving intuition. The poet defines and imitates nature—the movement of spirit in substance: "thou . . . Who art in all things, though invisibly."

Words are constantly generating, informing, and shaping experience that, if this were not true, has "neither being, forme, nor name." Experience, at the same time, is constantly modifying verbal patterns, forcing words into new combinations to accommodate it. This principle, in simple terms that belie the complexity of its conception, is the foundation of Vaughan's poetics. What appears in his elegy as "empirical" is actually a kind of gloss upon an underlying text. The natural world that Vaughan casually explores is, at first, a verbal construct. Its beginnings may be discovered in the third stanza of George Herbert's poem "Peace":

> Then went I to a garden, and did spy
>   A gallant flower,
> The Crown Imperiall: Sure, said I,
>   Peace at the root must dwell.
> But when I digg'd, I saw a worm devoure
>   What show'd so well.[3]

By his own third and fourth stanzas, Vaughan has shifted texts to work from lines 8–14 of Herbert's "The Flower."

> Who would have thought my shrivel'd heart
> Could have recover'd greennesse? It was gone
>   Quite under ground; as flowers depart

> To see their mother-root, when they have blown:
> Where they together
> All the hard weather,
> Dead to the world, keep house unknown.[4]

In neither of these borrowings, nor in most of the hundreds of others noted in the editions of W. A. Lewis Bettany and L. C. Martin, does Vaughan recreate Herbert's use of language. Instead, he draws upon the language Herbert uses, selectively, to generate and inform his observation. In general, as in the examples above, Herbert's metaphor becomes Vaughan's matter. Herbert's "Peace" is a parable. Its garden and flower stand for ideas. In Vaughan's elegy, field and flower are literally meant. Yet underlying Vaughan's empiric surface and the ordinary words he speaks are the remains of prior verbal patterns, of metaphor, or extended meaning. Vaughan's imitation newly combines and transforms the firm design of Herbert's texts. But it counts on that design, as well. Resemblances in line and stanza structure are significant. Vaughan wants to reconstruct his world on the basis of a former order that he holds in mind. He wants a "gallant flowre" to stand for a gallant soul, now gone. But who can ignore what empirically shows so clear? The two are not the same at all. Plants die and are reborn. People die and are gone. A third condition, mediating these two, emerges by the nature of Vaughan's expression. His use of language, drawing upon residual verbal orders, creates loose, intuitive associations that are less than firm metaphor or an equating, yet more than a failure of relationships altogether. Former certainty descends into expectancy, but permits a hope where before there was but speechless despair.

Vaughan's unusual reliance upon prior texts, a cause for considerable criticism, curiosity and speculation among readers,[5] is in some respects anticipated by his versions of Ovid, Boethius, and the Divine Casimire, and derives—as a technique at least—from methods of translation and imitative composition commonly taught in the seventeenth century. As the poet suggests in "Ad Posteros," his early schooling consisted largely of learning Latin texts. Writing exercises, directed by Matthew Herbert, undoubtedly involved their literal English renditions. Skilled translation, however, was to emphasize rendition of the "sense" of a former author above strict adherence to the text.

Interpolation, the adding of new material that extends or comments upon the sense of the original, is a further step away from literal translation and toward imitation. Vaughan's translation of Boethius, *De Consolatione, Lib.* 2, *Metrum* 5—"Felix nimium prior aetas . . ."—begins rather literally:

> Happy that first white age! when wee
> Lived by the Earths meere Charitee. . . .

A particular sense of "prior aetas" is rendered, but the rest is a literal turning of Boethius's Latin to English syntax and octosyllabic couplets. By the eleventh line of Vaughan's version, however, limited interpolation comes into play. From "Somnos dabat herba salubres; / Potum quoque lubricus amnis; / Umbras altissima pinus" Vaughan derives:

> Their beds were on some flowrie brink
> And clear Spring-water was their drink.
> The shadie Pine in the Suns heat
> Was their Coole and known Retreat,
> For then 'twas not cut down, but stood
> The youth and glory of the wood.
>
> (*Works,* p. 83)

Hutchinson believes Vaughan added the last two lines of this passage because he loved trees.[6] Broader ideas of innocence "cut down," or youth slain, or a slain youth may as well have prompted the extension. Whatever the motive, the method of translation Vaughan pursued encouraged such practice. By it, the poet's own recognitions may be heard emerging, though modestly, from another, prior voice.

As students became proficient in two languages, they were taught to imitate classical texts, in Latin and then in English, according to an extension of loose translation or textual glossing called *parodia*. The writer was to retain select phrases and the overall structure of the original, while varying from the model in diction, subject and implication. We have already witnessed the broad effects of this technique in the transition from secular to sacred lyric sequences.

Parody is usually understood as a burlesque form of imitation, but for poetry of the seventeenth century that definition will not hold. More appropriate is Dryden's statement that parodies are "verses patch'd up from great Poets, and turn'd into another Sence than their Author intended them."⁷ What Dryden fails to mention is that the parodist works from texts in a given language to create a new text in the same language. His task, then, is not the render the original—or originals—strictly, freely, or by any other precept offered a translator. Rather, he critically interprets and redisposes given "matter" to suit and to comprehend a new subject, occasion, and intention. In this manner, following Horace's *Ode* 1.2 point by point but varying the model to fit an immediate occasion, Andrew Marvell composed his first published poem, "Ad Regnum Carolum Parodia." George Herbert's "A Parodie" is a looser conversion of the love "Song" written either by John Donne or William Herbert, third earl of Pembroke, into a sacred poem. Vaughan parodies his own translation of Boethius, *De Consolatione, Lib.* 2, *Metrum* 5 in "The Retreate":

> Happy those early dayes! when I
> Shin'd in my Angell-infancy.
> Before I understood this place
> Appointed for my second race,
> Or taught my soul to fancy ought
> But a white, Celestiall thought. . . .
>
> (*Works,* p. 419)

In this poem Vaughan creates a vision of his remotest past by extending the "public" sense of Boethius's "prior aetas," through the "white age" of his own earlier rendering to a former time, before the Fall or before some onslaught of civil decadence, which is realized as the soul's invisible "infancy." Here, suspended angellike between then and now, heaven and earth, the shady pine forest Vaughan laments as slain in his translation reappears, transformed, as a vision of "that shady City of Palme trees" sighted once by Moses in the heart of the promised land. The thing itself, held in memory, suggests an idea. Now the idea becomes a type of the original. By placing Boethius's poem, Vaughan's translation, and "The Retreate" side by side, we can see that original meaning emerges through the processes of translation and *parodia.*⁸

Like his Elizabethan predecessors, Vaughan understands

that the poet's basic task lies not in the invention of subject matter, or in the formulation of the ultimate argument the language of his subject bodies forth, but in the disposition of the material he is given. He can be pleased by mere craft. For example, in the poem "To Mr. M. L. *upon his reduction of the Psalms into Method,*" Vaughan praises the metrician for being a poet, for transforming and ordering the irregular and sometimes irrational piety of David:

> You brought his *Pslams* now into *Tune.* Nay, all
> His measures thus are more than musical.
> Your *Method* and his *Aires* are justly sweet,
> And (what's *Church-musick* right) like *Anthems* meet.
> You did so much in this, that I believe
> He gave the *Matter,* you the *form* did give.
> (*Works*, p. 628)

Vaughan is not praising applied "Method" above the spontaneous "Aires" it modifies, but a double music where both method and inspiration, form and matter merge by likenesses in an anthem that constitutes a new reality, "more than musical." At the heart of this appreciation, as at the center of the Rosicrucian argument, lies the idea of transmutation. Nature, the interrelation of spirit and matter, "transcends Nature" when its changes correspond to and thus commit a final form. By a further correlate we are to understand that fallen or obscure nature is refined, purged of its "sins," and returned to something like its original perfection. How fascinating it is for the poet to recognize this "golden" world as not merely a subject of hymns and psalms, but also as a factor essential in determining the way they were composed. Of course, one must hear the anthem, the moving unison, for its efficacy is really the aim of the exercise. Then he should become a part and participate in the singing.

Vaughan maintains a vision of the regenerated world as a universal chorus[9] and works toward its realization by composing his own metrical psalms. Three versions appear in *Silex Scintillans.* Two of these, metrical paraphrases of Psalms 65 and 121, are relatively strict renderings—in the manner, presumably, of "Mr. M. L." More typical of his other lyrics is Vaughan's meditation upon or celebration of Psalm 104. It shows an energetic involvement with Scripture characteristic of the Countess of Pembroke's paraphrases, published in the immensely influential Sidney *Psalter*.[10] The countess's versions, anticipating the poetical descants upon simple plainsongs later written by Richard Crashaw, often merge the voice of the Psalmist with the voice of the prosodist meditating—singing in mind, alone—upon airs inspired directly, so it was believed, by God himself.

Translation and imitation were fundamental skills of Renaissance poets. Indeed, all scholars were encouraged to improve themselves by "perusing and rehearsing" the poetry of the masters, and by the 1640s contemporary poets—Sandys, Quarles, Herbert—were being added to the list of models for intralingual imitation.[11] The poet of *Silex Scintillans* purposefully advances techniques of imitation to an extreme beyond pedagogical expectation, but commonly taught procedures—gloss, paraphrase, *parodia*, meditative or strict metrical renderings of psalms—instruct the writer to retain words and phrases from his model in whatever new poetic "disposition" he creates, and this is initially and precisely what Vaughan does in the majority of his sacred poems. He does so, by one expressed account, in order to "tame" his own fierce blood, to temper and inform the shifting, ethically vague, and spiritually tormented little world in which he lives. In a poem addressed to Herbert, Vaughan proclaims:

> Dear friend! whose holy, ever-living lines
>   Have done much good
> To many, and have checkt my blood,
> My fierce, wild blood that still heaves, and inclines,
>   But is still tam'd
> By those bright fires which thee inflam'd;
> Here I joyn hands, and thrust my stubborn heart
>   Into thy *Deed*.
>   . . . .
> Settle my *house,* and shut out all distractions
>   That may unknit
>   My heart, and thee planted in it. . . .
>   ("The Match," *Works,* pp. 434–35)

The body of the poem "heaves and inclines," threatening to distract the reader's mind by visual impression. The phrasing and syntax that render order modify but do not eliminate that threat. For words and lines now join in the movement of a native pulse. Language here is "not dead, but full of *Blood* again, / I mean the *Sense,* and ev'ry *Line* a *Vein.*"[12] By the spirits of that blood, the poet recreates himself.

George Herbert's lines, among other literary resources, exist in Vaughan's mind and literally in the poems he writes as a seed or vital root exists in the ground. Through the earth, through the body's passionate blood, through the heart's desire, sorrow, anger, love, their sensible order moves, transforms, and is transformed. And, to be sure, it is heard—not only by the poet, but by his reading audience as well. Old voices echo in Vaughan's poetic rooms. Their language has been disjoined from prior contexts, rendered in new combinations, assimilated, and perhaps hidden, yet their lines are discoverable and other voices inevitably will be listened to as parts of Vaughan's. Recognition of the old in the new, like recognition of distinct lines in polyphony, is an act of discovery (nowadays editorially preempted) that Vaughan must have anticipated from his readers. For to recognize Vaughan's sacred sources, passages he (not to speak cryptically) prominently conceals, is to experience knowledgeably the literary imitation of life—the spirit/word moving in substance—crucial to his poetics.

Vaughan's most direct commentary on the general use of external voices may be found in his prose cento *The Life of Holy Paulinus.* He begins the translation of this *Life* with a series of "bright and flowrie *Encomiums*" taken from Ecclesiasticus 50:6–11. He calls these lines "most great (indeed) and most glorious Assimilations, full of life, and full of freshnesse," and with them, Bishop Paulinus can be described:

1. He was as the Morning-star in the midst of a cloud, and as the Moon at the full.
2. As the Sunne shining upon the temple of the most high, and as the Rain-bow giving light in the bright clouds.
3. As the flower of Roses in the spring of the year, as Lillies by the rivers of waters, and as the branches of the Frankincense-tree in the time of summer. (*Works,* p. 339)

Vaughan rightly calls these encomiums "Assimilations." They are created by the drawing together of material from various places, predominantly the canonical proverbs and psalms. Ecclesiasticus is described as a post-prophetic book. It does not rely upon the inspired voice of a single man, but admittedly contains a medley of voices compiled by "a man of great diligence and wisdom among the Hebrews, who did not only gather the grave and short sentences of wise men, that had been before him, but himself also uttered some of his own. . . . When as therefore the first [writer] died, leaving this book almost perfected, Sirach his son receiving it after him left it to his own son Jesus [Joshua], who, having gotten it into his hands, compiled it all orderly into one volume, and called it Wisdom, intituling it both by his own name, by his father's name, and his grandfather's. . . ."[13]

Vaughan is thus offered the apocryphal, assimilated wise sayings, dark sentences, parables, prayers, and songs of Ecclesiasticus as a precedent, a mode of composition that might be approximated in his own postprophetic age. For Vaughan, the synthesis of voices is a kind of historical reconstruction, carried out in a particularly personal way. The living man is literally the creation of near and remote ancestors. His very being, rightly seen, confirms a continuity. Just so, the inner man, that living spirit, is a synthesis of near and remote *books*—those places where spirit is communicated. In the poems of *Silex Scintillans* their sanctified fragments, woven together like talismans, create the voice and identity of the inner man at prayer:

> O thou that lovest a pure, and whitend soul!
> That feedst among the Lillies, 'till the day
> Break, and the shadows flee; touch with one Coal
> My frozen heart; and with thy secret key
>
> Open my desolate rooms; my gloomie Brest
> With thy cleer fire refine, burning to dust
> These dark Confusions, that within me nest,
> And soyl thy Temple with a sinful rust.
>
> Thou holy, harmless, undefil'd high-priest!
> The perfect, ful oblation for all sin. . . .
> ("Dressing," *Works*, p. 455)

In lines 2 and 3 above, Vaughan collapses two sentences from

Song of Solomon (2: 16, 17) to recreate an epithet for Christ. In lines 4 and 5 he paraphrases two lines from Herbert's "The H. Communion":

> And hath the privie key
> Op'ning the souls most subtile rooms.

Line 6 begins with an adaptation of the eleventh line from Herbert's "The Starre"—"Then with thy light refine." Lines 9 and 10 are derived from the Anglican Communion Service: "Jesus Christ . . . who made there (by his one oblation, once offered) a full, perfect, and sufficient sacrifice, oblation, and satisfaction, for the sins of the whole world."[14] These scriptural, poetic, and liturgical voices may not sound themselves clearly to readers today, but they would have been recognizably distinct to Vaughan's contemporaries.

The voices informing the measure of Vaughan's lines bind the poet to a tradition of sacred literature through which he must firmly and consciously have wished to express himself in the act of revealing, to all, the bond. The synthesis, as a mosaic in which the parts are simultaneously discrete and integrated, creates a sense of living history—all time at one time. This linguistic microcosm, the voice of the inner man, centers not upon the mind where all might be rendered comprehensive and complete according to some prior ideal, authority, or model, nor upon extremities where all is sensation and response, physical and discrete. The center, rather, is the heart—that most subtle of "rooms," the soul's inmost home, where the capacity to love must be restored. The poetry of *Silex Scintillans* is both about the heart and spoken from it.

True nature, Thomas Fuller states in his contribution to *Pulpit Sparks, or Choice Forms of Prayer by Several Reverend and Godly Divines* (1659),[15] is found in the "thoughts of all our hearts." Issuing from this place, where a world of words and empirical nature are seemingly one, is an expressive mode, "extempore" and varied. The expression derives from particular experience or occasion, yet it is patterned and communicative since it involves combinations of words derived from "constant" prayer forms. Here is one brief excerpt from a sentence that winds interminably on, merging various idioms, tight and loose, for three full pages: ". . . true, Lord, the law in our minds . . . our light, clearly knows and chearfully acknowledges all and every one of thy commandments for pure, and just, and holy; but the law in our members, our darknesse, our flesh, our old Creature breaks them daily in thought, word, and deed." The heart, thus speaking forth, is the repository of an awareness, a perception of two natures or "laws"—one fully complete and the other, all shattered. Its own nature, neither divine nor bestial—though seeking to mend the second by the first—is "human." The question that renders Fuller's prayer fearfully disjunctive and breathlessly extensive is whether this nature is acceptable to God or worthy of some sudden reform.

Like Fuller's varied prayer, and like the book it comes from, the verbal fabric of *Silex Scintillans* may be characterized preliminarily by the idea of mosaic synthesis. So may certain of Vaughan's poems that set out to define types. "Son-dayes," for example, is a poetic formulation of the days of days. The poem is composed entirely of independent phrases, a number of which have been identified from Herbert's "Prayer" and "Sunday."[16]

> The Pulleys unto headlong man; times bower;
> The narrow way;
> Transplanted Paradise; Gods walking houre;
> The Cool o'th' day;
>
> The Creatures *Jubile*; Gods parle with dust;
> Heaven here; man on those hills of Myrrh, and flowers;
> Angels descending; the Return of Trust;
> A Gleam of glory, after six-days-showres.
>
> (*Works*, p. 447)

This most curious collaboration depicts the "thoughts of all our hearts," each distinct, contained in a single form that moves toward, and finally achieves a balanced line, a unity, a symmetry. The multiple description is at once a succession of outer voices drawn into agreement and a mirror of an inner, spiritual identity some fragments of which, otherwise disembodied and unidentified, coalesce in the formulation of the stanza. Vaughan's dedication to admitting other voices is ultimately a way of self-awareness, for the spirit, that "other" within him, is manifested by such receptivity. Sundays then are at once an external event, "the Churches love-feast," and an inner event, the lamp that lights one man "through his heap of dark days."

Similar in construction is Vaughan's poem on the night of nights.

> Dear night! this worlds defeat;
> The stop to busie Fools; cares check and curb;
> The day of Spirits; my souls calm retreat
>   Which none disturb!
> *Christs** progress, and his prayer time;
> The hours to which high Heaven doth chime.
>
> (*Works,* p. 522)

The stanza is a succession of disjunctive, descriptive clauses, arranged asyndetically to portray not only a contrast between earthly and heavenly realities but the poet's secluded position as well. The night when spirits live and fools cease their business is for Vaughan, alone, a "calm retreat," a time suspended between mortal and eternal realms. In this passage Vaughan notes with an asterisk the scriptural texts he draws upon: Mark 1:35 and Luke 21:37.

These poems display the mark of a "baroque" sensibility that flourished briefly in mid-seventeenth-century English literature. Its governing precept, "All in One," is sounded again and again: in Sir Thomas Browne's incredible *Garden of Cyrus,* where an infinite variety of phenomena is contained in the quincunx; in *Paradise Lost,* where a single event contains the seed and pattern of all sequent events; in so many of Richard Crashaw's poems, where a single paradox multiplies and extends to fill all conceivable time and space; and in Marvell's beautiful poem "Ros" where the exiled soul, a drop of dew, turns in upon itself to create an inner cosmos, reflecting the heavens from which it fell while nourishing the earth it has fallen to preserve.

Ideological tensions between a world order imposed from without, consistent with the order of God or *eidos,* and a natural order unfolding from within, consistent (ultimately) with "reason" and applied mathematics, tensions that dominate the seventeenth century, are swelled to such a peak by events of the war and interregnum that unity between disparate positions becomes a far more important consideration than the single-mindedness pursuit of either. And however bewildered philosophers may be to see tenets of Plato and Descartes twined round each other in a single sentence, such syntheses were being urged upon the thinking public in the form of syncretist ideologies—Hermetic, Paracelsian—and poetic theory is in tune with the movement.

Remarks on an interregnum poetics are disparate. Typical of the times, there is no overriding authority of the stature, say, of Sir Philip Sidney. But if one can be content with fragments, none should be surprised to hear of a new, collaborative "skill" being advanced to restore an old "muse"—that singular vision of things as they should be, or as they once were, which Sidney himself considered the poet's central inspiration. None should be surprised to hear Thomas Fuller attributing the eloquence of the English language to its capacity for assimilating other languages: "He who mingles wine with water, though he destroys the nature of water, improves the quality thereof."[17] Ben Jonson was a great poet, Fuller next advises, by merit of his "elaborate wit." "He would sit silent in learned company, and suck in (besides wine) their several humors into his observation. What was *ore* in others, he was able to refine to himself."[18] Shakespeare, by Fuller's characterization, is one "in whom three eminent poets may seem in some sort to be compounded": Martial, Ovid, and Plautus.[19] This is, so to speak, alchemical criticism. The course of poetic art, as of language itself, is a process of pillaging and compounding, destroying and refining. The poet is no singularly inspired prophet, but neither is he a mere copyist. He is, rather, capable of drawing various idioms, tempers, humors, and voices together in a new and comprehensive way.

A remark more commonly remembered now and perhaps more consequential at the time is Sir William Davenant's definition of "wit." Likened to a spider's web, the poet's creative capacity is manifested as a subtle and various pattern, spun out from the center of himself, loose, flexible and delicate, yet capable of grasping and holding all the diverse "gifts" afforded by "Nature" within its lines.[20] Earlier in the seventeenth century, it is commonly generalized, a poet's wit is understood to be his inspired or angelic intelligence, his ability to see and make associations not commonly seen or naturally made. After the Restoration, again speaking broadly, "wit" comes under the definition of refined, reasonable, common sense. Davenant suggests a mid-century idea for the term, and it must be said that his definition, though it suggests something of both earlier and later views, is essentially distinct from either. Davenant uses a patterned figure from nature's common store, which reasonable Augustans might approve, to define the tough fibers of intellective strength upheld by an earlier poetics. Thus his definition demonstrates the assimilative force he understands wit to be. It is the natural web that gathers all estranged substance within itself. It is like a divine power in this respect, yet its manifestations are observed within the framework of natural and inherently sensible procedures.

Davenant's consolidating precept is represented with more precision, if less enthusiasm, by Abraham Cowley.

> In a true piece of *Wit*, all things must be,
>   Yet all things there *agree.*
> As in the *Ark,* joyn'd without force or strife,
> All *Creatures* dwelt: all *Creatures* that had life.
>   Or as the *Primitive Forms* of all
>   (If we compare great things with small)
> Which without *Discord* or *Confusion* lie,
> In that strange *Mirror* of the *Deitie.*[21]

Nature is still the Deity's mirror, but the reflection now is "strange." The empirical surface appears, for Cowley as for Davenant and Vaughan, fractured and fragmented. Yet all can be drawn together again, for everything is of a common origin. That original, figured as the microcosmic Ark and sanctified by the very terms of the reference, underlies the face of things, resides in the hearts and hopes of all, as some primal harmony or symbiosis that the poet is capable of recognizing and imitating. Central to Cowley's understanding is the insistence that unifying form is not "forced"—like edicts, say, of a civil or ecclesiastical authority. It is not imposed as a concept that distorts or denies experiential reality, but emerges as a natural principle of agreement or native concord.

Vaughan's fidelity to poetic precepts such as these is manifest in the very language he employs, the "assimilations" linked in a manner of his own disposing, and the spiritual concord and continuum he means to achieve by it. "Thy richer *Verse*," his brother acknowledges, "creates all *Poets*, that can but *reherse*" (*Works*, p. 38). Vaughan renders explicitly his ties with the past, but he does not, as Restoration poets commonly will, give over individual control of form as sustained by earlier seventeenth-century mannerist poets like Donne, or the versatile classicist Ben Jonson. Vaughan's ties with past texts, if we observe them lineally and from our own distance, represent an inner heritage that he must bring to life. Scripture stands as the original, inspired word. Church Fathers are its types, translators or rehearsers. Vaughan, a further step removed, contemplates, disturbs, assimilates and reforms the tradition within his own life and lines.

By terms of this sacred prescript the idea of "One containing All" may be located at the borders of time and (as its words persuade individual experience) at the heights and depths of any moment in time. The idea stands as the vision of a perfectly harmonious world before the Fall and as an "angel-infancy" before birth. It stands as the promise of a perfectly restored world at time's end and as the body's resurrection after death. It stands as the promise of a vital spirit, a "secret *Greenness*" locked in the womb of earth, and as a primitive humanity or potential new life locked within the heart's "rockie" walls. It stands in the serene concord and movement of the farthest stars and in the highest reaches, momentarily sustained, of the contemplative mind.

By this double axis Vaughan designs a remote frame for the madness, violence, and malevolence erupting upon the surface of earth and threatening to dissolve coherences altogether. At the midpoint of the axes, their solitary connection, is the poet. He stands frighteningly distant from the invisible, secret reality he can imagine and reconstruct, and frighteningly near a brute actuality that contemporaries such as Thomas Hobbes are beginning to postulate as "true." His head aches, his "fingers Itch, and burn to take / Some new Imployment.... Thousands of wild and waste Infusions / Like waves beat on my resolutions." Against the onslaught

    I School my Eys, and strictly dwel

> Within the Circle of my Cel,
> That Calm and silence are my Joys. . . .
> ("Misery," *Works,* p. 473)

"The Circle of my Cel," literally the retreat at Newton, is also the circle of the conscious self. Its border, like the wall of old Brecon town, both defines and constricts identity. Vaughan's urge is to animate this little world, to extend its reality in time. "True hearts," he is aware, "spread, and heave / Unto their God, as flow'rs do to the Sun" (*Works,* p. 436). To do so, Vaughan must create a durative, lyric mode spun unforced from the harmonious center in a way that neither denies nor accedes to the thousands of empirical "infusions," but accommodates them.

[4]
Natural Music

> ... there is something in it of Divinity more than the eare discovers. It is an Hieroglyphicall and shadowed lesson of the whole world, and Creatures of God; such a melody to the eare, as the whole world well understood, would afford the understanding.
>
> —Sir Thomas Browne, *Religio Medici*, Part 2

> ... while this world
> In wild *Excentricks* now is hurld,
> Keep wee, like nature, the same *Key*,
> And walk in our forefathers way.
>
> —H. Vaughan, to T. Lewes, Rector of Llanfigan, near Newton, evicted in 1650

The image Vaughan creates of himself in "Misery" is one of singular steadfastness walled in against all hostility. As in the image of the Cross described earlier—alone amidst seething crowds—there is a saddening helplessness to his rigor. Though he is facing his own misery by refusing easy literary escapes to an ideal world, integrity is enforced by external conditions, not by inner assurance or understanding. And confinement occupied by fear, anger, and the rule of its own stern bulwarks does not produce receptive introspection and inner development. If nothing enters, nothing escapes and nothing changes. Thus

Vaughan has in one respect willed the "rocky walls" around his heart that become the topic of his lament. The circle must break, expand, contain, and then be reformed. So, from retired seclusion, a cry secretly yet determinately emerges. Then the unvisited voice grows in anxiety and passion.

> Open my rockie heart, and fil
> It with obedience to thy wil,
> Then seal it up, that as none see,
> So none may enter there but thee.
>
> O hear my God! hear him, whose bloud
> Speaks more and better for my good!
> O let my Crie come to thy throne!
> My crie not pour'd with tears alone
> ....
> But with the bloud of all my soul,
> With spirit-sighs. . . .[1]

The desperate expression of these lines, the need for a way to approach "thy throne," the need for a truth and stability now exiled to remotest quarters by "wild *Excentricks*" of the world, resounds the major challenge to traditional Renaissance poetics. The challenge is rationally met, for one example, by Henry Reynolds; his *Mythomystes* (1632/3) is the most sustained theoretical argument to be written by any of Vaughan's contemporaries.

> What concernes [the poet] now so neerely as to attend to the cultivating or refining, & thereby advancing of his rationall part, to the purchase & regaining of his first lost felicity? And what meanes to conduce to this purchase can there bee, but the knowledge first, and love next (for none can love but what hee first knowes) of his Maker, for whose love and service he was only made? And how can this blind, lame, and utterly imperfect Man . . . hope to approach this supreme altitude and immensity, which
>
> > *In quella inaccessibil luce,*
> > *Quasi in alta caligine s'asconde,*
> > [In that inaccessible light,
> > Is self-hidden, as though in a remote mist]
>
> but by two meanes only: the one, by laying his burden on him that

on his Crosse bore the burthen of all our defectes, and interpositions betweene us and the hope of the vision of his blessed Essence face to face heereafter; and the other, by carefull searche of him here in this life (according to Saint *Paules* instruction), in his works; who telles us—*those invisible things of God are cleerely seene, being understood by the things that are made....*²

For knowledge of what to love, or at least the language of that regard, prescriptions from places such as Reynolds's treatise are entirely agreeable to Vaughan. Draw upon the texts of the past, Reynolds advises: "seeke and take from the hands of the fittest teachers." Ambrose, Nazianzen, Origen and Augustine are mentioned, among others. But how is one to love? In what manner or style can poets incite and convey thoughts of the heart? Love lyrics of the past, secular or sacred, had lesser distances to span. What extended form can now be offered to approach, through the intercession of Christ and the "translucent" example of things made, a supreme altitude and immensity?

The comments on poetics surveyed in chapter 3 fail to specify a particular style or lyric mode of setting language in motion. To recall Davenant, "subtle webs" may be spun out in many ways, depending on where perimeters are conceived in the "real" world. Neither is Henry Reynolds particularly concerned with literary type or style. But he does offer some interesting models when he talks about searching the "Misteries of Nature."³ Inquire of those, he urges, who lived nearest the time of the gods. Original wisdom is from Egyptian priests. Then there is Zoroaster, who conveys the *"seriem naturarum universi* ... the series or concatenation of the universall Natures, from a no degree of matter, to him that is above or beyond all degree, gradually extended." Then, for lyric precedent and authority, attend the singers—Orpheus and David. "There is nothing of greater efficacy then the hymns ... if the fitting musick, intention of the minde, and other circumstances which are knowne to the wise, bee considered and applyed." This comment, like *Mythomystes* in general, is somewhat arcane. However, Vaughan's achievements in prosody are as much dependent upon such Neoplatonic ideas of cosmic order, natural hierarchy, and the supposed form of ancient hymns as they may be akin to "extemporaneous" prayer forms like Fuller's or the temperamental, inspired speech of itinerant ministers like Fox and Powell. From both resources he achieves a "fitting musick."

On first hearing, the declamatory aspects of Vaughan's style usually predominate. Readers confront an expansive, variously accented, actively flowing line that moves restlessly upon ordinarily restrictive stanza patterns or forges, of its own momentum, longer strophic forms. What one hears resembles, nearly, the shifting rhythm and fluid cadence of speech or written prose. Syntactic structure appears the formal determinant, more so than musical rhythms—measured patterns of sound and stress—which underlie any schematic rendering of prosaic sense. Subtle turns of accent, internal rhyme and syntactic stops within a line, changing line lengths, extraordinary stanzaic or monostrophic patterns, and even broken rhymes—obvious features of Vaughan's lyric style—are set like variations upon theme, recitative upon continuo, against residual, measured or "harmonic" norms in which the poems ordinarily are resolved.

As an example of this unusually compounded style, the third stanza of "Resurrection and Immortality" follows.

<pre>
                             3
        Then I that here saw darkly in a glasse   51
               But mists, and shadows passe,
        And, by their owne weake *Shine,* did search the springs
                 And Course of things
               Shall with Inlightned Rayes   55
                 Pierce all their ways;
        And as thou saw'st, I in a thought could goe
               To heav'n, or Earth below
        To reade some Starre, or Min'rall, and in State
                   There often sate,   60
               So shalt thou then with me
                 (Both wing'd, and free,)
        Rove in that mighty, and eternall light
               Where no rude shade, or night
        Shall dare approach us; we shall there no more   65
                 Watch stars, or pore
            Through melancholly clouds, and say
                 Would it were Day!
        One everlasting *Saboth* there shall runne
        Without *Succession,* and without a *Sunne.*   70
                                        (*Works,* p. 402)
</pre>

Natural Music 85

Some of the characteristics of this style are already familiar. For instance, the long sentence that constitutes all but the last two lines of the stanza is generated by an obvious paraphrase of I Corinthians 13:12—"For now we see through a glass, darkly." The sentence is concluded by an italicized adaptation from Deuteronomy 28:67—"Would God it were morning!" Furthermore, Vaughan's concluding couplet clearly echoes Revelation 22:5—"And there shall be no night there; and they need no candle, neither light of the sun; for the Lord God giveth them light: and they shall reign for ever and ever."

In addition to mere substance, these biblical voices, drawn easily into the lines, transforming speech to firmer measure and in turn transformed as rendered by the first-person speaker of the stanza,[4] offer authority and direction to Vaughan's argument. By characterizing present time through the Old Testament voice of Moses, from Deuteronomy, and by sounding the past and future through New Testament citations, Vaughan achieves a justification for the effusiveness and urgency of his lines. The earth and the "Body," now as in times before Christ, lie beneath a veil of ignorance, despairing and "melancholly" yet stirred by the yearnings and admonitions of prophets' voices. The future, as the New Testament past, holds the reality of a manifest God. These alignments underlie the overt argument of the poem—the promise of resurrection to the body. The logic here is loose, or associative, and the historical sense cyclic. An event occurred. Another event, like it, will occur to you.

The internal lines of the stanza, rendered exuberantly, suggest a passage on spiritual ubiquity from the books of Hermes Trismegistus[5] that Vaughan may have heard in his brother Thomas's 1648 paean to Cornelius Agrippa:

> Now I am earth, and now a star, and then
> A spirit—now a star and earth again;
> Or if I will but ransack all that be
> In the least moment I engross all three.
> I span the heaven and earth and things above,
> And—which is more—join natures with their love.[6]

Vaughan's recollected astral ecstasy and "Min'rall" descent requires scriptural paraphrase to frame, direct, and make sense of such mercurial, atemporal vision. The imaginable movements of Vaughan's spirit have their beginning and end in the texts of revealed religion, but the journey itself is indeed winged and free. Without the fixed props of a cosmic or angelic hierarchy or the stabilizing influence of established liturgy, the thrust of spiritual passion to span earth and stars must be accomplished in a new, direct, immediate way—here by a series of kinetic images set moving by a volatile and continuously mobile song.

The substantive material of Vaughan's stanza, drawn in from other places, is in itself sufficiently comprehensible. But the poet's rendering of his subject—the lyric style of the poem— appears so complex as to be nearly free of form. The lines, varying in length and visual placement, do not seem to belong together. The poem is rhymed—*aabb,* as are forty-five others in *Silex Scintillans*—but in alternate couplets there is enjambment. Consequently, whatever measure may suggest itself in given lines gives way to the cadence of the sentence. While he pauses, frequently, within a line, Vaughan extends syntax to master variable line lengths and placements as well as the potential aural stop of end-rhyme. Forged is a cadence more fluid, subtle, less conspicuously repetitious than anything the verbal music of prior English verse had rendered.

The lines may be scanned syllabically. By numbering the syllables for each line, according to the rhyme order of the stanza, Vaughan's rhythmic paradigm and its imitations appear:

$10^a\ 6^a\ 10^b\ 4^b\ 6^c\ 4^c\ 10^d\ 6^d\ 10^e\ 4^e\ 6^f\ 4^f\ 10^g\ 6^g\ 10^h\ 4^h\ 8^i\ 4^i\ 10^j\ 10^j$.[7]

A repeating structure is established by the six-line pattern 10/6, 10/4, 6/4—the first *i* line is irregular—and concluded by two identical *j* lines.

The movement of thought and syntax relies, to a limited extent, upon the broad structure of Vaughan's underlying form. The first six lines are syntactically self-contained and are concluded with a semicolon. But the next six lines are not so restrained. Vaughan interposes the parenthetical line 62, "Both wing'd and free," to oblige his pattern and proceeds with his thought until the middle of line 65. Tension between the repeated pattern and the movement of thought and syntax can be perceived, but one's sense of sentence movement clearly dominates, until the final couplet. There, the endlessness projected by overt statement is caught in an epigrammatic stasis. The *s* sounds of the couplet alliterate; the opening word "One" rhymes with the end words "runne" and "Sunne"; the lines are of equal length; they constitute a self-contained syntactic unit; and the final line is both balanced—as "without" is repeated—and steadily measured. Thus it echoes line 51 and frames the stanza.

Vaughan uses this concluding harmony, sustaining the metrical paraphrasing of a passage from Revelation, less to complete his poem than to adjourn it with aural as well as biblical authority. A transformation is promised, revealed, and lyrically demonstrated, but its actual accomplishment is relegated to the future, or to the end of time. So Vaughan's more natural cadences shift to a traditional measure. The poet sets a quotation from Daniel 12:13—*"But go thou thy way untill the end be, for thou shalt rest, and stand up in thy lot, at the end of the dayes"*—between "Resurrection and Immortality" and the next poem, "Day of Judgement," and having underscored his theme of promised resurrection, continues to involve seven stanzas of Common Measure in a single, sinuous sentence.

Vaughan's tendency to override closure in pursuit of an idea or in exploration of a figure, thought, or theme, and the resulting serial order of poems is not yet a concern. Such developments, however, are not to be unexpected, given the expansive potential of the lyric style he is developing. A phrase from Vaughan's *The Mount of Olives,* or *Solitary Devotions* aptly designates the style.

> I say then, do not we see that these *birds* and inferior *creatures* which in the *spring* and *summer* continue here very merry and *musical,* do on a sudden leave us, and all *winter*-long suffer a kind of death, and with the *Suns* warmth in the *youth* of the year *awake* again, and *refresh* the world with their *reviv'd notes*? For the singing of birds is *naturalis musica mundi,* to which all *arted strains* are but *discord* and *hardness.* (Works, p. 177)

Here Vaughan is admiring a "natural music" whereby the creatures sound their universal theme of regeneration. Nature's annual cycle, likened to death and resurrection as well as a return to youth, is the reality lying behind assertions of a music of the world—a form embodied and displayed here, in the sounds and miraculous lives of "inferior *creatures.*" The cycle, a composed form, and the various, spontaneous "notes" that are actually experienced, are linked by a warmth generated outwardly by the sun, inwardly by the heart, and mutually by *anima mundi,* as Boethius renders Plato's term—a spirit conjoined with ultimate harmony and inspiring the multiple voices that celebrate it.

Vaughan gives the concept of natural music cosmic dimension as he praises the incantatory quality of Mrs. K. Phillips's inspired lyricism;

> Say wittie fair one, from what Sphere
> Flow these rich numbers you shed here?
> For sure such *Incantations* come
> From thence, which strike your Readers dumbe.
> ....
> So *Lodestones* guide the duller *Steele,*
> And high perfections are the *Wheele*
> Which moves the lesse, for gifts divine
> Are strung upon a *Vital line*
> Which touch'd by you, Excites in all
> Affections. . . .
>
> (*Works,* pp. 61–62)

The high "Wheele" of cosmic perfection is a numbered, musical pattern for lesser, worldly cycles, and the poet plays upon, imitates, and recreates the link between. Her flowing "Incantations" are vital embodiments of invisible, natural continua—lines of magnetic attraction or astral influence that join celestial with mundane reality. The reader is stunned, dissolved, and ultimately transformed by her song.

Remarks such as these bring Vaughan's apprehension of natural music, its origin, generation, and effects, close to Neoplatonic (or better, neo-Greek) theories of music and poetry that were conveyed by Boethius, regenerated by Florentine academicians, sustained in the French academies of the sixteenth century,[9] and were relatively commonplace in humanist poetics of seventeenth-century England.[10] In the works of the "musical humanists," remote Pythagorean explanations of the physical universe in terms of number, measure, and harmony take on a new immediacy and importance. If the Creation is conceived as a divine ordering of matter, and if order, measure and harmony are accepted as analogues, a broad basis for ideas of the "music of the spheres" as well as an inherent, concordant form of the world and its creatures will follow. A special kind of poetic measure and movement may then be derived as necessary, since the poet imitates nature in his song.

According to Boethius, the "music of the universe" is a system relating everything "high" with everything "low" and holding the entire creation together. Celestial music, though not actually heard, must exist since all movement creates sound. There is an established order of modulation in celestial revolution, he explains, "for some [stars / planets] are borne higher and others lower, and all are revolved with a just impulse, and from their different inequalities an established order of their courses may be deduced."[11] From apparent disproportion, then, an underlying symmetry is derived. The courses of the stars "are joined together by such mutual adaptation" that nothing more united and harmonious could be imagined.

In the phenomenal world, such harmony unites the four elements in a single "body and mechanism," and brings the variety of seasons to a unity—the year. By and within this natural consonance, potentially destructive "excesses" are tempered by their relationship to others: "Each part brings its own contribution or aids others to bring theirs. For what winter binds, spring releases, summer heats, autumn ripens; and the seasons in turn bring forth their own fruits or help the others to bring forth theirs."[12]

The music of nature implies a harmony in the human microcosm: "For what is that which unites the incorporeal activity of the reason with the body, unless it be a certain mutual adaptation and as it were a tempering of low and high sounds into a single consonance? What else joins together the parts of the soul itself, which in the opinion of Aristotle is a joining together of the rational and the irrational? What causes the blending of the body's elements or holds its parts together in established adaptation" but music?[13] If Vaughan's "Resurrection and Immortality" is read in light of this definition, the mercurial speech-song by which "soul" relates to "body" may be understood as a demonstration of natural music.

By Boethius's conceptualization, natural music is at once a vertical or chordal form, relating what is above with what is below, and in time a movement or succession that unites otherwise discordant or discrete events. Translated to a musical composition for voices, as such concepts later were by residents of Baïf's Academy of Poetry and Music, we get experiments such as a "natural *musique mesurée*" that combined the "intertwining" voices common to polyphony with a "syllabic homophony"—the latter derived from the humanists' belief that ancient music was monodic (single-voiced) and achieved by coordinating parts so that each syllable is sung by all voices at the same time. As Frances Yates suggests, such *"rythme d'ensemble"* produced a decidedly new musical effect.[14] Typically, and regardless of the number of actual participants, four vocal parts were used. In the more comprehensive treatises these parts could represent the four elements and seasons, as well as the four internal humors and external characteristics of man.[15] Thus Renaissance musical art is wed to "nature."

Boethius's third point concerns the harmonic union of rational and irrational aspects of the human microcosm expressed in "the musick of man's voice." The implications of this point are least explored by the academicians. Most often, they relegate such inner "tuning" to the category of music's effect upon listeners. Even with their concession to the idea that original vocal music—the songs of Orpheus, Amphion, David—was a rhythmic monody, relying upon words as much as upon measure and harmonic form, the theoreticians held Pythagorean metaphysics in such high regard that their example had little lasting effect on poetry not meant for musical setting.[16] Efforts to discover rules for ancient meter, to adopt quantitative norms for poetic lines, to restore the lost measure of David's divine poem—all of which were tried and the last of which appealed to Vaughan—ordinarily advanced the art of musical number or "method" above the expressive capacity of the texts it was supposedly rendering by nature's rule. But Vaughan's friend Thomas Powell proclaimed the music of man's voice as the most significant form of natural music.[17]

A natural music of the human voice was of considerable

interest, as well, to a group of Florentine scholars, poets, and composers called "the Camerata." For them, musical modes (scales), monody, oratorical techniques, and means of expressing and exciting emotion in general were primary objectives. Symbolic lessons composed and delivered by harmonic forms were subordinated to dramatic means of delivery. Chordal structures were used for accompaniment, while the singing itself varied between declamation and melody. As Gretchen Finney explains, "the total effect was that of talking in harmony."[18] The aim, by testimony of the composers themselves, was to recreate the natural, serial rhythms of speech and vertical, "symbolic" harmonies simultaneously. Operatic recitative is a living example of such intent. Music was, indeed, humanized.

Richard Hooker anticipates this lyrical expressiveness when he explains, in building a case for psalm singing, the "admirable facility which music hath to express and represent to the mind, more inwardly than any other sensible mean, the very standing, rising, and falling, the very steps and inflections every way, the turns and varieties of all passions whereunto the mind is subject." Anglican culture, then, was not without conceptual preparation for the liberating effects brought on by Italian musical example in the seventeenth century.[19] Airs and songs for lute and voice, for plays, and for masques became far less restricted by repetitive tunes and stanza forms. Varied and longer lines, extended oratorical, speculative and argumentative passages in rhythms near to speech, quick shifts of accent, and lyrics shifting from one stanza form to another were now realizable.[20] One respectable place to witness these effects is the text of William Cartwright's "The Royall Slave," a blend of masque and drama with "Ayres and Songs" set by Henry Lawes and "Appearances" designed by Inigo Jones. Vaughan knew the play, in a textual version that provides at least printed example of the new, loose, lyric style. He had nothing but high praise for it.[21]

The most liberating theory of all, though the least concerned with actual methods of lyric composition, equates the vocal or verbal imitation of nature with *furor poëticus*.[22] Simply put, this is the "poet's passion" that inspires incantatory lines, songs, or longer odes. Expression commences at the point where ordinary speech breaks into measure, as in a chant. Cadence here is not imposed by art, which directs and composes from the basis of external principle, but asserts itself from within as the poet responds to urgings of a harmony that is inwardly conceived.

Vaughan typically uses the distinction between natural and "arted" styles as a context for exploring and describing an appropriate lyric cadence. In a poem "upon . . . Gondibert," for instance, he sees Davenant's example as saving other poets from the deadly dross of artifice.

> Th' has taught their *Language,* and their love to flow
> Calme as *Rose-leafes,* and coole as Virgin-snow
> . . . .
> Like to the watrie Musick of some Spring,
> Whose pleasant flowings at once *wash* and *sing.*
>
> (*Works,* p. 64)

The waters of the phenomenal world, responding to native impulse just as birds sing and flowers spread and heave toward the sun, provide an incantatory *cantabile* that poetic style can be like, or likened to.

The comparison between poetic cadence and the flowing continuities of water-music, inspired perhaps by mechanical "singing fountains" or, conversely, perhaps inspiring such devices, becomes increasingly popular in mid-century literary commentary.[23] It is given additional dimension in Vaughan's tribute to the French writer Jean Ogier de Gombauld. His prose-romance is described as a "Journall of deep Mysteries" wherein the soul moves on a "Nocturnall Pilgrimage" through dark interior groves and lands of solemn, green shades.[24] The book is praised because the *"matter"* of spiritual pilgrimage is appropriately rendered in a *"stile"* that Vaughan explains by analogy:

> Just so have I known
> Some *Chrystal* Spring, that from the neighbour down
> Deriv'd her birth, in gentle murmurs steal
> To their next Vale, and proudly there reveal
> Her streams in lowder accents, adding still
> More noise and waters to her Channel, till
> At last swoln with Increase she glides along

> The Lawnes and Meadows in a wanton throng
> Of frothy billows, and in one great name
> Swallows the tributary brooks drown'd fame.
>
> *(Works,* p. 49)

The figure of moving waters represents spiritual or psychic life in time. It is the linear, durative mode linking a former unity or composed state (the original "*Chrystal* Spring") with a final, comprehensive harmony—an ocean of forms contained in one element. It is a process of becoming, of assimilating all "tributary" variety, of fulfilling potential. At the beginning, what was fixed becomes volatile. At last, the volatile is reformed and fixed. Caught within this scheme, yet urging and directing it, are (to maintain rhetorical diction) "tropes." These are moments of heightened awareness, billowing waves like insight suddenly perceived and given temporary form. Such moments are recreated in Vaughan's poems by rapt, musical phrases, measured and aurally harmonious lines often reminiscent of an original "lost felicity" and portending the final "supreme immensity."

In retrospect, the work of art resembles a tapestry that is at once the sum of all its parts and, by its symbolic comprehensiveness, more than that mere sum or multiplicity. As Vaughan explains— by compounding his metaphor—nature becomes more than nature, "plot" becomes allegory, what is mutable becomes more lasting, and time approaches eternity,

> for we
> In th' same peece find scatter'd *Philosophie*
> And hidden, disperst truths that folded lye
> In the dark shades of deep *Allegorie,*
> So neatly weav'd, like *Arras,* they descrie
> *Fables* with *Truth, Fancy* with *Historie.*
> So that thou hast in this thy curious mould
> Cast that commended mixture wish'd of old [*utile dulci*]
> Which shall these Contemplations render far
> Lesse mutable, and lasting as their star. . . .
>
> *(Works,* p. 49)

The natural music of Vaughan's own execution, not unlike the style he has been describing, is a curious mixture containing aspects of strict measure—the symbolic, cosmic harmony sought by academic humanists—and aspects of a ranging, expressive, dramatic vocal line as developed by the Italian Camerata or more radically conceived as *furor poëticus,* the antithesis of formal art. It is determined by what is Christlike in man, the spirit, sympathy or "warmth" that joins high with low, what is past with what is to come, and the rational self—otherwise locked in its rocky cell—with the irrational. Its analogues or models are from the book of God's works: the "Misteries of Nature." Theoretically, natural music both moves and composes, "sings" and "washes," pleases and instructs, fitfully toils and continuously anticipates final transformation and completion.

Vaughan can pattern his lyrics in expectation of ultimate metamorphosis, and at times he astonishes the reader, at the end, with portents of new life. "Quickness," for example, is based on the contrast between temporal and eternal life. Of the former,

> Thou art a toylsome Mole, or less
> A moving mist
> But life is, what none can express
> *A quickness, which my God hath kist.*
> (*Works,* p. 538, lines 17–20)

The apostrophe concluding the passage mirrors and contains the sounds of prior lines, yet it exceeds them by a distinct, framing alliteration and firm, final stresses. As a name or definition that exceeds mortal expression, it stands aurally near yet by the italics visually apart from the "moving," preceding lines. As the anxious, hopeful, yet clouded mind waits and watches for some redeeming illumination, so the poet prepares for and sometimes attends moments of heightened awareness by creating a loose, continuous linear network that can pursue and aurally approximate an absolute, invisible truth.

Conversely, Vaughan can draw upon the recollected "music of the spheres" in order to generate a poem. The opening lines of "The World," astonishing to so many readers—

> I saw Eternity the other night
> Like a great *Ring* of pure and endless light
> All calm, as it was bright,

—are set apart from the couplets of the ensuing stanza by the sustained *a* rhyme. The triple rhyme, extending a moment of lucid ascendancy that belongs to no real context whatsoever, is countered by the casual, reflective tone of the lines and by their quiet cadence. The poise and containment of finished iambic meter, toward which these lines lean, is broken by the stresses at the beginning of each line. Vaughan thus achieves a consciously varied rhythm that must move forward in anticipation of balance and completion. Without such urgings and irregularities of the spoken voice, "The World" would be merely an epigram. As it is, the near-sacrosanct clear vision recollected from some "other night" is drawn into motion, to descend and inform more mundane complexities. So the poem continues, drawing upon the form and initial brilliance from which it moves.

> I saw Eternity the other night
> Like a great *Ring* of pure and endless light
>   All calm, as it was bright,
> And round beneath it, Time in hours, days, years
>   Driv'n by the spheres
> Like a vast shadow mov'd, In which the world
>   And all her train were hurl'd. . . .
>   (*Works*, p. 466)

As these lines clearly display, the external design of "The World" is irregular and visually complex. But by extended and attentive listening, a rhythmic underlay similar to that in "Resurrection and Immortality" can be heard. By syllabic scansion the complete stanza reads $10^a\ 10^a\ 6^a\ 10^b\ 4^b\ 10^c\ 6^c\ 10^d\ 4^d\ 10^e\ 4^e\ 11^f\ 5^f\ 10^g\ 4^g$. With the exception of the hyperextended lines of the f couplet, Vaughan again sets ten syllable lines against those of six and four syllables. A variation on this pattern, containing an internal suggestion of its formal origins, is found in "The Morning-watch." In this poem Vaughan achieves a more overt peristaltic rhythm by grouping his shorter lines together.

> O Joyes! Infinite sweetnes! with what flowres
> And shoots of glory, my soul breakes, and buds!
>   All the long houres
>   Of night, and Rest
>   Through the still shrouds
>   Of sleep, and Clouds,
> This Dew fell on my Breast;

> O how it *Blouds*,
> And *Spirits* all my Earth! heark! In what Rings,
> And *Hymning Circulations* the quick world
> Awakes, and sings;
> The rising winds,
> And falling springs,
> Birds, beasts, all things
> Adore him in their kinds
> Thus all is hurl'd
> In sacred *Hymnes,* and *Order,* the great *Chime*
> And *Symphony* of nature. Prayer is
> The world in tune,
> A spirit-voyce,
> And vocall joyes
> Whose *Eccho is* heav'ns blisse.
> O let me climbe. . . .
>   (*Works,* pp. 424–25 lines 1–23)

The pattern of "The Morning-watch" seems to form itself from within—as if Vaughan found his measure after an initial improvisation and then repeated it to sustain the poem. The cause for such an impression is the continuous syntax and pulsing cadence that masters verbal and visual disjunctions so completely that the poem appears to have no line or rhyme scheme and no stanzaic division at all. But, after it has been once repeated, an incredibly challenging eight-line form is discernible: *10^a 10^b 4^a 4^c 4^d 4^d 6^c 4^b.*

The static form of "The Morning-watch," characterized by the now-familiar alternating line lengths and by a dispersed rhyme scheme, may be traced to Renaissance patterns for hymns or metrical psalms.[25] Though there are other possible sources, Vaughan suggests this "cosmic music" by beginning *Silex Scintillans* with a "Preface to the following HYMNS" and, in the lines above, by referring to "*Hymning Circulations*" and "sacred *Hymnes.*" Vaughan is not writing in set hymn form, however. Instead, by drawing measured lines and rhymes into the expansive network of his vocal cadence and syntax, he is writing *upon* the hymn, as if its form were his subject matter. The conventions of words-set-to-music, which can be derived by "seeing through" apparent disproportions of the lines, creates an undersong of symbolic measure shadowing forth, in Sir Thomas Browne's words, "something of Divinity more than the ear discovers."[26] The poem as a whole may be seen as "an Hieroglyphical lesson of the whole World, and Creatures of God," for while the pattern of the hymn is swept into a volatile "*Symphony* of nature," Vaughan's own *naturalis musica mundi* reveals the form it is inspired by, obscurely contains, and ultimately desires to achieve.

Instead of recreating the newly "arted strains" of a psalmodist by fitting his words into conventionally prescribed measures and stanzas, Vaughan fits prosodic conventions to the natural music of his words. Perhaps it is because of this manner of composition that "mistakes" are frequently heard in his verse. As already noticed, two syllables are missing from a line in "Resurrection and Immortality." And a couplet in the opening stanza of "The World" contains one syllable too many in each line. The third division of "The Morning-watch," lines 17–23 above, displays a far more astonishing error. The rhyme scheme formalized in lines 1–8, and repeated again at the end, is *abacddcb*. In the third division, however, the scheme is abbreviated and altered to read *ab(x)ccba*. The *a* rhyme is dispersed by the unrhymed line "The world in tune," and a line has been omitted. In this instance Vaughan's formal irregularity may be understood as a kind of aural emblem. It suggests that prayer, with all its "vocall joyes" and echoes of heaven's bliss, is still of this world and of this imperfect man. And although the poet must *know* the way to perfection—"The world in tune" could have been written "The world in *rhyme*"—he has not attained it and cannot justly represent his morning-watch as equal to the perfect harmony of heaven. Likewise, the "*Symphony* of nature" is (though near) still short of the heavenly model it celebrates. Yet the sweeping progress of Vaughan's poem nearly drowns the "error."

Elsewhere Vaughan argues by demonstration that singularly harsh irregularities of nature can be reformed and harmonized as they are drawn together in consort. So, as the harsh, echoic words in the following passage from "Christs Nativity" are transformed and completed by a chorus of voices—

> Awak, awak! heark, how the' *wood* rings,
> *Winds* whisper, and the busie *springs*
>   A Consort make;
>   Awake, awake!

(*Works*, p. 442)

—Vaughan's initial rhyme scheme is restored in the closing eight lines of "The Morning-watch."

George Herbert provides Vaughan a precedent for the emblematic or thematic use of unrhymed lines and metrical irregularities,[27] and informing both poets' markedly un-English practice may be the harmonic irregularity that is traditionally found in Celtic aural forms. The convention for breaking a harmonic scheme, called *hiraeth* by Welsh musicians and singers, "serves to emphasize a sense of passionate yearning . . . a longing for that which ordinary life can never give."[28] This is precisely the tone underlying Vaughan's ecstatic jubilation in "The Morning-watch." Anticipated by the broken rhyme of line 19, the poem concludes in shrouded, ardent prayer:

> O let me climbe
> When I lye down! The Pious soul by night
> Is like a clouded starre, whose beames though sed
> To shed their light
> Under some Cloud
> Yet are above,
> And shine, and move
> Beyond that mistie shrowd.
> So in my Bed
> That Curtain'd grave, though sleep, like ashes, hide
> My lamp, and life, both shall in thee abide.
>
> (*Works*, p. 425)

Since Vaughan does not acknowledge an interest in rural music and poetry until late in his life,[29] the importance of local lyric traditions for the poetry of *Silex Scintillans* is difficult to determine. It is certain, however, that Vaughan's loose measure and continuous line court musical irregularities and are sufficiently flexible to contain them. The broken rhyme, the hyperextended line, a harsh, grating sound are signs of mortal infirmity that art may "tune" and try to hide. By admitting such faults, breaking the force of affected forms, Vaughan contributes to the various, self-expressive medium that can seek to effect a natural, a true redemption. As the poet instructs his own verse, this process is demonstrated.

> Be dumb course measures, jar no more; to me
> There is no discord, but your harmony.

> False, jugling sounds; a grone well drest, where care
> Moves in disguise, and sighs afflict the air:
> Sorrows in white; griefs tun'd; a sugerd Dosis
> Of Wormwood, and a Deaths-head Crown'd with Roses.
> He weighs not your forc'd accents, who can have
> A lesson plaid him by a winde or wave.
> ....
>   Therefore while the various showers
>   Kill and cure the tender flowers,
>   While the winds refresh the year
>   Now with Clouds, now making clear,
>   Be sure under pains of death
>   To ply both thine eyes and breath.
>   As leafs in Bowers
>   Whisper their hours,
>   And Hermit-wells
>   Drop in their Cells:
> So in sighs and unseen tears
>   Pass thy solitary years,
> And going hence, leave written on some Tree,
> *Sighs make joy sure, and shaking fastens thee.*
>
>   (*Works*, p. 491)

In this example, the measure of Vaughan's opening lines is fractured by the internal stops of the fifth line. In line six, the ten-syllable restraint is broken. The lyric proceeds through eight-, five-, four- and seven-syllable lines to restore its original form at the end. As "*Sighs make joy sure,*" the varied cadence of Vaughan's song portrays its own regeneration from within. By resisting and then rejecting the "sugerd Dosis" of "forc'd accents," Vaughan works through affliction to create a form that contains and cures it. The remedy of nature is performed by such contraries. To complete the process, however, to conclude his poem and thus restore its body, Vaughan must turn to an external text. In this case, a line from Herbert's "Affliction (5)"—"We are the trees, whom shaking fastens more"—is paraphrased and italicized.

Vaughan breaks the pulsing movement of his poem to project an affirmative stasis that answers the complaint of his opening lines and restores their measure. In doing so, he wants the reader to know that his closing text is external—that it comes from somewhere beyond the natural world of winds, waves, showers, wells, and even mortal tears, though these forms can variously transcribe it. The words are from a holy man, and *his* text is the scriptural account of Christ's "way of the cross." The processes of nature and of mortal life, cycles of killing cures, seem to continue in infinite redundancy. But by divine analogy, or rather divine authority, the end and final redemption is made sure. Parallel patterns thus correspond in the final paraphrase. At the same time, Vaughan's music yields in closure to the fundamental measure its natural cadence has drawn upon, broken, and concealed. Vaughan adjourns his solitary incantation by revealing its formal potential and by joining in harmony with a text that can allow him, at least, momentary rest.

[5]
Natural Magic

I cannot allow Poetry to be more Divine in its effects than in its causes, or any Operation produced by it to be more than purely natural, or to deserve any other sort of wonder than those of Musick or of Natural Magick.

—William Temple, *Miscellenia*, 2, "Of Poetry"

Nature . . . is another kind of art, which, insinuating itself immediately into things themselves, and there acting more commandingly upon the matter as an inward principle, does its work easily, cleverly, and silently. Nature is art as it were incorporated and embodied in matter, which doth not act upon it from without mechanically, but from within vitally and magically.

—Ralph Cudworth, *The True Intellectual System of the Universe*, 3: xxxvii, 9.

The forces of nature around me reveal themselves with a mysterious urge.

—Paracelsus

Nature (speaks): God has given me power to resolve the four elements into their quintessence. . . . I resolve them for my own purpose, and thereby bring about all generation. By my heavenly mysteries I produce perfect works, which are justly called miracles. . . . By my virtue and efficacy I make the imperfect perfect, whether it be a metal or a human body. I mix its ingredients. . . . I reconcile opposites, and calm their discord. This is the golden chain which I have linked together of my heavenly virtues and earthly substances.

—John de Meung, *The Hermetic Museum*

"There is Musick in heaven and Musick on the way thither." The proposition was deliberated by Thomas Powell and his young friend Henry Vaughan while Brecon rang with noises of banged mortars, blue aprons, boys, pigs, dogs, and drums. They agreed. There is a music of the stars, an archetypal hymn, implicit in the idea of a coherent though remote cosmology. This is a music that can be inferred (the consequence of movement is sound) but we do not hear it. There is, too, a natural music in the movements of the created world, a sensed display of form in the primitive lives and voices of the creatures or the rhythms of waters flowing as they have from the beginning of time. This can be intuited, as things seen and heard suggest, by certain consistencies or patterns of movement. Standing between, modulated by the sensations and astral wheelings it alone can correlate, is a natural music of the human voice. This is authentic speech-song, arising as the expression of the poet mortally loosed from the inferable world of perfect harmony yet containing a concept of that form—knowing it in a way unverified by mere experience, yet seeking its manifestations in the visible world. Vaughan is always drawing upon, and toward, that mysterious resource, as one is said to be interiorly motivated or responsive to insight.

The poet's response to extraordinary form, the "true Hymn," increases his awareness of the distance between the present and a perfect state. But an affinity, without which there would be no response at all, is also proved. Vaughan, unconvinced of the values or inevitability of an alien perspective, deadened by its remoteness, and compelled by his sense of likeness to another life, releases lyric expression from arbitrary, "arted" rigor and recasts it in patterns that recreate his restless quest for the original, exemplary form of poetry and song—the shape of a life undamaged or redeemed. This is why the primitive forms of life so appeal to Vaughan, and why he claims them as examples. They offer a conception of the world as it was first created, and thus, indirectly, an image of himself in an ideal state. Movement toward that image, or identity, is a creative act inspired by the performance of nature and by the idea of the original creation, the making of the cosmos. Achievement of the ideal would be tantamount to breaking the "Circle of my Cel," the alien solitude enforced by fallen circumstance, and reformation as a new person—the first person, reborn.

Details which have been explored in previous chapters may now converge to preface Vaughan's endeavor. The return to Newton farm, his birthplace, may be reseen not as the defeat of a courtier's ambition but as an unwilled foreshadowing of the inner quest for renewal. Vaughan's dread fascination with the coincidence of thought and deed in physical battle precedes a perspective upon the Creation, when mind and matter, word and world, were one. The poet's decision to become "the Silurist," member of an ancient Celtic tribe, is consistent with a desire to become like those who lived nearer the time of the gods. Vaughan's verbal borrowings, paraphrases, and assimilations signify his desire to bring new life, or presence, to ancient voices that inspire him, ritualize his entrance to their sanctified fellowship, and facilitate his need to create a comprehensive and singular identity by compounding aspects of exemplary personalities. Vaughan's use of others' language may thus be regarded as a manifestation of the quest for rebirth as well as a way to achieve that end. As he can neither deny nor escape the present, he makes the past a part of it. In the company of the dead, their voices and perspectives distinct yet merging with his own, he can reassess, define, express, and in this sense create changes in his own condition.

Vaughan's likely association with the Rosicrucian movement and his early researches in the art of medicine are conducive to the task in another way. The Rosicrucian utopia, we have heard, is a society reformed in a manner analogous to alchemical transmutation. The Brotherhood's vision of global reform is to be accomplished, one may understand by the analogy, by the private metamorphosis, regeneration, or "awakening" of each constituent. Alienation from a former life or culture becomes the first step, the "separation," in an ascetic and radical transformation. At the end, like words in a single poem, all are rejoined. Then, private experience becomes common experience, the basis for a new world order. A secret or invisible "college" becomes the new community. The final poem in *Silex Scintillans,* for a significant example, combines medical, scriptual and pastoral idioms to this effect.

> ... then give thy saints
> That faithful zeal, which neither faints
> Nor wildly burns, but meekly still

> Dares own the truth, and shew the ill.
> Frustrate those cancerous, close arts
> Which cause [dis]solution in all parts
> . . . .
> Incline each hard heart to do good,
> And cement us with thy sons blood,
> That like true sheep, all in one fold
> We may be fed, and one minde hold.[1]

The broad, sociological aspect of Vaughan's theme depends upon a process of transmutation that, though based on a concept of individual reform, cannot be considered an exclusive occurrence, reserved for a chosen few or belonging only to realms of occult dreams, visions, or subconscious urgings. The process should be understood, rather, as a kind of universal law that happens or can happen to all people and all things, though (unlike gravity, for instance) requiring capacities of mind and spirit as well as mere matter for its operation. It is a capacity for health, Vaughan might explain, that can be encouraged in all who will to be well, though only some may be able to understand and transmit the "cure."

"God hath discovered unto us certain secret-natural universals," Vaughan records, "by whose help most Diseases are easily known and cured" (*Works,* p. 579). The operations of these universals (that is, the modes of being they assume and by which they are discovered) occur on several analogous if not identical planes. On one is the process of spiritual regeneration, most often claimed as the "true work" of alchemy and hermetic medicine. On a more immediate and presumably more accessible level is the hidden structure of change in the biological and chemical world, which may be used to comprehend the internal functions of the body. A mediating correlate is the full trajectory of the experience of love. This is the key to health, as love binds higher and lower powers and effects miracles or cures. The regenerate spirit brings health to the body because of its love to do so. The nature of love, which Vaughan knows mainly as it is expressed in the successive and cumulative form of lyric sequences, is therefore transposed to a new key in *Silex Scintillans*—a key traditionally amenable to pastoral themes. Love, as nature's operative, is the instrument of conversion to a true or native state of being.

Natural Magic 105

Vaughan's medical researches provide explicit paradigms for the operations of nature. Verbal diagrams and sequences abound, attempting to define and explain the process of transmutation. But more important, the medical texts exemplify a way of thinking that Vaughan adapts and manifests, both in discrete poems and in the overall dimensions of his book. In the limited sense, analogical patterns of thought typical of the literature Vaughan read and translated permit correlations among rational, emotional and physical pathways to rebirth, new identity and health. In the larger sense, completeness of character is consistently implied as the condition of true health is variously prescribed. Authors like Henry Nolle insist that the "nature of the whole Heaven" and that of the biological and chemical creation *must be* "consentaneous with the nature of man" (*Works*, p. 577). Otherwise, there is no universal law at all, or none that can be "discovered unto us" to relieve estrangement and disease.

The purpose of this final chapter on poetics, the end of a preface to *Silex Scintillans,* is to explore the formal cause of Vaughan's poems in light of a structural common denominator he held as secret, natural, and universal. To do so, it will be necessary to survey, albeit briefly, a tradition that may at first appear extra-literary and therefore beside the point. This is true in the sense that "universal law" is greater than any expression or application of it, and therefore deserves a formula or history independent of specific phenomena derived from or "proving" it. But literature—poetry in this case—is not merely an aspect of the hermetic tradition from which Vaughan's medicine derives. It is *the* "alchemical" medium. Nowhere else is the "philosopher's gold" refined. Nowhere else does a universal medicine, the "jewel much to be wished for and worthy the looking after" (*Works*, p. 578) propound itself. For nowhere else do the mind, spirit, and experience of a man achieve or have a chance of achieving complete expression and being.

Vaughan's "natural magic," first manifest as the perceived world achieves verbal reality, is a serial conception of experience within which disparate responses to change first cease to appear as arbitrary and at last may be comprehended. It is neither a corollary produced by application of prior assumptions (like a "belief in miracles") nor an idiosyncratic taxonomy, but a synthesis of doctrine and empirical detail made possible and rendered by the power of human expression. The world it best explains is the one it imagines and recreates. But this literary reality is bound by a network of necessities and inner workings; a *concept* of these mysteries can at last explain only why things must be as they are—not how they could be otherwise were conditions somehow different, or perfectly consistent with a desired model. The poet, like the alchemist, can make Nature "speak." But she will speak in no way that violates her mode of operation, nor promise what cannot be performed.

Patterns of explanation or expectation in Vaughan's poems arise from nearly visceral responses to or acknowledgments of something directly encountered. As Vaughan's subtitle—*Sacred Poems and private Ejaculations*—suggests, the poems are of two general sorts. "Ejaculatory" poems begin suddenly, with strong, exclamatory or interrogative phrases:

> And do they so? have they a Sense
>   Of ought but Influence?
> Can they their heads lift, and expect,
>   And grone too?
>
> (*Works*, p. 432)

The tensions of experience prior to composition release, with apparent spontaneity, formative questions, speculations, theories, and at other times admonitions, invocations, and thanksgivings. These inevitably produce transformations of the matter or the experience at hand. Other "sacred poems" begin as meditations, with an image or composition of place:

> Sad, purple well! whose bubling eye
> Did first against a Murth'rer cry;
> Whose streams still vocal, still complain
>   Of bloody *Cain*,
> And now at evening are as red
> As in the morning when first shed.
>
> (*Works*, p. 523)

Vaughan's conclusions, in both cases, are typically abrupt. A moral application, a biblical paraphrase or quotation—some form of measured, epigrammatic closing—will most likely be found. Vaughan's endings are attempts to reach a truth that emerges only gradually, with reluctance and pain. His poems, like those in a typical love-sonnet sequence, are largely about failed attempts. But failures caught in the attitude of self-admonition and prayer forge fresh starts.

> Heark, how he doth Invite thee! with what voice
>   Of Love, and sorrow
> He begs, and Calls; *O that in these thy days*
>   Thou knew'st but thy own good!
>   Shall not the Crys of bloud,
> Of Gods own bloud awake thee? He bids beware
>   Of drunknes, surfeits, Care,
> But thou sleep'st on; wher's now thy protestation,
>   Thy Lines, thy Love? Away,
>   Redeem the day,
> The day that gives no observation,
>   Perhaps to morrow.
>
> (*Works,* p. 444)

Guiding the interior progress of Vaughan's poems,[3] shaping his errant, natural music less firmly than a model hymn yet as surely as the spirit hymns inspire, is the secret pattern and lesson of nature, metamorphosis. Its most apparent traces—ranging, shifting observations linked by odd resemblances and driven by a desire for transformation, resolution, and understanding—evolve at times as a variety of exegesis where scriptural meaning is derived from natural phenomena. In "The Proffer," for example, little black insects become "poys'nous, subtile fowls," "the flyes of hell," and finally the "seeds of wickedness" of Matthew 13:25. This series resembles the stages of allegory, where literal figures pass through intermediary stages into tropological forms. Inversely, scriptural images may stand as heuristic analogies for empirical events. The "seers . . . drest in shining white" from Revelation constitute an "immortal shape" to which physical refining or whitening is "conformable." Hence the invocation:

>   . . . then shine and spread
> Thy own bright self over each head,
> And through thy creatures pierce and pass
> Till all becomes thy cloudless glass,
> Transparent as the purest day

> And without blemish or decay,
> Fixt by thy spirit.
> . . . .
> A state agreeing with thy minde,
> A state thy birth and death design'd:
> A state for which thy creatures all
> Travel and groan.
>
> ("L'Envoy," *Works*, p. 542)

Both of these processes are engaged in Renaissance emblem literature that calls for visual examination of an engraving, extrapolation of its "hidden" meaning, and the turning of this sense to a verbal motto or sequent poem, which is frequently followed by scriptural paraphrase or quotation. The verbal or scriptural "design" in turn explains why visual details are what and where they are. This kind of complex reading, which depends on reciprocal relations among different modes of expression and levels of meaning, is like the complete experiencing of an event that Vaughan desires to achieve. The object of initial attention gradually reveals the word or sense that (as far as emblems are concerned) preceded and accounts for its composition. Correspondingly the stone "silex," by natural magic, becomes "cloudless glass." What we first need to know about Vaughan's understanding of natural processes is that he proposes to extend the prospect of literary construction everywhere, as far as he can. To renew is to reclaim—to reclaim, in this case, aspects of the old idea that the world is nature's "book."

Correlations of word and world were commonly encouraged by ecclesiastical tenet and had been important to church practice. Richard Hooker sets the "experiential" stage for Anglican devotion by asserting that "if the natural strength of man's wit may by experience and study attain unto . . . ripeness in the knowledge of things human . . . what reason have we to think but that even in matters divine, the like wits . . . may grow unto much perfection of knowledge? . . . The truth is, that the mind of man desireth evermore to know the truth according to the most infallible certainty which the nature of things can yield. The greatest assurance generally with all men is that which we have by plain aspect and intuitive beholding."[4] Hooker applies this "truth" as a justification for Church ceremonies and ceremonial artifacts:

Now men are edified, when either their understanding is taught somewhat whereof in such actions it behoveth all men to consider, or when their hearts are moved with any affection suitable thereunto; when their minds are in any sort stirred up unto that reverence, devotion, attention, and due regard, which in those cases seemeth requisite. Because therefore unto this purpose not only speech but sundry sensible means besides have always been thought necessary, and especially those means which being object to the eye, the liveliest and the most apprehensive sense of all other, have in that respect seemed the fittest to make a deep and a strong impression.

This periphrastic prose arrives at Hooker's firm pronouncement that "Nature is no sufficient teacher [of] what we should do that we may attain life everlasting. The unsufficiency of the light of Nature" must be supplemented and completed by the light of scripture. The natural strength of man's wit must be "furnished with necessary helps, exercised in Scripture with like diligence, and assisted with the grace of Almighty God."

Hooker would have the impressed spectator, at church or in the world at large, proceed by a far more systematic catechism than Vaughan's. Though the poet would agree as a churchman on the point of human insufficiency, he usually permits the object of his attention to suggest *its own* interpretation instead of relying on external discipline to structure his response. Humbly, yet purposefully, he protests his "attendance upon Nature."[5]

The created world speaks to Vaughan in a way it could not to men who confined it in fixed systems of elements, qualities, humours, causes, or limiting principles an institution may find advantageous to impose. Vaughan does not see objects or creatures as fixed entities, but as active and interacting. Instead of quantified elements he sees vapors, dews, exhalations, sympathies, antipathies, distillations, combustions, corruptions, purifications, and subtly changing colors. He sees nature as a sequence of transformations. The form of his thought is determined by the way he perceives this natural movement. Vaughan's awareness of human nature and its potential and his interpretation of divine nature through scripture are linked analogically, associatively, to these initial responses. By knowing one, the other will be made known. A chain of analogies will naturally and thus necessarily unfold, aiming at a final paraphrase. But in order to see this, one must know how to say it. A grammar for change is requisite. Or, to invert Hooker's priorities, "we [need] not only sundry sensible means, but also speech."

We know that Vaughan's experience with civil and ecclesiastical violence during the 1640s placed him in contact with a "mutabilitie" he considered intolerable. The flux of the material and mortal world, the behavior of "matter" as it is mastered and corrupted by human nature, is clearly a degenerative process. Vaughan nonetheless sought to observe it—if only to isolate rare heroes and momentary virtues—and the dynamics of warfare are conceived in terms of optics: "The nimble *Eye*/Brings th' *Object* to *Conceit*." The language of alchemy is used in *Poems* to resurrect a typically degenerating love story. Lovers unite by means of "influence" and "sympathy," an "influxe" derived from stars untainted by mortal corruption. The poet is thus concerned, well prior to composing *Silex Scintillans,* with ways to talk about processes of corruption and generation.

Vaughan's linguistic choices sound unusual for English poetry, though any reader of Sidney, Fulke Greville, Donne, or Herbert will find the terms familiar enough. The difference lies in the way words are used. Vaughan's usage is less metaphysical and more speculative than that of earlier English poets. Or, to put it another way, the bonds of metaphor are strained and broken as distance between the poet and his subject increases. Vaughan must see something else clearly, and see its nature extended to still more things, in order to reconstruct coherent ground for "metaphorical" equivalence.

> Fair, order'd lights (whose motion without noise
>   Resembles those true Joys
> Whose spring is on that hil where you do grow
>   And we here tast sometimes below,)—
>
> With what exact obedience do you move
>   Now beneath, and now above.
> . . . .
> Musick and mirth (if there be musick here)
>   Take up and tune his year,
> These things are Kin to him, and must be had,
>   Who kneels, or sighs a life is mad.
>
>   ("The Constellation,"
>   *Works,* p. 469)

> Father of lights! what Sunnie seed,
> What glance of day hast thou confin'd
> Into this bird? To all the breed
> This busie Ray thou hast assign'd;
> > Their magnetisme works all night,
> > And dreams of Paradise and light.
> ....
> If such a tincture, such a touch,
> So firm a longing can impowre
> Shall thine own image think it much
> To watch for thy appearing hour?
>
> ("Cock-Crowing," *Works*,
> p. 488)

Vaughan is saying that if certain conditions are fulfilled, if these motions and behaviors are extended and confirmed, then here is what I can see and say of others and of myself. He is profoundly curious about how interrelationships occur, or can be claimed.

Though resemblances, "kinship," and resulting applications are of central importance in these poems, Vaughan means something, literally, by the terms he uses to describe and understand nature's activity. So did earlier Renaissance physicians and naturalists who modified the language they inherited from predecessors living in static, geocentric circumstances. To accomplish the modification, and thus begin to conceive of a world in motion, men like Giambattista della Porta (a favorite of Thomas Powell) turned to the vocabulary of alchemists and magicians. Alert to the dangers of this association, Porta dispels the darker connotations of his youthful science by aligning himself with "the most commendable Divines" and announcing his "detestation of the frauds of Divels and Witches." Then he asserts, "I think that Magick is nothing else but the survey of the whole course of Nature. For, whilst we consider the Heavens, the Stars, the Elements, how they are moved, and how they are changed, by this means we find out the hidden secrecies of living creatures, of plants, of metals, and of their generation and corruption."[6]

Renaissance "natural magic" derives from both the speculative and "the practical part of natural Philosophy, which produceth her effects."[7] Porta surrounds his researches with the detached interests of the Florentine Platonists. Pythagoras,

Plato, Zoroaster, Hermes, Plotinus, and others, newly Christianized or nearly so, form a venerable line of defense as the "magicians" of antiquity whose tenets forge a link between divine and terrestrial nature. If magic is the survey of all nature, writes Porta, it assumes a "knowledge and study of Divine things," for the "divers operations of Nature proceed from the essential forms of things. The form, as it is the most excellent part, so it cometh from a most excellent place; even immediately from the highest heavens, they receiving it from the intelligences, and these from God himself." Everyone knows that God "poured down by heavenly influence upon every thing his own proper form" and "commanded all things to bring forth seed" to regenerate this form from within. Since the Fall, astral intermediaries sustain the regenerative process. As *"Hermes* the learned" said, the stars, the Sun and Moon, issue and sustain the life-force of all things.

Porta constructs an ontology that his actual researches, so prefaced, can neglect. He is most excited by the *how* of things, the observed and imitable effects of divine causes. So one hears how a hen and a pheasant may gender together; how plants are changed, one of them degenerating into the form of another; how to preserve citrons without putrefying; how to extract quicksilver out of lead; how to extract essences out of salts; how to extract tinctures; how to make soap and perfumes; how to make spectacles; how to make water of air; how to part wine from water; or how to make sea-water potable. These "legitimate" investigations of nature are instituted for the practical and cosmetic benefits they may produce.

The brand of natural magic most attractive to Vaughan is identified by one text popular with the Platonists and one practical pursuit—hermetical physic. This synthesis of philosophy and theology, chemistry and medicine was taken far more seriously by its Renaissance propagators than Porta ever considered his book of wonders and natural secrets. Since the physicians claimed new and effective ways for changing the condition of human beings—in addition to animals, vegetables and minerals—hermetical medicine was in trouble most of the time. It was denounced by most traditionalist authorities, especially in England, and even today the name may evoke their imprecations. Literary criticism alone cannot dispel the confusion about Vaughan's Hermeticism. Or, so far, it has not. So, since the coincidence of the poet's medical researches and the composition of *Silex Scintillans* has already been marked as closely as possible, let us consider now the resources of Egyptian hermetic medicine and Renaissance hermetical literature written by Paracelsus and his followers to help account for what Vaughan had in mind when he regarded nature's operations and to help explain how his state of mind could affect both acts of observation and poetic expression.

Vaughan's translations of *Systema Medicinae Hermeticae generale* and *De Generatione* by Henry Nolle (a proudly acknowledged disciple of "the great Father and leader of the *German Philosophers*," Paracelsus) have an ancient and somewhat obscure origin toward which their author directs his readers. Nolle says of his *System* "It is termed *Hermetical Physicke,* because it is grounded upon *Principles* of true *Philosophy,* as the Physick or Hermes was" (*Works,* p. 549). And who was Hermes? "The Father and Prince of all true and loyall Philosophers," and founder of both chemical and medical sciences (*Works,* p. 600).

Nolle is repeating a popular attribution that gains a sense of authority in Clement of Alexandria's "Miscellanies." Clement believed that the Greeks usurped much of their philosophy from Egyptian and Indian "gymnosophists." As a textual ground for his argument, he describes an Egyptian ceremony wherein forty-two books attributed to Hermes are presented. Of these, thirty-six contain the "whole philosophy" of the Egyptians: the hymns to the gods; rules for kings; four books on the stars; principles of hieroglyphics; geography; ceremonies; sacrifices; ten books on the manner of worship; and ten "hieratic" books pertaining to the priesthood. The remaining six books are medical texts, separately treating anatomy, pathology, surgery and surgical instruments, drugs and medications, ophthalmology, and gynecology.[8] Clement's reference has usually been regarded as a fiction. The books he mentions are attributed to a god, and his description of them is insufficiently detailed. Furthermore, Western scholars from the Renaissance until this century have been partial to well-documented Hellenic origins for natural philosophy. Hippocrates and Galen are usually advanced as the early authorities on medicine.

Prior to Clement, Herodotus provides a descriptive account of Egyptian medical practice. "Medicine is practised among them on a plan of separation," he relates. "Each physician treats a single disorder, and no more: thus the country swarms with medical practitioners, some undertaking to cure diseases of the eye, others of the head, others again of the teeth, others of the intestines, and some those which are not local.[9] This information, which is followed by a detailed description of embalming, interestingly corroborates the specialist nature of Egyptian medical art implied in Clement's reference (and anticipates Paracelsus's insistence on medical case-study and Vaughan's accession to "separation" or individualized therapy). It may be appropriate to regard Clement's "Hermes" as the pseudonymous author or authors of a literature concerned with actual practices. This at least was the opinion of Georg Ebers, who believed he had found a papyrus of the hermetic book on drugs and medications mentioned by Clement.[10]

Recent translations of the Ebers papyrus and others reveal that contrary to most prior opinion, the Egyptians maintained "an almost entirely rational approach to medical problems, particularly in the field of surgery, based upon acute clinical observation and the development of sound empirical practice and procedure."[11] But these procedures operated in conjunction with sacred principles received from priests. Early empirical studies were made possible by the belief that nature is sanctified, and thus worthy of investigation. It was accepted that an immaterial force permeates the universe, relating the macrocosm and microcosm: "what is above, is below." This assumption led to a "system of logic based on analogy and similarity, that deduces identity and solidarity between two things from a resemblance of form, or of name, or from some entirely fortuitous allusion."[12] Vegetal and mineral substances were considered marked or "signed" in a way that indicated their essential medical properties. "Magical" cures, such as recommending yellow flowers as a remedy for jaundice, underlie the theoretical law of homeopathy—like cures like—that appears to dominate the Egyptian texts.

Egyptian medical practices were ordained by religious principles. They may have been pursued in association with religious ends. Preservation of the body is of course important in this life, but to Egyptian practitioners the same was true after death. "Just as the physician could by appropriate therapy postpone the destructive power of *wḥdw* [a fecal substance thought to cause internal corruption of the body] during life, so the embalmer by mummification, itself a therapeutic procedure although transcendentally conceived, could prevent physical decay of the body after death. Thus the word *srwḥ* means 'to embalm' in *The Book of the Dead*, but in medical context expresses medical treatment in general."[13] Restoration of the body and preparation for the resurrection of the body become mutually sustaining analogues. Much could be learned about physical structure from embalmers. By observing the process of decomposition, the action of internal diseases could be hypothesized. And the process of restoring a living man to health could reinforce a theology that asserted a "cure" for death.

This specific information on Egyptian hermetical medicine was not directly available to Renaissance scholars. Nor is much of it implicit in the Greek manuscripts translated by Marsilio Ficino and published as the *Pimander* of Hermes Trismegistus in 1471. Nevertheless, and perhaps by no coincidence at all, the rapid growth of interest in the *Hermetica* sponsored by Ficino's Latin translation was followed by a very vocal, problematic, anti-humanist interest in natural magic and hermetical physic. An intellectual climate saturated with idiosyncratic Neo-platonism encouraged the "magical" speculations of Cornelius Agrippa (1486–1535) and his younger contemporary, the staunch adversary of Galen, Philippus Aureolus Theophrastus Bombastus Paracelsus von Hohenheim. Merely saying his name suggests the storm of controversy he created. Paracelsus's interests in natural magic center upon chemistry and medicine—iatrochemistry, or in the author's own neologism, "spagyric" medicine. In this field, Paracelsus considers himself a hermetic physician.[14]

Renaissance humanists like Ficino revived and commented upon the pagan classics of Greece and Rome partly to find literary postulates for human nature derived from experience, not determined by scholastic principle nor deduced from ecclesiastical prescript. Scholastic methodology and the labyrinthine, invisible systems it had created for sacred as well as secular affairs were attacked, ignored, or modified to accommodate new thought, especially that of Plato. For men interested in experiential knowledge and inductive procedures, a dialogue such as the *Timaeus* was of great value. The hermetic texts at first suggested the universality of monotheism. Hermes was, Ficino applauds, "the first to discourse learnedly on God's majesty." Moreover, he foresaw the future judgment and the resurrection of the world.[15] Christianity appears in this context as a world religion, arising naturally from the experience of Egyptians, Greeks, and thus presumably all men.

Renaissance medical theorists like Paracelsus likewise invoked principles from the Neoplatonists and identified their interests with hermetic literature. They did so for reasons similar to those of the humanists. They sought a way out of the rigid determinism imposed by scholastic authority, a way around ecclesiastical dualism that denied value to material existence, and especially a way to amend hellenic medical theory that was governed by the concept of bodily "humours" and cure by "contraries." Generally speaking, Galenic medicine is based on the idea that four internal humours or bodily fluids—blood, phlegm, yellow bile, and black bile—must be kept in harmonious proportion in order to maintain health. The humours correspond to the four elements, are characterized by the four primary qualities of hot, cold, moist, and dry, reside in the four basic parts of the body, and yield four essential temperaments. An excess of one humour, resulting in sickness, may be remedied by application of an opposite. For the excessive heat of fever, apply a medicine with excessively cold properties. Nature is thus predetermined as exasperatingly quantified, simple, self-contained and "contrarious." According to Paracelsus's testimony, more patients were being killed than cured by the indiscriminate application of Galenic remedies.

In order to institute a change in the concept of health and theory of medicine, Paracelsus had to challenge the authority of Hellenic rationalism. The rhetorical force of his writing is aimed at the scholastics. It is wrong, he maintains, to impose mathematical or geometric patterns upon nature and human nature since they have no compelling power over what actually happens. Personal experience, clinical observation, demonstrable proofs from the laboratory, and the "light of Nature" constitute viable grounds for understanding. This argument for empiricism expands to contest philosophical dualism. As Egyptian priests and physicians had done before him, Paracelsus constructs analogies between divine and material worlds that aim at a sanctified and intrinsically dynamic vision of matter. Neoplatonic allies are helpful to him here[16]—Plotinus offers a systematic transition from divine to material existence in the form of a descending emanation or overflow from God; the hermetic books explain that the stars radiate a *logos* to the created world—and Paracelsus's less controversial ally is the book of Genesis. The Spirit moved upon the face of the waters to establish the elements, forces, and faculties of all things; the spirit of life unfolds in matter, perpetuating its initial charge to grow and multiply.

Growth, multiplication, and the generic continuity of living things are accomplished through cycles of transmutation. Paracelsus sees that substances are constantly engaged in a series of changes and renewals. The four standard elements are not fixed, but merge and emerge from one another. To account for this dynamism, and to modify Hellenic medical theory at the same time, three universal substances or principles are introduced from Arabic alchemy—mercury, or the potential of material to vaporize; sulphur, or the power of combustibility and the essence of changeability; and salt, or the principle of fixity and resistance to fire. For Western culture in general, "this was an advance in the limited but important sense that these principles relate to experience and therefore do not demand that nature must of necessity be simple and accord to some rigid scheme."[17] The earliest surviving alchemical texts, those of Zosimos (ca. 300), attribute the triad of vital principles to Hermes.[18] Once again, the interests of early empirical studies and hermetic literature appear to be related.

The "universal substances" designated in alchemical language as nominative categories actually function like gerunds, or emblems that excite an awareness of motion and temporal lines of change. When Paracelsus says "mercury," he sees the quick activity, the glimmering separations and reformations of quicksilver, and the volatile mists rising from the heated substance. He sees metal becoming liquid and then effervescing, becoming transparent. When he says "sulphur," he sees a substance that burns, the burning itself, the flame as it expands, contracts, and changes color, the transforming of one thing into another. When he says "salt," he sees what is left after burning—ashes or a liquid essence. From this he intuits the permanent, durable aspect of all bodies.

The central theme of Paracelsus's writing is the capacity of chemical processes to explain organic processes. On the basis of this comparison he argues that chemically prepared remedies, homeopathically applied, can bring the sick to health. Hellenic theory is thus opposed by the law favored in ancient Egyptian texts: "every like is cured by its like." Vaughan translates the famous recipe as "One wedge drives out another. Venemous bitings are allayd by Venemous Medicines" (*Works,* p. 230). Additionally, Paracelsus will be found maintaining that contrary to Galen, diseases are separate entities entering the body from without, and that internal diseases arise from a fecal substance, "tartar," which should be purged but is not. These particular points,[19] Paracelsus's analogical form of testimony, his examples of embalming as a prototype "conservation" of the body, and his implicit parallels between restoration to health and the resurrection of the body all have much in common with ancient Egyptian medicine.[20]

These distinctive features of hermetical medicine are both systematically portrayed in Paracelsus's writing and "read" as parts of a grand, tripartite paradigm of analogous chemical processes. Specific details produce medical theory only as they excite the unfolding of a universal allegory, the first stage of which is chemical separation. "The principle . . . of all generation was Separation. . . . [The inherent essence or inner 'seed'] of minerals brings each metal to its own nature. . . . Like macerated tincture of silver, so the Great Mystery, by penetrating, reduced everything to its own special essence. With wonderful skill it divided and separated everything, so that each substance was assigned to its own due form."[21]

The second stage has to do with "the Nature of Things" as they move through their life cycles. This durative aspect of the Paracelsian system is broadly formulated as a process of transmutation for all living things. The procedure is suggested by numerous analogies between laboratory observations, related technologies, and organic life. "Transmutation ... takes place when an object loses its own form, and is so changed that it bears no resemblance to its anterior shape, but assumes another guise, another essence, another color, another virtue, another nature or set of properties: as if a metal becomes glass or stone; if stone or wood becomes coal; if clay becomes stone and slate; hide, glue; rag, paper; and many such things."[22] Transmutation apparently follows a positive, or at least a useful pattern. Change is for the good, if the right procedures are observed. For human life, the soul or "astral seed" undergoes gradual changes to emerge from its physical confinement. The sinful body is "purged." Paracelsus's pattern of changes is tentatively set in seven steps, a "ladder of ascent," correlating matter with an astronomical ascendant as with spiritual ascension, which reads: Calcination, Sublimation, Solution, Putrefaction, Distillation, Coagulation, and Tincture. Parts of the scheme may be rearranged as observed data demands, but the beginning and end appear to be constant.

The third stage both completes a cycle and starts it over again. At the level of laboratory experiment, a process of "resuscitation" is advanced by which transmuted or "mortified" metals may be brought back to their original metallic body. The return involves a "heightening," strengthening, or general improvement of the original. If the process of "renovation and restoration" is repeated, whenever signs of deterioration occur or if the first attempts are not altogether successful, the metal becomes better and better.[23] The restoration of metals provides the base for a series of analogies: "To each thing may be again conceded that which had been taken from it and separated in mortification." The death of a man "is nothing else but the end of his day's work, the taking away his air, the evanescence of his balsam, the extinction of his natural light, and the entire separation of his three substances body [salt], soul [sulphur] and spirit [mercury], and the return to his mother's womb. For since the natural earth-born man comes from the earth, the earth, too, will be his mother, into which he must return, and therein lose his earthborn natural flesh, so that at the last day he may be regenerated in a new, a heavenly, a purified flesh, as Christ said to Nicodemus when he came to Him by night."[24] On a cosmic level, the physical universe is destroyed, purged, and all bodily forms are purified and resurrected. The world is thus born anew, and all processes are refined to a final stasis.

Paracelsus is compelled to explain the meaning of chemical and organic transformations. His greatest energy and enthusiasm is to be felt in the chain of analogies, the spontaneous transformations of experience, inevitably following the description of physical properties and mixtures. The observed phenomenon is not an end in itself, but the outer sign of an inner significance that he "alchemically" unleashes. According to Paracelsus, the physician's evolving explanation transpires according to the same "constellation" as the external event. That is, the same stars influence both—and both are "constellated" or pieced together in the same way. As a result of this assumption, a distinctive mode of exposition is required for the Hermeticists to write about mineral and organic distillation in a way that actually imitates the alchemical procedure. A given material, influenced by fire, moves through successive changes in apparent qualities as it is "spiritualized." And the loose, analogical structure of most Paracelsian paragraphs reveals an associative thought process that, urged by the physician's passionate witnessing, moves through similarities toward the comprehension of something quite different from the initial subject or sensory experience.[25] The hermetic epistemology is a series of transitions from one medium to another—from mineral to organic, from organic to human, from human to cosmic, from cosmic to mineral.

Generally speaking, Paracelsus regards observed phenomena as emblems or hieroglyphics that must be deciphered. Just as herbs have no medicinal value unless their "arcana" are distilled, just as quicksilver is no cure (indeed, it is lethal) until it is alchemically prepared, so the physician must move beyond appearances to comprehend the spiritual, essential significance and universal character of any physical event. And patients, the physician's readers, must understand that medicine works inwardly as well as outwardly. They should know the meaning of a medicinal process since the "foreconceit," guided and manifested by the spirit (desire, will), collaborates with the body in effecting a cure.

The association between Renaissance hermetic medicine and ancient Egyptian prototypes here becomes significant, since the tendency to regard natural phenomena as "hieroglyphic" derives importantly from responses to Egyptian traditions and artifacts. Don Cameron Allen traces the history of this view from Diodorus Siculus, Tacitus, Plutarch, Clement, and Plotinus through seventeenth century commentators like Sir Walter Raleigh. He makes a strong case for the popular *Hieroglyphica* of Hor Apollo as a primary contributor to the belief that Egyptian texts depict a kind of natural arcana, a set of pictorial signs containing hidden mysteries that seek to be verbalized.[26] The pictures were supposed to suggest their own proper interpretations, just as the emblems so popular in the Renaissance were contrived to do. Paracelsus's ties with ancient hermetic medicine may not be solely responsible for his view of a mysterious universe, but they clearly reinforce this view. Consequently, "reading into" and explaining an event is the only way to describe it.

Paracelsus insists that his procedures are empirical and exact. Some of his followers, including Henry Vaughan's brother Thomas, maintain the same outlook. Hermetical medicine in England, however, is generally more subdued and cautious in its claims. Aristotle, Hippocrates, and Galen ordinarily are integrated with the iatrochemists, and the scientists' insistence on empiricism is regarded at times with a wholesome scepticism. Sir Thomas Browne, for example, approves "the Philosophy of *Hermes*, that this visible world is but a picture of the invisible,"[27] but his discussion of the way nature's hieroglyphics may be read differs from that of Paracelsus. Browne explains his own empiricism as a relaxing of deterministic logic, as an attentiveness and a willingness to imagine the eventual coherence of nature's often obscure forms.

> I am now content to understand a mystery without a rigid definition in an easie and Platonick description. That allegorical description of *Hermes**, pleaseth me beyond all the Metaphysicall definitions of Divines, where I cannot satisfie my reason, I love to humour my fancy; I had as leive you tell me that *anima est angelus hominis, est Corpus Dei*, as *Entelechia; Lux est umbra Dei*, as *actus perspicui:* where there is an obscurity too deepe for our reason, 'tis good to sit downe

with a description, periphrasis, or adumbration; for by acquainting our reason how unable it is to display the visible and obvious effects of nature, it becomes more humble and submissive unto the subtilties of faith.[28]

Browne abjures the insistent righteousness of scholastic or empiric physicians and favors a contemplative mysticism. His way of understanding is demonstrated by the implied synthesis of the terms *Platonick, Hermetic,* and *allegorical* above. They have different origins and denotations, but he intends the same meaning for all three terms. The definition is not rigid, but loose. It is based upon analogy. The paradoxical "descriptions" that so please Browne—"Light is the shadow of God"—are violations of logic, syllogistic fissions, analogies of an allegorical as opposed to a metaphysical nature. They are not comprehended rationally, but "easily," intuitively, through imaginative rather than rigorously intellective means. For Browne, the effects of nature are circumlocutions that stand in relation to truth as the circumference of a circle relates to its center. Given the circumference, one can imagine the center; it is naturally intuited. Without it, the detail of the circle could not be. Just so, growing plants imply a seed, and the seed implies a vital principle (Paracelsus's "arcanum"). But the last is not to be seen independent of its manifest transformations.

Henry Vaughan's understanding of nature and experience will arrive at Browne's still curious quietude, but I do not believe he would have reached such moments of intellectual candor had not the experience of the medical empiricists been available to him. To find the limitations of the "light of Nature," he must pursue that light. Yet standing between Paracelsus's headlong conviction that he or any sensible man can see the truth of nature's "universals" and England's subdued Paracelsians such as Browne are powerful voices of opposition and precaution. Martin Luther's "doctrine" of original sin and Montaigne's persuasive scepticism, for example, scarcely can be ignored. As Hooker argued, human insufficiency requires the help of scripture. But human depravity, proved on the battlefields of the Continent and England as well, requires a miracle. To truly see, Paracelsus states, a man unencumbered by scholastic falsehood need only look around. But Jacob Boehme later argues, "It behooves the Doctor . . . to study the whole process ... then he may find the universal, provided he be born again of God."²⁹ This provision, and subsequent arguments that the inner and outer work of nature may be delayed, or rendered dubious by the intermittence of divine dispensation, at once make the Paracelsian tradition more appealing—since rebirth is the secret message of many of his treatises³⁰—and diminish its singularly empirical thrust.

Vaughan inherits Paracelsus's hermetical medicine through a number of intermediaries, principally Joseph Quercetanus (or Duchesne), Oswald Croll, and Henry Nolle. The first two appear as prime authorities in Nolle's treatises translated by Vaughan as *Hermetical Physick* and *The Chymists Key*. Nolle evidently adds very little to his sources, except for an unusual confession of his professional troubles with an arrogant, elderly mentor. In transition from Paracelsus to Vaughan, hermetical medicine undergoes a number of changes in detail and specific recipe that are of interest to medical historians.³¹ Of interest to literary study is the persistence of a distinctive style and the insistence of a broad, conceptual framework emerging from and containing the details. The processes of alchemy and theology are overtly intertwined, and consequently we are prepared and encouraged to read descriptions of laboratory procedure as shadowing forth a divine "entelechy." Thomas Tymme, the English translator of Quercetanus's *The Practice of Chymicall and Hermeticall Physick* (1605), prefaces the work as follows:

> It may seeme ... an admirable and new *Paradox,* that *Halchymie* should have concurrence and antiquitie with *Theologie,* the one seeming meere *Humane,* and the other *Divine.* And yet *Moses* ... tels us that the *Spirit of God moved upon the waters* which was an indigested Chaos ... [and] by his Halchymicall Extraction, Separation, Sublimation, and Conjunction, so ordered [the Creation]. ... Moreover, as the omnipotent God hath in the beginning, by his divine wisdom, created the things of the hevens & earth ... to serve the time which he hath appointed: so in the fulnesse & last period of time (which approacheth fast on) the 4 Elements ... having in every of them 2. other Elements, the one putrifying and combustible, the other eternal & incombustible, as the heaven, shall by Gods Halchymie be metamorphosed and changed. For the combustible having in them a corrupt stinking feces, or dross matter, which maketh them subject to corruption, shal in that great & generall refining day, be

> purged through fire: And then God will . . . bring all things to a christalline cleernes, & will also make the 4. Elements perfect, simple, & fixed in themselves, that al things may be reduced to a *Quintessence* of *Eternitie.* Thus . . . you see a *Paradox,* no *Paradox,* & a *Hieroglyphick* plainly deciphered.[32]

We are soon informed that the chemist's salt, sulphur, and mercury correspond to body, soul, and spirit—the elemental, intellectual, and celestial capacities of animals, vegetables and minerals. Within all of this triplicity, and standing as its final cause as well, is the divine Trinity.

A complex, universal metaphor is being composed here that, by accounting for the origin and culmination of all change, engages all processes of nature in a grand teleology. The world's body ultimately will be healed. The proof for this is to be seen in the chemical behavior of nature, which is effected by the chemistry of the creation and portends the last day, and the resurrection. To understand this pattern at a given moment, to see the links sustaining divine guidance of earthly change, one must read the "emblems" of nature aright. Thus Thomas Vaughan introduces *The Chymists Key* by advising that when Nolle "speaks of *Rain,* and *Dew,* I am contented to think he means *something else* then what is vulgarly so called" (*Works,* p. 594). *De Generatione* becomes a work of religious significance if its descriptions are understood as "philosophical figures." Such understanding is achieved, as Henry Vaughan translates, simply by contemplating the minerals, creatures, and other changing figures of the macrocosm:

> Let us (the divine mercy assisting us,) goe directly to the house of wisedome by the light of nature, that by the simple and peaceable contemplation of the creatures, and her operations in them, we may truly discover and describe unto others the perfect manner of generation, and so come not only to the certain knowledge of our selves, but learne also how to produce and prepare out of perfect bodies and substances such a medicine or medicines as will innoxiously and faithfully cure all diseases that are incident to our owne fraile bodies. (*Works,* pp. 602–3)

Vaughan is representing here an argument for empirical certainly, parenthetically aided by divine mercy. The parenthesis becomes a crucial factor in resolving a dilemma created when Hippocrates and Galen enter the Paracelsian context of Nolle's text. According to the hermetic belief, the physician *"must be the servant, not the Master of nature";* but *"according to the sentiment of* Hippocrates *and* Galen, *he must be a profound Philosopher, and expert, or well vers'd in the Art of healing"* (*Works,* p. 580). How can a philosopher, versed in a particular art and trained to think in terms of its precepts, attend the operations of nature as an impartial observer? How can he seek certain knowledge by watching, if he sees what his prior knowledge instructs? Paracelsus had excluded the Hellenic rationalists on these grounds, but Nolle seeks to subdue the problem of acknowledging them with a semantic distinction. "True Philosophy is nothing else, but a Physicall practise or triall . . . he onely is the true Physician, created so by the light of Nature, to whom Nature her selfe hath taught and manifested her proper and genuine operations by Experience" (*Works,* p. 581). This is not what the hellenic doctors mean, though Nolle believes he has glossed the point successfully.

A better synthesis is less articulated than assumed. The observer is part of the world he observes, and it is a part of him. Just as mineral transformations are motivated by inner virtues implanted by celestial power, so "Imagination *is a Star, excited in the firmament of man"* that affects its kindred spiritual faculty, reason. The imagination can be misled, since man's will is free and he is tempted, but the knowledge of "true and perfect medicines" can be received nowhere "but from God, whom we can serve by no other means in this life, but onely by piety" (*Works,* p. 579). The Christian doctor is therefore "inlightened" the same way that nature is. He does not impose his fancy or alien rational structures upon nature in order to read her mysteries. Rather, he is intellectually predisposed to perceive the true forms of nature as they also exist in his mind.

The "Hermetic Phylosophy" advanced by Nolle, having absorbed the rational expertise demanded by hellenic "sentiment" as well as the Christian teleology implicit in Paracelsus and explicit in Tymme's preface to Quercetanus, finally argues that a collaboration of the reason, imagination, and God may effect natural change. The hermetic physician turns to prayer.

Cogitations or thoughts, surpasse the operations of all Elements and Stars: for while we imagine and believe, such a thing shall come to passe, that faith brings the worke about. . . . Our faith that it will be so, makes us imagine so: imagination excites a Star, that Star (by conjunction with Imagination) gives the effect or perfect operation. To believe that there is a medicine which can cure us, gives the spirit of Medicine: that spirit gives the knowledge of it and the Medicine being known, gives health. (*Works,* p. 591)

Such miracles do not violate, but corroborate the law of nature as Vaughan's text portrays it. By asserting the efficacy of prayer, Nolle argues that the mind does not singularly alter the course of matter, but that understanding is a "realizing" only if one wants it to be. The spirit, desire (or that mode of conviction still called faith), is what effects transformations. The hermetic physician, using referential terms to comprehend an external operation, relates that highest ideas or forms excite "stars," and stars effect elemental changes. To derive an internal model, a self-reflexive analogy, read the terms aright. Cogitations, mental shapings of whatever experience, arouse the spirit of a man that, in turn, transforms idea into image or expression—as in the writing of a poem or the exercise of a regimen upon the body. Then, in time, renewal occurs. Expression clarifies and confirms the image. By this enlightenment the concept or prior idea is newly seen, better understood. Understanding thus parallels, succeeds, and precedes the course of actual expression, the one complementing and encouraging the other. The key to this serial operation is the "moving" spirit, nexus of word and world, composed both of form and substance, distinct from both but requiring something to operate by as well as something to operate upon or with. Spirit, in simplest sense, is therefore said to coordinate words and things. In an extended, more complex sense, it shapes one by the other. Capacity for mere reference becomes a genuinely creative act. And that phenomenon, named, is no more than natural magic.

Nolle presents some cases of "imaginative" healing, complementing the psychosomatic diseases he had earlier described as effects of an inflamed imagination, and offers one of the prayers from Oswald Croll's *Basilica Chymica* as an appropriate thanksgiving for the "efficacy of this natural faith" (*Works,* p. 592).[33] The results of these "rare Physical operations" are accepted as perfectly reliable data. In so determining, the

Natural Magic

hermetical physician establishes anticipations of experiential proof for parapsychological theses such as conversion and spiritual regeneration. This is the promise that inspires and haunts the poetry of *Silex Scintillans*. Vaughan anticipates and seeks that "certain knowledge" of himself that comes with the sense of having been touched. His reciprocations are constantly registered as microcosmic analogues to sense awareness. The inner world responds and is known in the same way as the outer.

> How rich, O Lord! how fresh thy visits are!
> 'Twas but Just now my bleak leaves hopeles hung
>   Sullyed with dust and mud;
> Each snarling blast shot through me, and did share
> Their Youth, and beauty, Cold showres nipt, and wrung
>   Their spiciness, and bloud;
> But since thou didst in one sweet glance survey
> Their sad decays, I flourish, and once more
>   Breath all perfumes, and spice.
>
> (*Works*, p. 441)

Key points of doctrine pertaining to future life are likewise subject to the proof, demonstrable in the present, of natural magic. The (truly) miraculous production of glass, among other examples, stands as experiential testimony for the resurrection of the body. Vaughan makes this point in his essay "Man in Darkness, or A Discourse of Death":

1. *For I know that my Redeemer liveth, and that he shall stand at the later day upon the earth.* . . . *Job* 19. 25–27.
2. *Thy dead men shall live, together with my dead body shall they arise.* . . . *Isa.* 26. 19.
3. *Behold (O my people) I will open your graves.* . . . *Ezek.* 37. 12–14.

And thus have we most full and absolute promises from the *divine spirit*, and from *Jesus Christ*, who is the *life of the world*, for the redemption of our bodies. Nor are we left destitute of very clear and inexcusable demonstrations of it in *nature*. We see mortal men when the *body* and *substance* of *vegetables* is consumed in the *fire*, out of their very *ashes* to make *glasse*, which is a very bright and noble *body*, how much more shall the Immortal and Almighty God . . . out of dust and corruption, raise us up incorrupt and glorious bodies? . . . Having then these *prolusions* and strong *proofs* of our *restoration* laid out in *nature*, besides the promise of the *God* of nature . . . let us so dispose of this short time of our sojourning here, that we may with joy and sure comforts expect that day of refreshing. (*Works,* pp. 175–77)

The processes of nature, inspired by and sustaining scriptural doctrine, serve as models for a regeneration of the spirit realizable in this life and physical resurrection in a next. They become, in an exemplary sense, the "Physick" that changes "sick Accessions into setled health."[34] They are "auxiliaries and consentaneous to our nature. Upon which very consideration, that famous principle of the *Hermetists* is grounded: *Every like is cured by its like*" (*Works,* p. 581).

This law of hermetical medicine, as far as Vaughan's own documentation reveals, is I believe the most useful expression of a principle underlying the poet's associative thought and the analogical structure of his poems. Individual lyrics seize upon immediate responses to events and, imitating nature's operation, move to transform transient sense into something durable and new. The capacities of lyric forms are expanded to contain a wide range of associations. "Affliction," for example, runs to forty lines in order to regard "Physick" in five analogous ways: psychological, natural, aesthetic, political, and celestial. "The Bird" requires thirty-two lines to explore the inanimate, the vegetal, the human, and divine implications of a single image. "The Waterfall," in forty lines, separates component parts of an initial hieroglyph—a stream about to cascade, the descending water, rings of water radiating at the base of the fall, the further progress of the stream—in order to discover such inclusive tropes as "a sea of light" and "those Fountains of life, where the Lamb goes." Since the shifting associations of the poems are suggested by the initial subject of each, no precise methodology, no fixed exegesis, applies in all cases. Nor is the length of a poem preestablished.

The precepts and procedures of hermetical medicine affect the form of Vaughan's poems by shaping the way he understands natural metamorphoses. Regeneration, the initial and dominant concern of *Silex Scintillans,* is a natural process; spiritual regeneration is approached and comprehended by drawing upon other and more immediately accessible modes of experience. But the system of analogy providing access to the inner world, bringing the theme of change as restoration, must stand the test of personal experience. Metals can be calcined and revitalized, we are told. The process is demonstrated, and so proved. "O that man could do so!"

> All things here shew him heaven; *Waters* that fall
>   Chide, and fly up; *Mists* of corruptest fome
>   Quit their first beds & mount; trees, herbs, flowers, all
> Strive upwards stil, and point him the way home.
> ....
> All have their *keyes,* and set *ascents;* but man
>   Though he knows these, and hath more of his own,
>   Sleeps at the ladders foot; alas! what can
> These new discoveries do, except they drown?
> ....
> Lord! thou didst put a soul here; If I must
>   Be broke again, for flints will give no fire
>   Without a steel, O let thy power cleer
> Thy gift once more, and grind this flint to dust!
>   (*Works,* pp. 461–62)

Vaughan despairs in his exile, in his separateness. The natural "physick" demonstrated variously in the greater world and discoverable through eyes of the hermetic philosopher affects him only intermittently. Momentary illumination, stirrings of an inner liveliness, are diminished and erased by time and mundane affairs. "Heaven hath less beauty than the dust. . . . And money better musick than the *Spheres."* The question here, put another way, is whether the cosmographic extensions encouraged by Hermeticism and employed to reconstruct nature's original, and therefore eternal, universal operation, have anything to do with an individual seeing himself complete, restored, or for human society to do the same. As the outer "mirror" is gradually reconstructed, as external analogues between one form of life and another are successively revealed, will the inner man be reflected in it? Is there any place for man in the world he can imagine and "alchemically" foster? These questions cannot be idly regarded. Only the complete work, the successive and retrospective experience of *Silex Scintillans,* can answer them.

Vaughan's poems are explorations and transformations of single images, events, scriptural passages, moments of insight or despair; as such, they are complete in themselves. But just as the processes of nature conjoin the lives of all created things, so these discrete entities, moved by a single spirit however volatile and variable, interrelate as parts of a grand design. A gradual yet constant metamorphosis is implicit in the hermetic paradigm. The durative process, the cycle set between Creation and the Last Day, is transmutation. And transmutations are steps to perfection. Vaughan would like this pattern for his "hagiography," *Silex Scintillans*. But since the script must emerge from experience, and his experience is that of a man who loves, the only way for Vaughan to know and confirm his theme, or find his place in a world rendered comprehensible by separations, dissolutions, radical refinements, and restorations, is to let the spirit take him through whatever changes it will. What but this passion could attempt the theme of regeneration, resurrection, and the life of the world to come? "Sure it was *Love,* my Lord; for Love is only stronger far than death" (*Works,* p. 415). Vaughan needs not to be reminded—of I *Corinthians,* 13—that the only work that can be perfected is the work of love.

The pattern of the lover's trial, played against and within the masque of nature's metamorphoses, will determine a sequence for the poems in Vaughan's book.

[6]
Silex Scintillans 1650:
"The Resurrection of the Dead"

I spent a third of the night in great anxiety on a most miserable journey ... and became night-blind on the bare moor; last night it was, on a long winding pitch-black road, like Trystan looking for his white slender love. Many a damp long-backed ridgy field I travelled, toilsome and wide.... The black headland lay dark in front of me, it was perplexing, as if I were locked in a dungeon, when utterly betrayed in battle. [But] The Son of Mary the Virgin, pleasant talisman of faith, does not sleep when it is time for high salvation; He saw how great was Ap Gwilym's plight, and God was merciful, He lit for me the rushlights.... Proud and sudden, the stars came out for me ... their glow was bright as sparks from the bonfires of seven saints ... our Father's sunny paths ... a cause of deep longing.... Praise to the pure light, like a bright path, the clover-flowers on Heaven's face, that came to my aid, though I was so late, like gilded frost, marigolds of the air ... they showed me carefully the valley and the hill.... Before I slept a wink, I came at day-break to my true-love's hall.
— Dafydd ap Gwilym, from *A Celtic Miscellany*

Soule's joy, bend not those morning starres from me,
   Where Vertue is made strong by Beautie's might,
   Where *Love* is chastnesse, Paine doth learne delight,
And Humblenesse growes one with Majestie.
What ever may ensue, ô let me be
   Copartner of the riches of that sight:
   Let not mine eyes be hel-driven from that light:

> O looke, ô shine, ô let me die and see.
>   For though I oft my selfe of them bemone,
>   That through my heart their beamie darts be gone,
> Whose curelesse wounds even now most freshly bleed:
>   Yet since my death-wound is already got,
>   Deare Killer, spare not thy sweet cruell shot:
> A kind of grace it is to slay with speed.
> —Sir Philip Sidney, *Astrophil & Stella*, sonnet 48

> The sun rises when morning comes, the mist rises from the meadows, the dew rises from the clover; but oh, when will my heart arise?
> —Welsh *penillion*, from *A Celtic Miscellany*

> I acknowledge one Baptism, for the remission of sins. And I look for the resurrection of the dead. . . .
> —Nicene Creed

"Moriendo, *revixi*;" by dying, I gain new life. Vaughan's motto: action generates no morbid or redundant response, but magically transforms its subject. Just as one who loves must love, however, the dying man has no alternative but to die. New life, then, is not a counterforce nor a metaphysical option, but what occurs (as a cumulative gain, the result of many recognitions) by the natural, radical act. To perceive this, attend the act. New life is the renaming of a studied dying. As a metaphor or simple linguistic transformation, the naming is inappropriate, impermissible. As a motto, Vaughan's statement is paradoxical. In lyrics the paradox can be celebrated; in lyric meditations the connection between one state and its apparent opposite can be explored. The sequence, *Silex Scintillans*, recreates the entire operation. But we, as readers, must recreate the book.

Vaughan's style and poetic form have been characterized by the making of various compounds and analogies and the transformations produced or attempted by such articulation. These characteristics reveal a serial conception of experience that the poet regards as secret (thereby appearing in proximate forms or sudden intuitions), sanctified, and universal. Whether in reasoning, meditation, or prayer, Vaughan thinks in terms of a physical and spiritual diagram, a cosmos of remote relatedness where lines of correspondence are not clearly drawn but which transpire strangely, quickly, or tortuously transpire. Associations are not fixed, but fluid—subject to change as they create change. As in the expression of Paracelsus and his followers, Vaughan frequently elides the logical subordination required for distinct levels of meaning. The nature of one subject shifts, imperceptively at times, into that of another; past and present merge; analogies that mold perceptions are caught in transitory states and limited by poetic closures that promote, as the poet often prays, a greater design or final "translation." That greater design becomes the subject now.

The disjunctive continuity of a lyric sequence, the tenuous analogy it allows between one experience and another, is essentially and obviously different from narrative and dramatic forms that subordinate variety, multiple possibilities and predicaments, moments of feeling or insight, to place, time, and an uninterrupted plot. Narratives have one beginning and one end. The sequence restarts, regenerates, again and again. It contains as many closings. Narratives necessarily develop an internal consistency or "logic" that prohibits some concerns and insists on others. The sequence is not compelled by the same degree of necessity or causality, and consequently—or potentially—it becomes a far more ranging, universal form. As such it relies on more remote, less immediately constraining schemes. It is hardly random, but judged by narrative standards, or approached in a readerly disposition used to narrative, the sequence is a "deconstruction." Signs of a comprehensive form are there, but the poems have been separated from it—severed from a prior, undifferentiated unity. As the experience represented by the sequence is essentially a transformation of the poet, a recovery of identity and wholeness, the experience of reading for us is a remaking of the comprehensive form, and a reseeing of ourselves in that act and in its final form. The magic, or polemic, of the genre aims at this effect. Step by step, "alchemical" reformation of the individual, according to Vaughan's strange friends the Rosicrucians, is the only reason for writing books.

At any internal point, the sequence maintains a balance or a kind of dialectic between the multiplicity of lyric parts, the trenchant variousness of experience, and the possibility of narrative. There may be a sure and meaningful way to dispose time and change—all that is historical instead of timeless and exclusive. But what is incontestably true, or truly felt at any given moment, must not be distorted or excluded by prejudging or guessing the outcome of a process that is still going on, and then using the guess to shape the occurrence. Each stage of the overall experience, as each day of a life, must be lived through.

On the initial reading, we are likely to focus attention on individual poems. All will be read, but some may appear more important or interesting than others. In a rudimentary sense, the sequence has been seen to serve as a type of "memory theatre" or device for locating important figures and ideas. Frances Yates reminds us that Petrarch, for his *Rime* as well as the *Rerum memorandarum libri,* was cited during the Renaissance as an authority on the art of memory.[1] In this regard, particular poems—or more rightly any remarkable, memorable statement—are of primary significance. The sequence itself is merely a place in and by which such items readily can be recovered. Of merely operative concern, then, are means by which the sequence is constructed.

For Petrarch and his followers, the means of sequential structure could be purely abstract (based on a system of symbolic numbers), calendrical (based on a system of recurrent dates or seasons), liturgical (following events of the church year), and typological or mythical (following the pattern of a prior story or combination of stories, as Petrarch uses Ovid's *Metamorphoses*). For these means to be effective, readers must recognize that key signals in the poetic text relate to systems outside the work itself. Given that recognition, the sequence of the external system, not the internal, various movements of words, will determine the order of the work. As will be seen, calendrical, liturgical, and typological sequences function in *Silex Scintillans.* Vaughan may also be employing a numerological sequence based on a recurring pattern of eight, the number for regeneration or resurrection, but I would be hard pressed to prove it.

The Petrarchan model, however, depends upon narrative and dramatic devices that are integral to the text. Most noticeable is a sustained persona or narrator: lover; star-gazer; or ingenuous spokesman, the poet himself. In the *Rime,* more so than the *Vita Nuova,* and in sequences of the English Petrarchans even more, the lyric persona specifies general kinds of a lover's circumstance. Narrative properties of setting, time and place, become more prominent and consequential to the affairs and aims of the speaker as they are more localized or individualized. Dramatic properties of plot derive from personalized circumstance as the speaker turns from saying "here is what always happens," the effects of which are known or predictable, toward "here is what happened to me," the effects of which require demonstration and explaining. Once sympathy for, or at least interest in the speaker is established, once his initial plight or immediate past is represented, his possible future becomes important. The opening predicament takes on a causal capacity, issuing us into extended time in anticipation of mediate and ultimate effects.

Narrative aspects of the sequence provide properties for a dramaturgy, the representation of an action in which the poet, represented as speaker, is the main actor. If one attempts an account of this action, or even thinks in terms of an evolving story while reading a lyric sequence like *Silex Scintillans,* individual poems cease being, exclusively, poems. Their integrity is being usurped by the idea of a serial operation, a preconception ("I look for the resurrection of the dead") that is sustained by the particulars of the text. For the action to continue in time, or come to life, we can but briefly abide lyric closure. An interval and sequent moment must occur, for without that differentiation all sense of time, movement, and drama is lost. But the aim of dramatic action is resolution, its own new unity, just as the aim of narrative is the reconciliation of all that is separate, different, of all the variety that the telling of a story propagates from a single motive. The sequence, then, represents an action that moves from one kind of unity—limited, alien, and defiant of change— through a separation of parts, multiplicity, then back to unity. It bears a theme of return, recovery, reform. In terms of the subjects of *Silex Scintillans,* the sequence supports a reconciliation of rival political factions, the restoration of the church, the reestablishment of the nation, the recovery of original identity and health by the return to an ancient concord of man, the creation and creator.[2]

The sequence is both a medium for statements of such

broadly ambitious themes and an operation—an act, an arranging, deliberately performed upon the poems—that moves the themes toward resolution. In its operative capacity, however, the sequence calls attention not to ultimate goals, truths, or conclusions, but to the way these are being pursued. The focal interest, as in the case of hermetic medicine, is the efficient cause—the moving spirit.

In retrospect, the basic structure and typology of *Silex Scintillans* can be reduced to a formula. Here is a version, in the idiom of the day, rendered by Oswald Croll and Paracelsus's English translator:

> The best Physicall Method, in order to thy Eternall welfare, is here observed; the maine scope and principall intention being first to rectifie the Archeus [heart/spirit] of the inner Man, that it may attract health from the heavenly Iliaster [source/donor], and distribute the same to all the faculties of thy soul, and members of thy body; then to profligate and chastise the peccant humors of thy outward and naturall man: and all through the Grace of God revealed in the great mysteries of the Incarnation, Life, Death, Resurrection, Ascension, Mediatorship, &c. of our blessed Lord and Redeemer Jesus Christ.[3]

The statement assumes deficiencies. You are not strong, nor in health. You suffer, for the heart is sick, detached. You lack complete being; you are dying. The principal restorative operation is interior: a psychological or spiritual recovery. Then the inner "regeneration" assumes other forms, bringing by a homeopathy or force of analogy health to the physical man whose mission it is to exemplify and further extend the restoration. Recall: Vaughan studied medicine while writing *Silex Scintillans* and then, his book sent out as minister to the inner man, he became a physician. The method is effected by divine grace, manifested in the pattern of Christ's life, death, resurrection, and "mediatorship."

Vaughan's narrative/dramatic sequence is experiential testimony, gradually confirming the formula. The poet's passion and quest are complex, clouded, perplexed by appearances and fears, delayed by a cold and solitary heart that holds, blindly, to static safety. But the heart will beat and move. The man will love, and the trajectory of his passion ultimately mirrors the course of nature's magical resurrection, since both are guided by the same mediator. Both achieve the status of structure by the same typology or schematic concept: "manifest grace."

Edward Thomas was, I believe (and reference to this kindred spirit is too appropriate to overlook), the first reader of *Silex Scintillans* to recognize that Vaughan "did not sever his mistress from the rest of his life."[4] The point is intended generally, for though Vaughan writes of his mistress's (his first wife's) death and composes poems on exemplary women—all in the 1655 Book II—the object of his quest is not expressly she. His aim is a radically new character, the original self redeemed and restored. Yet, perhaps no less than what he sought, it is the capacity to love and to endure that he achieves. As Petrarch petitions Love as a personified, external force, Vaughan overtly addresses the mediating Spirit. For this is the healing, unifying force that can render the seeker strong, at one with himself and his world. What Thomas says is that divisions of love according to its professed objectives are basically impertinent to Vaughan. For him human love "went side by side with the change that put the waterfall's murmurs and the flowers into eternity, and made the rain visibly come from God's hand." There is a common energy and kinetic scheme. So while the affairs of the heart move to fulfill a certain parabola, other forms of change, as they too are explored and exploited, challenge, encourage, and sustain the interior journey.

It begins suddenly, graphically. A bold and stunning engraving on the title page, centering prefatory poems to *Silex Scintillans I*, depicts a stony heart being struck by an arrow-entwined caduceus. The weapon is held by a human hand extended from a bank of clouds. A Latin poem, "Authoris (de se) Emblema"—"The Author's Emblem (of himself)," prefaces the engraving. But the personalized emblem, as the perception and expression of self, depends upon and contains certain prior texts. Vaughan's line "Caro, *Quod fuit ante* Lapis" suggests Ezekiel the prophet (12:19), whose words are not his own: "Thus saith the Lord God . . . I will give them one heart, and I will put a new spirit within you; and I will take the stony heart out of their flesh, and will give them an heart of flesh." The sub-text is essential. Both the Latin poem and Vaughan's "Dedication" address "My God, . . that didst dye for me," and the emblem itself reveals a human, fleshly countenance emerging from the mass of stone. Words of a mysterious divinity, conveyed by an ancient voice, revive, as the heart revives. But details of the emblem suggest other voices as well, modifications of such an original.

Vaughan's saintly mentor George Herbert surely is heard, shading the scriptural promise in versions of his own. The opening poems of "The Church," beginning with "The Altar," convey the popular figure of the heart as stone. And lines 89–95 of "The Sacrifice" resonate in the sense of "The Author's Emblem," lines 6–9. But the arrows of Vaughan's emblem invoke familiar, secular versions of Love's powers turned *apparatus belli*. The figure is virtually obligatory for opening a Petrarchan sequence (cf. *Rime,* sonnet 2). Given this setting, Vaughan's stony heart contains (inverts, "parodies") the unyielding lady of the *rime petrose,* "stony rhymes," whose narcissistic introversion can recreate itself, as in Petrarch's poems, by turning the lover's heart to stone. Vaughan sees his own isolation, his fatigue, his resistance to powers of love and change, in terms of the lady

> ché non la move, se non come petra,
> il dolce tempo che riscalda i colli,
> e che li fa tornar di bianco in verde
> perché li copre di fioretti e d'erba,—
>
> [who is not moved, except as a stone is,
> by the sweet season that warms the hills
> and turns them from white to green
> and clothes them with flowers and grass,—][5]

and against whose defense no mild love will succeed.

Vaughan's *petra,* however, is specifically "Silex"—Latin for flint as well as a common name for the "philosopher's stone" or essential matter,[6] and the caduceus, around which Love's arrows are twined, is the instrument of Hermes. These details extend the sense of the emblem to the realm of natural magic and beyond, to hermetic accounts of the Creation as a type of rebirth or resurrection. The process, as explained in Paracelsus's first *Book of Philosophy Written to the Athenians,* is a separation or distinguishing of unique and original form from the mysterious element that conceals it. A statue, he says, is hidden in the stone or wood from which it will be carved. And

> ... as the statue is not seen till the wast wood be cut away that so it may appear: So is it in the *uncreated mysterie,* that which is fleshly or sensible ... came forth and got to its own form and kind by a right and instituted separation ... not as if a house were built, but as a Physician makes a compound of many vertues, though the matter be but one.[7]

Paracelsus's text goes on to consider the "severall and various chips or fragments" that fall during the cutting. For Vaughan, as the stone is forced to reveal its hidden flesh, these fragments become flames flashing toward heaven, falling tears, manifestations (like the poems to follow) of a heart deeply moved by a force linked to the effector of all creation and scripturally, physically known by an "all-quickning bloud."[8]

A sense of quickness and vitality distinguishes Vaughan's engraving from more ordinary, static postures to be found in seventeenth-century emblem books. Though the "Dedication" considers it a past event, the emblem itself shows an ongoing action, unfinished, vague, a becoming. Likewise, at the end of *Silex Scintillans I* the poem "Begging" indicates that the "work" is not yet done. A second part must ensue. But Vaughan's prefatory material combines scriptural, amatory, and hermetic idioms to create a complex frame of reference for the living present. As in mannerist compositions, the framing is directive.

Visually, endless space surrounding the stony heart (itself suspended by no apparent device) is blocked and shaded to provide lines of perspective. Accompanying verbal contexts are like sight-lines: discrete, yet seeming to converge at a vanishing point of ending or origin. Physically, as represented by hermetic philosophers, "separation" is the first stage in a naturally evolving process that will culminate in a recombining and restoration. Emotionally, love's onslaught leads to stages of disengagement from self, movement toward another, and then return. And scriptural interpreters have regarded regeneration as a serial process. Similar to those above, at least in its initial degrees, regeneration begins with an awakening, an initiation, or in John Milton's term a "renovation" of the heart[9] based upon the law of nature and conceived in terms of natural transformations. Its sacramental counterpart, by Vaughan's association too, is baptism. Comprehension of the event is equivalent to a vision of Creation, and "The Morning-watch" (*Works*, p. 424) celebrates such a revelation. This leads to further, purifying effects of repentance and confession and reaches a penultimate awareness that prior steps of the mediator, phases of the prototype life of Christ, have been traced. A typological and liturgical sequence, moving toward "Easterday" and "The Holy Communion" suddenly becomes apparent. Its aim, through a sacramental merging of seeker and guiding Spirit, is an inner restoration of the man in his original image.

In an extended sense, doctrinally proclaimed, the liturgical and typological sequences look forward to transformations external to any individual life. As Augustine summarizes the scheme,[10] resurrection of the body is to be expected at the end of time if inner regeneration is achieved in time, or in a lifetime. Vaughan's opening poem, "Regeneration," is therefore followed by the series "Death," "Resurrection and Immortality," and "Day of Judgment." As E. C. Pettet has explained,[11] these poems mirror a series of visionary prophecies on the Last Things appearing at the end of *Silex Scintillans, Book II* (1655). But Vaughan's immediate point, as we know, has to do with an experiential analogy—the body's recovery from sickness. The time of his two-volume sequence is the time of an actual twofold transformation: from inner deadness to life; from outer sickness to health. These conditions diminish, realize, and anticipate pledges of the Creed: the resurrection of the dead and new life in the world to come.

A conception of the entire work is established at the onset. Vaughan's point of departure indicates where he will seek to conclude. The text attends the transition, the moving metamorphosis as it occurs, moment by moment, to the first-person hero of his own hagiography.

Unlike George Herbert, who instructs his reader at "The Church-porch" prior to entering the ecclesiastical world of *The Temple*, Vaughan offers no rule for reading and no structural division beyond the prefatory material. Experience will be our guide, as well as his. Vaughan says as much in the preface to his *The Mount of Olives: or, Solitary Devotions:* "I have purposely avoided to leade thee into this little Book with a large discourse of Devotion, what it is, with the severall Heads, Divisions, and sub-divisions of it, all these being but so many fruitless curiosities of School-Divinity, *Cui fumus est pro fundamento*" (*Works,* p. 140). Vaughan would agree with Thomas à Kempis's remark "On the Imitation of Christ": "I would far rather feel contrition than be able to define it."[12] This is not to say, however, that definitions are not forthcoming.

1

We enter the world and time of *Silex Scintillans* in late spring, frosty and chill, on a day eclipsed and dark, as witness to a crime that is not a crime. The paradoxical nature of setting and action is sustained to give "Regeneration" characteristics of a waking dream (or dream of awakening). The speaker, in deliberate yet unplanned violation of mortal and rational norms, breaks into reverie—a mediate level of consciousness allowing him a capacity for errant narrative as well as perspective on images of the innermost self. The poet spies on interior mysteries forbidden by codes of the ordinary and reasonable world. The lover, his senses enlivened by the sights, becomes aware of another.

Eight temptingly emblematic scenes[13] are chronicled in "Regeneration": a road *"Primros'd,* and hung with shade"; a mountainous path; a pair of scales at the mountain's peak; a fresh field; a grove of trees; a fountain; a bank of flowers; and a rushing wind. Of these, the first pair serve, explicitly, to separate manifest nature from the poet's inner nature. Surly "winds and clouds" of sin erect a dark (but aerial, penetrable) barrier between the restorative season, an old-calendar designation that places this new-year narration near Easter, and an interior winter: the modern new year. By traversing the mountainous path and taking some measure of himself at its pinnacle, Vaughan distantly acknowledges a darkness, a coldness, that is not inflicted upon him but is strangely part of himself. The recognition gives him a fresh perspective. Sudden voices call him to new vistas. The ensuing scenes of the poem are only glimpsed briefly, but all belie an alienation pronounced in the opening stanzas. They are all in a way springlike, refreshing;

furthermore, the scenes appear to suggest meanings. Shadowy associations between thoughts and appearances, or between conscious ideas and images of the unconscious, are caught but then attenuated.

At the end of the poem another rushing wind is heard:

> But while I listning sought
> My mind to ease
> By knowing, where 'twas, or where not,
> It whisper'd; *Where I please.*

Vaughan's paraphrase of John 3:8 ("The wind bloweth where it listeth") identifies the mysterious figure as the breath of the Spirit and offers a scriptural analogy for the poem's experience in the story of Nicodemus. Upon hearing the doctrine taught by Jesus—"Except a man be born again, he cannot see the kingdom of God"—the astonished, literal-minded Nicodemus responds: "How can a man be born when he is old? Can he enter the second time into his mother's womb, and be born? . . . How can these things be?" Vaughan is equally puzzled and amazed. His poem is a chronicle of restless curiosity and anticipation. Newness and strangeness are reflected in descriptive terms, especially in verb forms: "Storm'd thus"; "Sigh'd I upwards"; "I wonder'd much." "Regeneration" concludes with a quotation in the sensuous, veiled language of another lover. *"Arise O North, and come thou South-wind, and blow upon my garden, that the spices thereof may flow out"* (Cant. cap. 5, ver. 17).

Vaughan comments upon his failure to understand the lesson or to interpret the mysteries of "Regeneration" in the following poem.

> But as thou sawest that night
> Wee travell'd in, our first attempts
> Were dull, and blind. . . .
>
> ("Death," *Works*, p. 400)

By addressing the reader with his confessed perplexity, Vaughan creates a link between the two poems and begins the narrative sequence with a search motif. This budding drama is given a specific place in "The Search," the sixth poem of *Silex Scintillans I*, which begins:

> 'Tis now cleare day: I see a Rose
> Bud in the bright East, and disclose
> The Pilgrim-Sunne; all night have I
> Spent in a roving Extasie
> To find my Saviour. . . .
>
> (*Works*, p. 405)

The poem proceeds to recapitulate a night-watch that has been completed at the time of this narration—a roving ecstasy wherein the soul awakens from its bodily prison and is released to a new life of meditative searching. The five opening poems preceding "The Search" dramatize and reflect upon soul's nighttime pilgrimage.

The night-watch is a meditational form that Vaughan uses to advance his narrative. But the narrative develops in a spiraling line, repeating and elaborating certain figures, departing from and approaching a central theme; *moriendo, revixi*. As an initial flexion, the form and purpose of the night-watch are more than integral to the total design. In a limited sense, this out-reaching and introspective prayer-form provides a synopsis of *Silex Scintillans I*.

Vaughan derives his idea of the night-watch in part from Jesuit texts. As stated in chapter 2, his "Praise of a Religious Life by *Mathias Casimirus*" represents a version of the watch that stresses illuminating perceptual effects. Further comment particularly applicable to "Regeneration" appears in a translation from the Jesuit Nieremberg's *De Arte Voluntatis*, done during Vaughan's "sicknesse and retirement" and published as "Of Life and Death." Here, the stress is on restorative physical effects.

> As those that travell in rough, uneven mountainous roades are alwaies gasping and weary, which makes them sit down often, to recover their spent breath, and refresh themselves, that having reach'd the brow and crown of the hill, they may walk onwards with more delight, and be at leasure to feed their Eyes with the beauteous prospect, and freshnesse of those green & flowry plaines which lye extended before them: So this troublesome and tumultuous life hath need of death, for its ease and repast, as a state in which it doth repaire and strengthen it selfe against the fair Journey and progresse of eternity . . . life is driven to be sustained by so many deaths, that is to say, the mortal life is necessarily preserved by sleep, which is the usher & *Masquerade* of death. (*Works*, pp. 284–85)

Can one learn about death by the analogy with sleep? Do such restorative effects occur? How? The narrative must portray, test, confirm prior texts.

To effect a separation, the night, death's masque, shrouds the body. The soul, Vaughan continues, watching through this deathlike prolusion, marks its time to slip away. Released from strictly physical demands and confines, the subject moves, not rationally but by a kind of music, through a strange, painful, solitary dissolution characterized by sighs and tears, and modeled upon a hermetic view of nature's magic and a complex scriptural archetype that Vaughan documents in *Solitary Devotions*. The "Admonitions for Morning-Prayer" cite examples of the Saints of the "Primitive Church" who "used to rise at midnight to praise the *Rock of their Salvation with Hymns* and *Spiritual Songs.*" They sang like the Psalmist David, groaning and weeping through the night. And even "*Christ* himself in the day-time taught and preach'd, but continued all night in prayer, sometimes in a Mountain apart, sometimes amongst wild beasts, and sometimes in solitary places." Following these models and an admonition from Chrysostome, Vaughan urges his reader: "When all the world is asleep, thou shouldst watch, weep and pray ... for as the *Dew* which falls by night is most fructifying ... so the tears we shed in the night, make the soul fruitful" (*Works*, p. 143). The development of the watch is almost the equivalent of a healing process. To make it so (in the sense of restoring, regenerating, "making fruitful") Vaughan typically advances an analogy from the world of nature. But does the analogy convey a valid perception?

To return to the first lines of "Regeneration";

> A Ward, and still in bonds, one day
>   I stole abroad,
> It was high-spring, and all the way
>   *Primros'd*, and hung with shade;
> Yet, was it frost within. . . .

The Ward, speaker and actor of the poem, is like the soul still in bondage to the body yet able to make this journey through a strange and furtive release. The action of release, here resembling the sudden entrance to a waking dream, imitates the departure of a vital spirit at the time of death. This gives the act

The Resurrection of the Dead 145

its dangerous characteristics; a radical extension would be suicide. A violation of conscious, critical life is being committed. The circle of rational resistance that alienates the man, confines him to a "cavalier" role of opposing and manipulating nature, is being broken. The break is followed by a kind of collapse, introspection, and then an increasingly energetic, dramatic account of the soul's detachment, ascent, and encounter with vivid, fragmentary scenes. These scenes belong to neither a material nor a mental world, but to an intermediate medium, subtly emblematic and therefore enigmatic.

The initial release is determined neither physically (as actual death) nor mentally (as an act of will). It appears to be caused by a force external to nature, like a blow struck by an unseen adversary. But by the night-watch the release can be prepared for, as sleep is the condition for dreams.

"Regeneration" ends in a petition, "let me die before my death," that sets the stage for the ensuing dramatic dialogues "Death" and "Resurrection and Immortality." Both of these poems maintain the separateness of soul and body characteristic of the night-watch. "Death" is structured as a dialogue between soul and body. This is followed by a debate in which "Soule" instructs "Body" in the spirit that will preserve it after death. It is argued that the spiritual release of the night-watch exists as a proof for eventual bodily regeneration. Therefore, death in a literal sense is not what it appears to be. It is not a destruction, but a recreation.

> And as thou saw'st, I in a thought could goe
>   To heav'n, or Earth below
> To reade some *Starre*, or *Min'rall*, and in State
>   There often sate,
>   So shalt thou then with me
>   (Both wing'd, and free,)
> Rove in that mighty, and eternall light
>   Where no rude shade, or night
> Shall dare approach us; we shall there no more
>   Watch stars, or pore
> Through melancholly clouds, and say
>   *Would it were Day!*
>   (*Works*, p. 402)

Resurrection of the body, promised by the intimate "we" of

these lines, anticipates the subject for the next poem, "Day of Judgement." The text from Daniel 12:13 is set as a link between the two poems: "But go thou thy way untill the end be, for thou shalt rest, and stand up in thy lot, at the end of the dayes." One returns to the night-watch at the end of "Day of Judgement" by means of a quotation from I Peter 4:7—"Now the end of all things is at hand, be you therefore sober, and watching in prayer."

Though Vaughan's dialogue poems are not intensely dramatized, they project a deeply felt conflict. By the body's nightly "death," the soul can be released to seek its Saviour. Since the body must "die" for this to happen, its blood seen as ice and its form reduced to dust, how can it too be born again? The soul answers such questions academically at first— "Nothing can to *Nothing* fall"—and then in the language of the hermetic physician: "thou only fal'st to be refined again." Yet how is such "refining" accomplished? The soul in its meditation can move from heaven to earth, "reading" a star and then mineral matter. Thus, it demonstrates a connection between the spheres of stars and stones of earth. The soul asserts that such a link proves "a preserving spirit doth still pass/Untainted through this Masse." Such is the language of natural philosophy, and it helps to show the way. But the experience of the soul is in fact a release from the demands of the body, so why should it sustain an interest in the affairs of a corpse? Vaughan must fall back on the promise of Judgment Day, the mystery of the Second Coming, to satisfy the questions and fears of the body.

Upon conclusion of the watch, Vaughan assumes the posture of Old Testament prophets, like Daniel, to await the Second Coming as they did the first. But he has less direct assurance than they. The daylight world is like a corpse to him. The spirit has fled; churches, empty houses, show no vital signs. The poem "Religion" reflects on Old Testament documentation of the commerce between God and man. Divinity used to be expressly portended by natural figures; men discovered winged angels in their own tents. Some of the scenes from "Regeneration" are given Old Testament parallels here,[14] but the vitality of this past time and territory now appears lost. The theme of the fallen world, the fallen Church, the corrupt and dying body of nature, is portrayed in an extended metaphor of poisoned waters and relates "Religion," "The Search," "*Isaacs* Marriage," and "The Brittish Church." As the Church has been pillaged and abandoned—it is now "the food of wild boars"—Vaughan's only restorative hope lies in private prayer.

Vaughan's sequence on the effects of the Civil War, the fallen Church and the ransacked, poisoned body of the world develops as an expanding set of analogies generated by the content and debate of the dialogue poems. On the levels of political and ecclesiastical morality, however, one cannot wait until the end of time for the "resurrection of the body," the reuniting of spirit with the manifest world. By this decision the quality of mortal life would be forever damned. The urgency Vaughan feels on this matter is heard in the Body's call to the wandering Soul, 'Come back. Inhabit the sick world and make it well.' As the pilgrim Sun returns at dawn, the night-watch ends and the soul does return, but empty-handed. The Savior has not been found, nor is there any "balsam" for the body's mortal wound.

The body's call for some sign of assurance, some notice of its imminent health, can be satisfactorily answered only if the soul is first cleansed and restored. The soul must move from its own separateness to some coherent unity. It is time "to get thee wings on, and devoutly climbe/Unto thy God." In the "White dayes" of "*Isaacs* Marriage," Genesis 24, the love-struck soul succeeded in this ascent through an active zeal and the accommodation of nature's example.

> Thy soul . . . did flye
> Above the stars, a track unknown, and high,
> And in her piercing flight perfum'd the ayer
> Scatt'ring the *Myrrhe,* and incense of thy pray'r.
> So from *Lahai-roi's* Well some spicie cloud
> Woo'd by the Sun swels up to be his shrowd,
> And from his moist wombe weeps a fragrant showre,
> Which, scatter'd in a thousand pearles, each flowre
> And herb partakes, where having stood awhile
> And something coold the parch'd, and thirstie Isle,
> The thankful Earth unlocks her self, and blends,
> A thousand odours, which (all mixt,) she sends
> Up in one cloud, and so returns the skies
> That dew they lent, a breathing sacrifice.
>   Thus soar'd thy soul. . . .

(*Works*, p. 409)

Vaughan's style demonstrates the meaning of his volatile emblem. Like the sentence that refuses rest, rejecting even the period-stop—"So from *Lahai-roi's* Well ... Thus soar'd thy soul"—to continue its analogy and argument, Vaughan portrays universal health as a continuous process of ascents and descents. The "Marriage of all states" is no fixed or static relationship, but a series of exchanges whereby the restored soul refreshes the body, the body breathes the soul forth on its celestial flight, and "the thankful Earth" lives, dies, and lives.

This process dramatizes the efficacy Vaughan anticipates from his night-watch. To see the scheme in its full effect and in terms familiar to Vaughan, scriptural precedents need to be correlated with another restorative model that is documented in the hermetic books. The night-watch or regenerative dream appears in the first book of Ficino's collection, and was widely known to Renaissance readers—Vaughan included.[15] In "The Pymander" the novice Hermes relates an evening prayer upon his vision of rebirth: "I wrote in my self, the bounty and beneficence of Pimander; and being filled with what I most desired, I was exceeding glad. For the sleep of the Body was the sober Watchfulness of the minde; and the shutting of my eyes the true sight."[16] As a dreamer released to his dream and guided by Pymander (the Mind), Hermes transcended his corporeal bonds. This initial act of the soul's separation is fraught with dualistic pronouncements. The soul seeks a victory of true intelligence over the evils and delusions of the world and the body, just as the lover seeks a perfect, transcendent, and in this fixed sense, unearthly union with his beloved.

To the extent that he sees the world as corrupt and evil, and as his yearning for an ideal love develops, Vaughan is congenial to this version of Platonism that urges abandonment of the material world as a prerequisite for a new spiritual life. His soul's escape is advised by an ominous voice—

> Search well another world; who studies this,
> Travels in Clouds, seeks *Manna,* where none is.
> ("The Search," *Works*, p. 407)

—and the exhortation is heeded on three specific occasions in the early course of *Silex Scintillans.*

The Resurrection of the Dead 149

The second or durative stage of the hermetic watch is described as Hermes asks Pymander to "tell me of the ascent by which men mount; tell me how I may enter the new life." Pymander answers:

> First of all, in the resolution of the material Body, the Body it self is given up to alteration, and the form which it had, becometh invisible; and the idle maners are permitted, and left to the Demon, and the Senses of the Body return into their Fountains, being parts, and again made up into Operations. And Anger and Concupiscence go into the brutish, or unreasonable Nature; and the rest striveth upward by Harmony. And to the first Zone it giveth the power it had of increasing and diminishing; to the second, the machination or plotting of evils, and one effectual deceipt or craft; to the third, the idle deceipt of Concupiscence; to the fourth, the desire of Rule, and unsatiable Ambition; the the fifth, prophane Boldnes, and the head-long rashnes of Confidence; to the sixth, Evil and ineffectual occasions of Riches; and to the seventh Zone, subtile Falshood, always lying in wait; and then being made naked of all the Operations of Harmony, it cometh to the eighth Nature, having its proper power, and singeth praises to the Father with the things that are, and all they that are present rejoyce[17]

This is at once a purgatorial vision of spiritual restoration after death, and the outline of a meditative ascent, through zones representing the spheres of the cosmos, to divine enlightenment. The process is analogous to Paracelsus's observation of matter moving from "calcination" through purifying stages to "tincture" or essential "color."

Hermes instructs his son Tat in the relationship between the above scheme and the doctrine of regeneration in the book "Of Regeneration." "You said that no one can be saved until he has been born again," Tat reminds his father, and requests an explanation of this doctrine. He is ready for the lesson, as he has now alienated himself wholly from the deceptions of the world. Hermes replies, "I would, O Son, that thou also wert gone out of thy self, like them that dream in their sleep." The state of wisdom, the knowledge of Good and of God's omnipresence, is achieved at a distant point where the limits of intellection and manifest nature fuse, at the fixed border of the universe that encloses all the mutable spheres. Here, regeneration comes in the manner of illumination, an understanding of the permanence that is eternal life. Hermes finally teaches his son the hymn "of praise to the Father," to be sung when the incorporeal spirit of the seeker reaches the sphere of stars.[18]

The third stage of the hermetic watch concerns the awakened soul's return to rest within the body. This development is inconsistent with the soul's anticipated union with God and at odds with a literal rendering of some of the hermetic passages. The regenerate soul is victorious over the material body, and should stay that way. But Renaissance readers like Everard and Henry Vaughan's brother Thomas could frequently find their ways around the sometimes vague dualism of the *Hermetica*. For example, a passage from Stobaeus's *Hermetica*, 1. 41.1—

> οὗτός ἐστιν [ὦ τέκνον] ὁ ⟨περὶ⟩ τῆς ἐκεῖσε ὁδοῦ
> ἀγών[ος]· δεῖ γάρ σε, ὦ τέκνον, πρῶτον [τὸ σῶμα [πρὸ τοῦ 15
> τέλους] ἐγκαταλεῖψαι, καὶ] νικῆσαι ⸢τὸν ἐναγώνιον βίον⸣, καὶ
> νικήσαντα, οὕτως ἀνελθεῖν.

—is rendered in the first book of Everard's collection (p. 4) as:

> This is, O Son, the Guide in the way that leads thither; for thou must first forsake the Body before thy end, and get the victory in this Contention and Strifeful life, and when thou hast overcome, return.

The sentence builds to the decisive term ἀνελθεῖν: 'go up,' or 'ascend.' By whatever process of choice or textual corruption, Everard accepts a second meaning, 'go back,' and the sense of the dialogue is rendered ambiguous if not entirely changed. The final step of the enlightened soul no longer appears to be union with God, and a *contemptus mundi*, but return to the world.

Efforts to reform the hermetic scheme are even more apparent in Thomas Vaughan's readings. In his essay "Anthroposophia Theomagica," Thomas treats the hermetic "Pymander" as a parallel to Scripture by relating Genesis—"darkness was upon the face of the deep," and "the Spirit of God moved upon the face of the waters"—with the words of Hermes' guide: "Pymander, informing Trismegistus in the work of creation, tells him the self same thing. 'I am that Light, the Mind, thy God, more ancient than the watery nature which shone forth out of the shadow.' "[20] The "Light" of the original creation, the hermetic God of enlightenment, is then interpreted as the immanent spirit responsible for the regeneration and growth of all things. Personal attainment of this new life is discussed in "Lumine de Lumine."[21] "You ... will be regenerated by water and the Spirit, these two are in all things. They are placed there by God himself, according to that speech of Trismegistus: 'Each thing whatsoever bears within it the seed of its own regeneration.' " The seed, or potential, is brought to life by starlight and dew. "There is not an herb here below but he hath a star in heaven above; and the star strikes him with her beam and says to him: Grow."[22] The star's beam descends to earth in a shroud of dew. The drop of dew, enclosing "star-fire," is the "astral balsam and elemental radical humidity which . . . is restorative of both spirits and bodies."[23] Henry Vaughan recounts the process, in precisely these terms, in his *Solitary Devotions* and in "The Morning-watch."

Thomas Vaughan considers the seed, star, and dew as literal phenomena of a distinctly hieroglyphic character. The seed is a latent capacity within all matter, an inherent idea of regeneration. The star-fire is the spirit of God, enlightening the soul at the pinnacle of its ascent. Dew, related to the primal waters upon which life was created, is the active medium for divine light, a bond between heaven and earth functionally akin to Christ. Through this medium the body may be "touched" with the idea of its own permanence or essential quality, and thus "restored." The philosophical and empirical hermetic traditions are here intertwined to create a hybrid version of the night-watch, a process analogous in its overall pattern to the "chemical allegory" advanced by hermetical physicians. The action of physical dissolution and subsequent refinement of spirit works toward a final restoration of the "mortified" body. Vaughan quotes Paracelsus as an authority on the night-watch,[24] and the poet's understanding of the restorative scheme is undoubtedly colored by his interest in hermetical medicine.

Underlying the hermetic version of the watch, and perhaps the Christian spiritual dream as well, may be an ancient Egyptian ritual known as the "therapeutic dream." This precedent is none too firm; but it is interesting. As Paul Ghalioungui relates:

Egyptians spent, on occasions, one or more nights in the Tem-

> ple.... Sleep, like Death ... was, according to their conception, a reversible state during which the soul delved in the *Nun,* the dwelling of the Dead, as the Sun dives at night in the primordial Ocean.... [the] soul could travel and act.... When sleeping in the Temple, the Egyptian could try and obtain contact with the gods by means of magic formulae, and interrogate them. His principal aims were knowledge of his future, of the dangers that threatened him, and of the evil spells that were following him. But, according to Sauneron, he also sought thereby a cure to his ailments, and the practice of this therapeutic incubation, which is usually attributed to the Greeks and is thought to have been introduced only late in Egypt, was therefore of Egyptian origin. He agrees, in that respect, with Diodorus Siculus who attributes the principle of the healing dream to Isis.[25]

The soul's cure fills the "incubating" body, restoring it to health and providing a genuine, experiential sign of the resurrection to come.

Vaughan, proceeding by devotion and colloquy rather than by magic formulae and interrogation, seeks this very sign and prays for such immediate, healing effects. And if the body can be restored from sickness to health, perhaps the process can effect some analogous change in the body of the world, the body ecclesiastical and politic. On this less personal level (and in terms not quite platonic) we might understand that a "philosopher king" returns to restore and maintain his "republic," not by a man-made term set to his education, but because it is within his nature to do so. The isolated intellect sacrifices its love affair with Truth, since the process promoting its ascent continues in descent. The mortal body is sustained by such cycles, at the expense of static, ideal love.

In outline form, the night-watch begins as preparation for spiritual release. It proceeds in an ascent through purgative "spheres" or stages of enlightenment, the last of which designates a return to the first. This schematic approach to regeneration informs the structural continuity of *Silex Scintillans I* in two ways. It defines and limits the entire book, and it designates intermediate settings or "compositions of place" involving the watch that punctuate the book in its early stages and may be used to frame intervening poems. The theme of regeneration, restoration of spirit and body, man and the world, takes initial shape within this form.

2

The night-watch is brought into focus a second time by a chilling, numbly anticipatory composition of place that stands apart from the main stanza of "The Lampe" (*Works*, p. 410).

> 'Tis dead night round about: Horrour doth creepe
> And move on with the shades; stars nod, and sleepe,
> And through the dark aire spin a firie thread
> Such as doth gild the lazie glow-worms bed.

The admonition *"Watch you therefore, for you know not when the master of the house commeth, at Even, or at mid-night, or at the Cock-crowing, or in the morning,"* Mark 13:35, stands at the end of this poem. We are moving through a second night in which the incipient themes of the fallen world, of social and ecumenical corruption, are personalized.

The initial experience of *Silex Scintillans I* is filled with eager anticipation. There is a dreadful hope of contact with the source of the poet's ardor and a bewildered awe at signs of "the master's" presence. Now dead night and outer horrors isolate the man, again. But Vaughan's scriptural citation reduces and ejects that first, headstrong enthusiasm. The diligence "to watch" is external, unassimilated. Vaughan needs to be cared for and commanded, for even though "The Lampe" and "Man's fall, and Recovery" are poems on his own redemption, their conviction is premature. Their sense of special priviledge is not well founded. Both poems are really about separation. In order to feel redeemed, Vaughan must see himself as unlike other things and other people—unlike the lamp, which will burn out; unlike his Old Testament fathers whose labored pilgrimages he abridges (so he wrongly supposes) in one short leap, on one brief night's excursion.

"Man's fall, and Recovery" is a summarized scriptural calendar and teleology documenting the loss of angels and other intermediaries between heaven and earth. A single "holy one" remains, to whom the poet clings. History becomes a personal statement in this poem. But Vaughan extends his concept of spiritual existence to include a calamitous "fall" only to arrive at the ensuing "Recovery" (notice the capitalization). In this context he appears an alien boy-saint, born in the wrong age and trapped by unfortunate circumstance:

> I'm Cast
> Here under Clouds, where stormes, and tempests blast
> This sully'd flowre
> Rob'd of your Calme, nor can I ever make
> Transplanted thus, one leafe of his t'awake,
> But ev'ry houre
> He sleepes, and droops, and in this drowsie state
> Leaves me a slave to passions, and my fate....
>
> (*Works*, p. 411)

Sins or the "fall," so goes the complaint, are not my fault. For I've been robbed. I am *not being taken care of*.

The first vision of love, an awakening of the senses, has come and gone. Its absence has a disintegrating, regressive effect. Vaughan feels more than ever removed from the assuring calm of his "eternal home," and blasted by the unkind mortal world where he has awakened, transposed. So, he closes himself up. "Man is such a Marygold"[26] that unless the beams of love are always with him, he shuts and hangs his head. The character of Vaughan's love is shy, childlike, subject to rapidly shifting extremes. Dante's testimony (*Vita Nuova,* 12) following Love's greeting is similar and perhaps instructive: "I closed myself in my room where I could lament without being heard; and here, asking pity of the lady of courtesy and calling, 'Love, help your faithful one,' I fell asleep like a little boy crying." Petrarch (*Rime,* #39) sees himself as a child fleeing the rod. No place is far enough away from the one who has dispersed all his senses and then left him, once more, with a heart cold as a stone.

At this stage of the sequence Vaughan feels, likewise, abandoned—"left alone too long,/Amidst the noise." The striking force of love weakens self-control, fragments his sense of character. Who is he—The ward? The soul in flight? The slave to passions? The diligent pilgrim?

> O knit me, that am crumbled dust! The heape
> Is all dispers'd, and cheape;
> Give for a handfull, but a thought
> And it is bought;
> Hadst thou
> Made me a starre, a pearle, or a rain-bow,
> The beames I then had shot
> My light had lessnd not,
> But now,

> I find my selfe the lesse, the more I grow. . . .
> ("Distraction," *Works,* p. 413)

The man reflects on self-disintegration. The poem imitates the form of the collapse. Yet there is direction to this apparent anarchy. Vaughan feels himself receding, growing "lesse," moving in retrograde and inwardly while he circles with petitions and complaints "my hard heart, that's bound up and asleep."

This "retreate" is soon to be acknowledged and meaningfully rendered, but Vaughan approaches self-diminishment, sight of himself as a youth and then as a child, critically and defensively. He knows he should be rational, in control, and quickly delivered from painful solitude and confusion. Who, in all sorrow, would abide such a state? So, the emblematic stony heart is reviewed. The point is to transform it. Stone becomes the rough mountain of "Regeneration;" it could become the hill of "Mirrhe, and Incense" (in "The Brittish Church") where the Lord of love now resides; but it is a subterranean vault to which "Love only can with quick accesse/Unlock the way" ("The Showre," *Works,* p. 412). In "Mount of Olives" the rock is reseen as the sacred hill where the Savior "wept once, walkt whole nights on," and was slain. But the memory of Olivet and Calvary, at this point, releases a sense of abandonment and despair. Here love left the world and whatever call to life the place may traditionally inspire prompts in Vaughan only "sighes and teares" ("The Call," *Works,* p. 416).

Access to love is blocked by the Passion, a mystery that Vaughan conceives as central to his quest. His character of the Redeemer, "To make us more, thou wouldst be lesse" ("The Incarnation, and Passion," *Works,* p. 415), echoes the complaint "I find my selfe the lesse, the more I grow." But the parallel is inexplicit. Less than an analogy, it frames no new perception. The matter is shrouded by self-concern, which must be broken down. At first, Vaughan focuses critical attention on the warfare that has racked the land and Church, which has ended his own youthful hopes and taken the life of his brother. Who ordains the slaughter? Depravity can be externally placed with ease, "But 'twas my sinne that forc'd thy hand," Vaughan murmurs. Then, without pause or lament, comes outrage and rationalization.

Following a legalistic model from Romans 5:18—"As by the offence of one the fault came on all men to condemnation; So by the Righteousness of one, the benefit abounded towards all men to the Justification of life"—Vaughan attempts several times to interpret an act of love as an act of logic. The necessity of reform is treated likewise in this endeavor to form a reasoned understanding of himself.

> Thus hast thou plac'd in mans outside
>   Death to the Common Eye,
> That heaven within him might abide,
>   And close eternitie;
> Hence, youth, and folly (mans first shame,)
>   Are put unto the slaughter,
> And serious thoughts begin to tame
>   The wise-mans-madnes *Laughter*;
> Dull, wretched wormes! that would not keepe
>   Within our first faire bed,
> But out of *Paradise* must creepe
>   For ev'ry foote to tread;
> Yet, had our Pilgrimage bin free,
>   And smooth without a thorne,
> Pleasures had foil'd Eternitie,
>   And *tares* had choakt the *Corne*.
> Thus by the Crosse Salvation runnes....
>   ("Thou that know'st for whom I mourne," *Works*, p. 417)

These lines provide explanations for the loss of an exterior and immediate spiritual presence as well as the loss of innocence and youth. But the mind is barely able to conceal embittered premonitions ("Dull, wretched wormes!") of a more genuine response.

The difficulty here is not one of authority, but of acceptance and conviction. Vaughan tries to understand his dismal state by aligning it to the parable of the sower with his tares and corn. To the same purpose he paraphrases the story of the son whose prodigality was required in order that he desire his home ("The Pursuit," *Works*, p. 414). But these voices of the New Testament way, "by the Crosse Salvation runnes," are less assuring than the image of a calm that lies in "our first faire bed" of the paradise lost. So instead of a chronicle forward in time, as the causally oriented intellect would command, Vaughan is compelled to move backward in a review of his past. The allure is security of conceptive innocence. By an awareness of its continued presence, he might redeem this pure aspect of love. Yet first glances at the fragments of the past record, with lucid sorrow, the frailty of the man at present:

> Yet have I knowne thy slightest things,
> A *feather*, or a *shell*.
> ....
> Yea, I have knowne these shreds out last
> A faire-compacted frame
> And for one *Twenty* we have past
> Almost outlive our name.

The nature of Vaughan's search changes in these poems from "roving ecstasy" to an intense yet tender yearning for an earlier time. The poet seeks to be capable, if not of love, at least of openness and receptivity. There he could be gentle and gently submissive; then he could relieve the cross and pain that present times relentlessly put upon him. The retreat is, however, part of love's plan. Passionate experience calls for this secondary disposition, just as disintegration of the initial man (or matter) prepares for the natural magic of reform. And the archetypal death-which-is-not-death, the Passion of Christ, merges with images of a martyred youth in Vaughan's self-reflecting elegy. As it begins, tears appear from the heart of stone.

> Thou that know'st for whom I mourne,
> And why these teares appear....

By such addition, in the poet's terms, "crumbled dust" may be given form. By one account, the first man thus was made.

3

Serial associations can be sustained only so long, and the reader's problem is knowing when to pause in the course of events. Perhaps for our convenience, but expressly for his own recapitulation and self-appraisal, Vaughan punctuates the lyric continuum a third time in the setting for "Vanity of Spirit" (*Works,* p. 418):

> Quite spent with thoughts I left my Cell, and lay
> Where a shrill spring tun'd to the early day.
>   I beg'd here long, and gron'd to know
>   Who gave the Clouds so brave a bow,
>   Who bent the spheres, and circled in
>   Corruption with this glorious Ring,
>   What is his name, and how I might
>   Descry some part of his great light.

Vaughan's recollection of the recurrent form of his recent experience, linked with natural signs and the image of an imminent sun, creates the figure of a "glorious Ring" that appears here for the first time. A motif, rather than a change of viewpoint or direction, now alerts us to a new movement in the book. The metaphoric values of the ring will be explored in ensuing poems; its inclusive, structural implications are apparent when, six poems away, Vaughan's habitual meditations are performed as "The Morning-watch" and "The Evening-watch."

In the first of these, the rings of morning light are radiantly described. In the companion piece, a dialogue between Body and Soul, Vaughan elaborates on the effect of his symbolic departures and returns. The body, weak and sleepy, asks questions at prayer time. How many hours until day? How long must I sleep until *my* regeneration? In response to the irrelevance of mortal hours, the soul draws a lesson from the figure of a vast and eternal circle analogous to the one portrayed in "The Morning-watch." The circle becomes a "plain watch" that "winds All ages up. . . . The last gasp of time / Is thy First breath, and mans *eternall Prime*." By this analogical magic, the soul argues that we approach Judgment Day in retrograde. Time, in moving forward, is actually circling around to its beginnings; the last day will be the first, and man will return to "Angell-infancy" and the Garden.

The circular figure that enacts the paradox of time's timelessness is given various levels of meaning in the poems preceding "The Evening-watch." The pattern relates to Vaughan's search for childhood, and it is given cosmological dimension in the spheres or rings of the universe. The aim of the seeker is rebirth. If temporal progress is actually circular, Vaughan's continuing search obligingly moves in memory around to the bright innocence of the child, and then further to the physical limit and starting point of creation, the eighth, starry sphere of the cosmos.

The beginnings of this journey, schematized in the hermetic prospectus for the night-watch and falteringly attempted in the opening poems of the book, are encountered in "Vanity of Spirit" and "The Retreate." Prior to introspection, the poet meditates on external places: the creatures, the earth, and the underground "womb" of the world.

> I summon'd nature: peirc'd through all her store,
> Broke up some seales, which none had touch'd before,
>   Her wombe, her bosome, and her head
>   Where all her secrets lay a bed
>   I rifled quite, and having past
>   Through all the Creatures, came at last
>   To search my selfe, where I did find
>   Traces, and sounds of a strange kind.
> ("Vanity of Spirit," *Works*, p. 418)

The movement is from an outer to an inner reality, suggesting the transition from ordinary to an extraordinary, dream-like sensibility of the watch. On an exterior level the search yields only a set of stones covered with undecipherable hieroglyphics—cryptic images on an ancient tomb.[27] Like the scenes in "Regeneration," these stone "creatures of earth's womb" are suggestively meaningful, but their mystery remains undisclosed, *"since in these veyls my Ecclips'd Eye / May not approach thee."* But by the power, or "logic" of hieroglyphic suggestion, Vaughan moves to discover a less darkly mysterious vision of his childhood days in the well-known poem "The Retreate":

> When on some *gilded Cloud*, or *flowre*
> My gazing soul would dwell an houre,
> And in those weaker glories spy
> Some shadows of eternity.
> (*Works*, p. 419)

Premonitory, shadowed sensations of eternal life urge the poet to meditations on death, and on the stars that glow like memories of lost souls and act to inspire and guide the living. In the elegy "Come, come, what doe I here?" Vaughan prays to be entombed like the dead youth he laments,[28] and awake with his spirit in the starry ring. "Midnight" follows as a meditation on the stars. In "Joy of my life!" the eighth sphere of the universe is identified with God's Saints and the youthful soul Vaughan laments to have lost. The star-soul guides the mortal poet—"How in thy absence thou dost steere / Me from above!"—and Vaughan's vision begins to appear as a shadowed Epiphany. The lamented youth is becoming a type of Christ.

In an epitaph to "Midnight," the words of John the Baptist, another of Christ's forerunners, anticipate the process of rebirth: "I indeed baptize you with water unto repentance, but he that commeth after me, is mightier than I, whose shooes I am not worthy to beare, he shall baptize you with the holy Ghost, and with fire" (Matthew 3:11). Vaughan (with the Hermetics) apprehends such fire as celestial. He surveys the stars, in their "watches," and wishes that his soul could be with them, shining with like ardor. He prays to be transformed by these refining flames, but in his present state he will be touched by water only—water descended from the stars and bearing a sign of fire. The unearthly image of burning liquid, blood-red and quick, combines with the natural figures of dew and flowers to create a testament of regenerative growth, "The Morning-watch."

> O Joyes! Infinite sweetnes! With what flowres
> And shoots of glory, my soul breakes, and buds!
>   All the long houres
>   Of night, and Rest
>   Through the still shrouds
>   Of sleep, and Clouds,
> This Dew fell on my Breast;
>   O how it *Blouds*,
> And *Spirits* all my Earth! heark! in what Rings,
> An *Hymning Circulations* the quick world
>   Awakes, and sings. . . .
>
> (*Works*, p. 424)

The morning-watch ecstatically affirms the soul's return from its astral ascent. Illuminated by the sun's first rays, it breaks open like a flower. Then down weeps a dew, also a sacramental figure, to inhabit and "spirit" the sleeping body. Vaughan's imagery here, like that of his engraving, suggests the very first activities in time, the workings of a divine spirit upon primal matter. As the original process of generation inspires this vision of regeneration, a cycle of nature is fulfilled. As the nature and power implied in Christ's first generation—

> I have been
> As far as *Bethlem,* and have seen
> His Inne, and Cradle; Being there
> I met the *Wise-men,* askt them where
> He might be found, or what starre can
> Now point him out. . . .
>
> ("The Search," *Works,* p. 405)

—is now revealed through reference to the "Sun" and to his second birth by baptism, a scriptural pattern is fulfilled.[29]

We have reached the first of two transforming moments in *Silex Scintillans I*; for Vaughan's perception of it, both natural and sacramental rites are necessary. By watchful ascent, the soul is enlightened and the body is refreshed. The "Son" is revealed, and all the world comes to life. The lover, for his symbolic death and ardent climb, is rewarded with a sign and touch of grace. He responds with full assent.

This series of poems is sustained by emotional intensity, metaphoric continuity, the "narrative" of the night-watch, and by a distinctive structural integrity. The sense of ritual made explicit in the "Watches" is implied by consecutive formal repetitions. "Come, come, what doe I here?" and "Midnight" use a rhyme scheme found nowhere else in the book. The first is patterned *ababccdeed,* and in the second this form is expanded by six lines rhymed *ffghhg.* Together, the poems constitute a prayer for second birth, or baptism. "Content," "Joy of my life!" and "The Storm" are all composed in eight-line stanzas rhymed *ababcdcd.* This is a rare form for Vaughan but, significantly, it repeats the stanza of "Regeneration."[30] In "The Morning-watch," the eight-line scheme is varied to read *abacddcb.* It appears that as the first sacrament is approached, as various dimensions of devotional experience are being consolidated by the inclusive figure of the ring and the cyclic pattern of the watch, a latent formal symbolism is likewise stressed. Eight, the number of the cosmic sphere to which the soul in reverie ascends, designates regeneration in traditional numerology.[31] Vaughan appears to be restoring another ancient hieroglyphic, perhaps in hope that the magic of "numbers" will secure the balm he has received and the bond between earth and stars that has come alive to him.

4

Dante sought an explanation of Beatrice through dream visions. Petrarch saw Laura as a pure soul of Paradise to be approached as the soul goes from earth to a star (*Rime*, 28; 109). Sidney devotes a section of his sonnet cycle to Astrophil's nocturnal meditations on Stella (sonnets 30–40), Drummond and Habington both use the dream vision, and Vaughan's own Amoret is momentarily apprehended through celestial influx and sympathy. The vision and touch of a manifest spirit, the object of Vaughan's translated passions, owe something to the sonnet tradition—not only in the general manner of its achievement but also in the particular placing of this episode in the sequence. Following the first encounter with love and the effects of denial and retreat to other subjects—ecclesiastical turmoil for Vaughan; heroic virtue for Sidney; public life for Petrarch; "screens" for Dante—one is led to expect a vision of the Ideal. Vaughan is particularly close to Sidney in the timing of the event, and the affairs that follow it in *Astrophil and Stella* generally anticipate those of *Silex Scintillans I*. There will be a formal attempt to subdue the body and achieve union with the beloved on an ideal or platonic level. The union will be approached and celebrated, but the joy will be of brief duration. Demands of the passions, of the body, will again be heard and will consume the lover's attention. Book I will end upon the plains of earth, but Vaughan has more of the story to tell than Sidney. Like Petrarch, like William Drummond, he will compose a second volume. But let us return to the trials of the first.

"The Morning-watch" contains, as "The Evening-watch" foreshadows, the fulfillment of Vaughan's watchful meditations, but the pattern of his book is not complete by this means. This dawn is not a final truth in itself, but an emblematic event loyal to another still mysterious law of ascents and returns. The emotive yet veiled imagery of the poem projects the imminence of another revelation—the body and blood of Christ—that does not take place. And the structure of the lyric is flawed. An unrhymed line—"The world in tune," line 19—in the complex but otherwise sustained scheme of the poem quietly demonstrates that this earth-bound hymn is but an imperfect echo of another song. And so the poem ends with the soul's petition for cleansing and ascent to the veil of stars, where the true hymn might be listened to and learned. "The Evening-watch" contains a prayer for the body's peaceful rest as it sinks to the dust of earth. This introduces a series of funeral poems, beginning with the elegy "Silence, and stealth of dayes!"

> ... 'tis now
> Since thou art gone,
> Twelve hundred houres, and not a brow
> But Clouds hang on.
> As he that in some Caves thick damp
> Lockt from the light,
> Fixeth a solitary lamp,
> To brave the night
> And walking from his Sun, when past
> That glim'ring Ray
> Cuts through the heavy mists in haste
> Back to his day,
> So o'r fled minutes I retreat
> Unto that hour
> Which shew'd thee last ...
> ....
> I search, and rack my soul to see
> Those beams again. ...
>
> (*Works,* pp. 425–26)

These lines recapitulate the poet's meditative watches and affirm a grim historical occasion for their occurrence. The calendrical sequence of the book is localized by a symbolic reenactment of burial services held on "that hour which shew'd thee last," some fifty days before the time of this narrative. Though the event has a literal significance, its details are obscure. Vaughan may be reflecting on the funeral of his brother William,[32] but as we will see, the death of a child plays an important part in the later development of the book.

Literal detail appears deliberately lost, just as Vaughan's elegies are deliberately untitled. Attention is not to be focussed on the isolated event, but on its symbolic dimension. Vaughan is recreating a myth, which he will imitate in the course of his own transformation. The sequence of symbolic deaths undergone in *Silex Scintillans I* exerts a transformational power over the poet's life, like the power of metaphor over ordinary language.

"Separation" and a fragmenting of identity come first. Three aspects of character, or self-images, ensue: the man of the present; a youth; a child. The self-concern of the man, his desire to control rationally the currents of his inner life, is broken down by an initial kind of dying. Next, as concluded in this series, the young man dies and is interred. Later, the child is gently spirited to heaven. Each of these deaths represents a stage in the interior retreat, a process of losing self-consciousness. The level of violence, at each point, lessens. Reliance on forms of external ritual increases, as if Vaughan were being moved by no conscious act or will. At last, the final and first vestiges of the individual, of remembered and thereby conscious constraint, are gone—when the child is gone. By this, the soul is free of the body, ready to assume the identity of another, ready for transcendent union with the redeemer. By this, the "elemental" self, lying beneath manifest and mutable forms, may be revealed, rejoined, and restored.

Dramatic action is now no longer developed as a matter of intermittent attacks and willful retreats. Vaughan sees himself as becoming part of a process that moves with the inevitability of a ritual. The poems in this series, composed mainly as elegies, reflect the "Order for the Burial of the Dead" from the Book of Common Prayer. As the first rites for burial are followed by a choice of psalms,[33] Vaughan's elegy "Silence, and stealth of dayes!" is followed by three lyric hymns. The Lesson at burial services, taken from I Corinthians 15 beginning with "Christ is risen from the dead, and become the first-fruits of them that slept," is paraphrased in the opening lines of Vaughan's "Buriall":

> O thou! the first fruits of the dead
> And their dark bed,
> When I am cast into that deep
> And senseless sleep. . . .
> (*Works*, p. 427)

As the entire burial service is informed by the death of Christ, these poems surround and contain "The Passion." And the poet concludes his meditation on Romans 8:19, "And do they so?," in the manner of the Collect for the burial of the dead.

Within this liturgical atmosphere and scheme, Vaughan contests the idea of a strict separation of soul from body with his awareness of a sympathetic tie that renders such division, however desirable, impossible. The poet, seeing his own death as he reflects upon another's interment, projects himself into a choir of souls and stars in "Church-Service": "O how in thy Quire of Souls I stand . . . A heap of sand!" The exclamation is worthy of the thought's remote fantasy. A body (let alone my own) moved to that celestial place? The body is interred, dissolving—"It is (in truth!) a ruin'd peece. . . . And scarce a room but wind, and rain beat through." The hermetic physician would remind us that "essences released in dissolution return to tangible forms after they are refined." Such is the nature of "sublimation." The churchman would nod acknowledgment that the body has received the balm that will preserve it. Vaughan adds the prayer:

> Thou great Preserver of all men!
>   Watch o're that loose
>   And empty house,
> Which I sometimes liv'd in.
>   (From "Buriall," *Works*, p. 427)

The body, dust in the tomb of the world, groans for its redemption. The unbodied spirit, buoyed by an effective yet transitory "breath" of guidance from a vital God, ascends and moves as a star. The poet relives the experience in "Chearfulnes":

> Lord, with what courage, and delight
>   I doe each thing
> When thy least breath sustains my wing!
>   I shine, and move
>   Like those above. . . .
>   (*Works*, p. 428)

In the manner of the hermetic seeker, himself an idealistic lover, Vaughan cries for his own translation: "O that I were all Soul! that thou / Wouldst make each part / Of this poor, sinful frame pure heart! / Then would I . . . A Consort raise / Of Hallelujahs" and dream of the country beyond the stars, that angelic territory of the hymn "Peace," which follows. The poet clearly wishes to transcend forever the corpse he has gently but firmly buried. He wants to die, thus to love. But as the Martyr's blood, transformed to dew, distilled to tears, has already descended from this land beyond the universe, so the dreamed projections of the soul begin their inevitable descent in "The Passion"—

> I would I were
> One hearty tear!
> One constant spring!

—toward a terrestrial end in "And do they so?":

> I would I were a stone, or tree
>   Or flowre by pedigree,
> Or some poor high-way herb, or Spring
>   To flow, or bird to sing!

As quickening influence fills the lives of the creatures, drawing them toward its common source and end, so the mortal life of the poet undergoes another awakening. This time it will lead to ethical reform under the guidance of an enlightenment descended from stars, the shining dead, and "spiriting" within him now.

Vaughan's prayers and hymns on the death of the body and the resurrection of the spirit, framed by the "Church-Service" for burial of the dead, offer additional certainty to the liaison and lesson of "The Morning-watch." Vaughan returns to mortal wakefulness sure that "there's a tye of Bodyes!" Those who are unenlightened will dissolve, spirit and body, to clay. Their love will languish, self-centered and unfulfilled, "for things thus *Center'd*, without *Beames*, or *Action* / Nor give, nor take Contaction." But Vaughan, struggling here to express mercurial associations, sees that

> Absents within the Line Conspire, and *Sense*
>   Things distant doth unite,
> Herbs sleep unto the East, and some fowles thence
>   Watch the Returns of light....
>
> (*Works*, p. 429).

These lines explain a native responsiveness to light by a "sense" or spirit presence that circulates through the creation, engaging creatures above and minerals below the earth's surface in watchful anticipation of transformations to come. But there is more to this activity than simple waiting. The creatures are actually growing in health and self-fulfillment. As William Harvey writes, apropos of Vaughan's appraisal of vital "circulations": "In as much as it [the blood] is a *Spirit,* so it is the *Fire* . . . the *Sun* of the *Microcosme,* and *Platoes Fire:* not because (like ordinary fire) it *shineth, burneth,* and *destroyeth:* but because it doth *conserve, nourish,* and *encrease it self,* by a free perpetuall motion."[34] Plato's fire, nature's regenerating balsam, sets an example that is clear to Vaughan. But he is too overcome with ardor and anxiety to participate in such terrestrial ideas. No more delays, Vaughan cries, "O brook it not! thy bloud is mine, And my soul should be thine" (*Works,* p. 433). He will school himself like a saint and die for his beloved. He wills to burn, and shine.

5

Vaughan has done with "watching." In "The Relapse," "The Resolve," "The Match," and "Rules *and* Lessons" (*Works,* pp. 433–39), he adopts a more positive, active role in the divine love story unfolding about and within him. Experience thus far has convinced him of an immanent spirit inscribing nature's transmutations with purposeful form. Inspired by this example, drawn in by sacramental overtures, he moves from witness to participant in the metamorphoses of "The Morning-watch." Vaughan now makes positive identification of the immanent urgency he then felt by introducing the figure of a divine grain or seed.

>   . . . let this grain which here in tears I sow
>   Though *dead,* and *sick,*
>   Through thy *Increase* grow *new,* and *quick.*
>   ("The Match," *Works,* p. 435)

The seed thus sown, Vaughan will nourish it with resolutions, "Rules *and* Lessons." He will draw out the lesson of nature and quicken it toward the end.

Past experiences tighten into aphoristic antidotes for all relapses, "sullen, and sad Ecclipses," which dim the poet's sight and halt his progress. Vaughan makes "The Resolve," coldly honest, to follow the "ancient way" and "narrow path": "Tell youth, and beauty they must rot, / They'r but a *Case.*" With new-found austerity he renounces his secular poetry. The follies of youth become pure poison, and a pact is made with a "Dear friend," George Herbert, whose "ever living lines / Have done much good / to many, and have checkt my blood, / My fierce, wild blood that still heeaves, and inclines, / But is still tam'd" (*Works*, p. 434).

Control, rigid discipline, is the lesson Vaughan draws from Herbert's example, and this sequence of poems shows the model clearly. "Rules *and* Lessons" is based on Herbert's "The Church-Porch," and by its set of sometimes inspired, sometimes harsh admonitions, Vaughan shapes the processes of nature with catechistic imperative and design.

> When first thy Eies unveil, give thy Soul leave
> To do the like; our Bodies but forerun
> The spirits duty; True hearts spread, and heave
> Unto their God, as flow'rs do to the Sun.
> ....
> Walk with thy fellow-creatures: note the *hush*
> And *whispers* amongst them. There's not a *Spring,*
> Or *Leafe* but hath his *Morning-hymn;* Each *Bush*
> And *Oak* doth know I AM; canst thou not sing?
> ....
> *Mornings* are *Mysteries;* the first worlds *Youth,*
> Mans *Resurrection,* and the futures *Bud*
> Shrowd in their births: The Crown of life, light, truth
> Is stil'd their *starre,* the *stone,* and *hidden food.*
> ....
> To highten thy *Devotions,* and keep low
> All mutinous thoughts, what business e'r thou hast
> Observe God in his works; here *fountains* flow,
> *Birds* sing, *Beasts* feed, *Fish* leap, and th'*Earth* stands fast;
>   Above are restles *motions,* running *Lights,*
>   Vast Circling *Azure,* giddy *Clouds,* days, nights.
>
> When *Seasons* change, then lay before thine Eys
> His wondrous *Method;* mark the various *Scenes*
> In heav'n; *Hail, Thunder, Rain-bows, Snow,* and *Ice,*
> *Calmes, Tempests, Light,* and *darkness* by his means;
>   Thou canst not misse his Praise; Each *tree, herb, flowre*
>   Are shadows of his *wisedome,* and his pow'r.
>   (*Works*, pp. 436–38)

As earth "stands fast," all creatures imitate the restless celestial motions, the running lights of heaven, by striving to overleap themselves. An innate chemistry, perceived in the bonds of analogy, drives all life toward a resurrection.

As Vaughan's own spirit-seed is nourished by forerunning examples of volatile duty, the torments of the body are acknowledged, admonished, and abandoned to steadfast darkness. The poem "Corruption" (*Works,* p. 440) recounts the bleak journey of earthly man, away from Eden, through Old Testament times when *"Paradise* lay / In some green shade, or fountain," to the brutal present where, loveless, "mad man / Sits down and freezeth on":

> He raves, and swears to stir nor fire, nor fan,
> But bids the thread be spun.
> I see, thy Curtains are Close-drawn; Thy bow
> Looks dim too in the Cloud,
> Sin triumphs still, and man is sunk below
> The Center, and his shrowd;
> All's in deep sleep, and night; Thick darknes lyes
> And hatcheth o'r thy people. . . .

Beneath the range of references captured by these lines—the curtain/veil drawn between heaven and earth; the rainbow/sign of deliverance now remote—the body sinks like a weight. Man, like some excrescence fallen below the "Center" of the universe, rages in idleness and curses in his sleep.[35] The resolved soul, now in the course of its purgation, will have none of this.

In the poem "Holy Scriptures," where "souls are hatch'd unto Eternitie," Vaughan seeks means for utter transcendence. Here lies the life of Christ, the "Key that opens to all Mysteries," waiting to be read and tracked. Had I each line inscribed in my heart, Vaughan suggests, I would write that book over again instead of these poems. As it is, he assimilates bright fragments, words and phrases, other voices, and by them he will translate himself. Disembodied, he would become the Word.

From the distance of prose commentary on his poetic accomplishment, Vaughan considers the pattern of his private experience as a "kinde of hagiography" (*Works,* p. 392) and as an ethical model for others. He addresses the matter in *Solitary Devotions:* "Neither did I thinke it necessary that the ordinary instructions for a regular life (of which theere are infinite Volumes already extant) should be inserted into this small Manuall, lest instead of Devotion, I should trouble thee with a peece of Ethics. Besides, thou hast them already as briefly delivered as possibly I could, in my *Sacred Poems*."[36] As L. C. Martin and others have noted, Vaughan may be referring here to the not-so-briefly delivered poem "Rules *and* Lessons." He may also have in mind the self-admonitions on everyday piety and ethics of a churchman without a church that appear after this sequence of resolves.[37] Private administration of the Eucharist, for example, is an issue in "Dressing" (*Works,* p. 456)—

> Give me, my God! thy grace,
> The beams, and brightnes of thy face,
>   That never like a beast
>   I take thy sacred feast,
> Or the dread mysteries of thy blest bloud
> Use, with like Custome, as my Kitchin food.

—and "The Law, and the Gospel" (*Works,* p. 466):

> Let me not spil, but drink thy bloud,
> Not break thy fence, and by a black Excess
> Force down a Just Curse, when thy hands would bless;
> Let me not scatter, and despise my food,
>   Or nail those blessed limbs again
>   Which bore my pain;
> So Shall thy mercies flow: for while I fear,
>   I know, thou'lt bear,
> But should thy mild Injunction nothing move me,
> I would both think, and Judge I did not love thee.
>   John Cap. 14. ver. 15.
> *If ye love me, keep my Commandements.*

Lines and references such as these make it clear that Vaughan seeks the ethically exemplary life he represents, through self-advisement, to others. Like his friend Thomas Powell, whose *Four General Heads of Christian Religion Surveyed & Explained* (1657) was being prepared at the same time as *Silex Scintillans,* Vaughan holds "Catechistical exercises" to be an "Architectonical Science, the Art of saving souls," based upon the universal

The Resurrection of the Dead 171

foundations of the Creed, the Commandments, the Lords Prayer, and the Sacraments.[38] But the crucial difference between the catechist and the poet lies in how a new life is comprehended. While Powell authorizes "frequent use of the Lords Supper" as the means to enforce "our watch; to descend to that most usefull and necessary duty of self-examination, or searching our own bosoms,"[39] Vaughan's sequence portrays self-examination, the search and the "watch" as necessary precedents to any significant ritual communion.

The matter of priorities here is, as we know, of vital importance to interregnum religious and political factions. I have remarked that Vaughan's prose expression often resembles the speech of itinerent Independents like Cradock, Vavasor Powell, and Fox. Now, he appears to be employing liturgical forms as the Independents used scriptural paraphrase—as a way of expressing and communicating inner experience, not as a way to enforce or predict it.

The host of "Manualls" printed during the interregnum, when the Anglican catechism was outlawed, in effect legislate against experience. Their authors (including Thomas Powell and to a lesser extent Vaughan in his *Solitary Devotions*) seek to impose forms of behavior, and then argue the reality of the forms by contrasting their exemplary products with only the most lamentable actions of unredeemed humanity. Empirical reality is said to be prescribed by Christian ethics. Behavior that errs from these bounds is unreal, mutable, yet capable of submitting to reform. It is wrong to say that Vaughan would dispute this last condition, but it is just as wrong to forget that in the poet's view the world moves neither errantly, ethically, nor logically, but magically. For Vaughan, rules, lessons, and liturgical rites are the desired consequence of native experience and natural example. One reforms character, not behavior. And reform is not caused by institutional or social rules or rituals, but by the mediating spirit within the heart.

Just as Vaughan reveals a thorough schooling in "Catechistical exercises," however, he clearly acknowledges and thinks in terms of a metaphysical diagram that distinguishes the unreal from the real, physical from the idea, this world from the next. And since in this series of poems he moves to dismiss the former in order to achieve the latter, the furthest reaches of that diagram must be represented more explicitly. To extend himself that far, to fully imagine death and transformation, mysterious images (the dew, the ring) must be sharpened and defined by a more comprehensible language and scheme. On one level of consciousness the man is preparing for a public, sacramental rite. On another, a strange, unearthly "grain" is sown in the private soil of the body. Effecting both of these activities, though, is an inner demand (no longer mere desire) for consummate love and transfiguration. Vaughan requires to be enthralled by another who exists for him in the hieroglyphics of his inner nature, then as the perpetrator of his resolutions, and next as the man-god revealed.

It may be useful to reconstruct this progress in terms of a typological sequence. The story begins with a winter awakening set in "high-spring" (the inner man is some steps behind his guide), where nightly meditations like those of Christ on the Mount of Olives are pursued. The poet seeks the light of a "Pilgrim-Sunne." Vaughan feels betrayed by the cruelty and crosses of the world; Christ, literally, is betrayed. Vaughan recollects services for the Burial of the Dead and finds himself facing "The Passion":

> How pale, and bloudie
> Lookt thy Body!
> How bruis'd, and broke
> With every stroke!
> How meek, and patient was thy spirit!
> How didst thou cry,
> And grone on high
> *Father forgive,*
> And let them live....
>
> (*Works*, p. 431)

The patience of the perfect man contrasts with Vaughan's reticence. Christ's incredible cry *"Father forgive"* is nowhere near Vaughan's hostile words for violent men or the pity he feels for his own violated life. But the poet, moved by a now "mild Injunction" to change, accepts what the form of this poem graphically, falteringly represents—the mortal cross. Consequently, following the series of funeral poems and the generally ascetic resolutions just examined, there comes a series

The Resurrection of the Dead 173

of confessional poems. These provide a liturgical transition to the formal celebration of communion on Easter Sunday (*Works*, pp. 451–59). There, at last, the resurrected God and the resolved soul will become one.

One gains historical perspective and meaning by reading *Silex Scintillans I* in light of liturgical and typological sequences. Without them, Vaughan's "plot" may resemble that of a primitive initiation rite the intention or aim of which, clarified by no particular system of cultural values, remains shrouded. Although as full constructions these sequences are external to the dramaturgy of the text, they are clearly assimilated, part by part, in the language of the poems and are thus adapted as expressive schemes. For Vaughan, at least, these systems explain the changes of feeling and perception going on within him. By allusive fragments he allows the gradual recognition that an archetypal life, its episodes condensed as in a creed, has been pursued from the beginning.

6

> You that do truly and ernestly repente you of your sinnes, and be in love, and charite with your neighbors and entend to lede a newe lyfe, following the commaundements of God, and walking from hence forth in his holy waies: Draw nere and take this holy Sacrament to your comforte, make your humble confession to almighty God.... (The Book of Common Prayer)

> Look from thy throne upon this Rowl
> Of heavy sins, my high transgressions,
> Which I Confesse withall my soul,
> My God, Accept of my Confession.
> ("Repentance," *Works*, p. 448)

The seed of Vaughan's resolved soul, propped by ethical rules and lessons, calls now for strength and recognition, forgiveness and grace, through penetential tears. Earlier elegiac lamentations, mournings at the urn of the dead, and still earlier tears shed in self-pity are here resolutely absent. Vaughan's thoughts are on "Christs Nativity" (*Works*, p. 442), the Passion—"O call to mind his wounds, his woes" (*Works*, p. 449)—and the "love-feasts" of Sunday communion (*Works*, p. 447) that will constitute the climax of *Silex Scintillans I*. The poet's inspiration is framed by "His holy ways," and ascent to that border is again sought passionately.

> ... give wings to my fire,
> And hatch my soul, untill it fly
> Up where thou art, amongst thy tire
> Of Stars, above Infirmity;
> Let not perverse,
> And foolish thoughs adde to my Bil
> Of forward sins, and Kil
> That seed, which thou
> In me didst sow....
>
> (*Works*, p. 446)

"Disorder *and* frailty," the poem quoted in part above, confesses personal failures of a special kind. "While I grow/And stretch to thee, ayming at all/Thy stars ... Each fly doth tast,/Poyson, and blast/My yielding leaves." A storm of lamentations may drive the flies of sin away, Vaughan continues, but these waters beat his tenderly aspiring soul to the ground at the same time. The poet's problems, like diseases or "venomous bitings," are alien to his essential nature. They must be purged by a "venomous medicine" that he clearly knows—"Birds, beasts, each tree/All that have growth, or breath/Have one large language, *Death*" (*Works*, p. 444)—but lacks the power to promote by himself. Vaughan keeps threatening to break forever from his "Cell of Clay." Now, wishing that his beloved would come quickly and do the "killing" for him, he confesses the weakness of his own attempts. The early progress of his book is summarized in a stanza:

> Thus like some sleeping Exhalation
> (Which wak'd by heat, and beams, makes up
> Unto that Comforter, the Sun,
> And soars, and shines; But e'r we sup
> And walk two steps
> Cool'd by the damps of night, descends,
> And, whence it sprung, there ends,)
> Doth my weak fire
> Pine, and retire,

>   And (after all my hight of flames,)
>   In sickly Expirations tames
>   Leaving me dead
>   On my first bed
>   Untill thy Sun again ascends.
>   *Poor, falling Star!*
>   ("Disorder *and* frailty," Works, pp. 445–46)

The insufficiency Vaughan talks about is not one of intent, but of intensity and natural capacity. Prayers, watches, resolutions, and knowledge of Scripture may be had without love, or without sufficient love. Vaughan blames himself for this. But his prayers, like volatile mists, arise and expand only to contract and descend again. They proceed according to a natural prospectus, a cycle that Vaughan acknowledges for its benefits but wishes to transcend. By heightening his ardor, he hopes, like the hermetic seeker, to break through the limits of the known universe or self and to witness what lies within, beyond. But only a supernatural stay could keep him there.

Vaughan's confessed "weak fire" advances the process of self-recognition and tells something about the casting of this sacred love story. Like Petrarch and Sidney, he pursues an ideal as the beloved. And like these predecessors who show that they are selfish, abjectly wanting their laurels and their stars, Vaughan is admittedly guilty of unresponsiveness. But in *Silex Scintillans* the "mover" is not unmoved: "Heark, how he doth Invite thee! with what voice/Of Love, and sorrow/He begs, and Calls." It is the lover himself, mortally defined, who now lacks the strength of his convictions.

George Herbert's main sins are scheming and rebellion. Vaughan, who begins his poem "Repentance" in imitation of Herbert,[40] confesses "wilful rebellions" among other heinous, generalized transgressions. But his real sin is a tender lassitude. It shows in his loose style, as "craftiness" shows in Herbert's, and is duly confessed as a tendency toward gradual, oblique, and sometimes guileful "growth."

>   Lord, since thou didst in this vile Clay
>   That sacred Ray
>   Thy spirit plant, quickning the whole
>   With that one grains Infused wealth,
>   My forward flesh creept on, and subtly stole

> Both growth, and power; Checking the health
> And heat of thine. . . .
>
> *(Works,* p. 448).

Vaughan confesses the tardiness he had resolved himself against in poems just prior to these, as well as to the stealth and halting steps witnessed from the first poem of the book. In doing so he sets himself against the natural, loose movement of his thought and style. He relies in a highly restrictive way on Herbert, on verse formalities in general, and on a schematized concept of purgation. Instead of nurturing the characteristic virtues of his own voice, Vaughan bends (and virtually disappears) beneath the formal yoke of literary and ecumenical authority. He is quite literally forcing himself, or moving to overcome himself, to become another, and if these poems reveal a lack of confidence in his own poetics and aesthetic resources, lack of confidence is what he is confessing. The intent of this series is to make personal needs and inadequacies clear, and then become distant from them. Although it takes considerable ability, confidence, and ambition to pursue the search this far, that very sureness or egotistic integrity must itself be purged—given up in the "Fifth Sphere" of the hermetic ascent as the man is "made naked of all Operations."

The rigors of ceremony purify by stripping away accidents or mortal habits of character. So, as Vaughan develops this phase of his sequence, the theme and thus the language and form of his poems changes. The poem "Faith" furthers an explanation.

> . . . when the Sun of righteousness
>   Did once appear,
> That Scene was chang'd, and a new dresse
>   Left for us here;
> Veiles became useles, Altars fel,
>   Fires smoking die;
> And all that sacred pomp, and shel
>   Of things did flie;
> Then did he shine forth, whose sad fall,
>   And bitter fights
> Were figur'd in those mystical,
>   And Cloudie Rites;
> And as i'th' natural Sun, these three,
>   *Light, motion, heat,*

> So are now *Faith, Hope, Charity*
> Through him Compleat. . . .
>
> (*Works*, p. 451)

Light, motion, and heat, kinetic and volatile, requiring Vaughan's "natural music" as means of expression, are here translated and stabilized. When Christ was revealed, as Vaughan expects he will again be soon, the emblematic or "veiled" mode was broken. Tropes vanished into "plain" talk; language becomes merely, or blissfully, schematic. With no further need for obliquity and delay, Vaughan approaches the climax of his book.

7

Vaughan's Easter Sunday celebration is a carefully staged event. Indeed, it must be if he is to achieve the transcendent vision called for by the "plot" he is pursuing. So, as Vaughan has assimilated other forms and voices into a natural music of his own, now he yields his aspirations and the form they take to laws of another life. To involve himself in communion, marriage with the beloved, Vaughan seeks representation in the pure soul of an infant emissary.

The communion ritual is prefaced by a short lyric poem, "The Burial of an Infant."

> Blest Infant Bud, whose Blossome-life
> Did only look about, and fal,
> Wearyed out in a harmles strife
> Of tears, and milk, the food of all;
>
> Sweetly didst thou expire: Thy soul
> Flew home unstain'd. . . .
>
> (*Works*, p. 450)

There is the "experience." In one brief, Jonsonian elegy, formally unlike any other of Vaughan's, yet told in a tone so intimate that one might wonder if a child of his had died, the soul's ascent transpires. The poet associates himself with the child in the poem "Admission":

> Wee are thy Infants, and suck thee; If thou

> But hide, or turn thy face,
> Because where thou art, yet, we cannot go,
> We send tears to the place. . . .
>
> (*Works,* p. 453)

And now, from his own terrestrial and mortal state, Vaughan celebrates the glories of "The Dawning" of Easter in his accustomed way.

> . . . as this restless, vocall *Spring*
> All day, and night doth run, and sing,
> And though here born, yet is acquainted
> Elsewhere, and flowing keeps untainted;
> So let me all my busie age
> In thy free services ingage,
> And though (while here) of force I must
> Have Commerce sometimes with poor dust,
> And in my flesh, though vile, and low,
> As this doth in her Channel, flow,
> Yet let my Course, my aym, my Love,
> And chief acquaintance be above. . . .
>
> (*Works,* p. 452)

At the climactic point of Vaughan's story, the bond between earth and heaven is again intensely personal, as well as ritualistic and personified. A child's soul has ascended; Christ arose on this day, his body resurrected. Vaughan, in heart and mind, will track the course of one to meet the other. He has several means to do so. Like the other creatures of the world, he participates in the vital sensations of the day. Like mercurial waters rising from the earth, his prayers exhale the figure of a disembodied soul. Like Hermes the seeker, he will make the final step of a purgative ascent to the borders of the universe and there sing hymns of glory to the Maker. Finally, in the role of communicant, Vaughan will approach the altar of the resurrected God and symbolically seal the marriage of his soul.

The stage for Easter is set as planets vanish, the veil of the stars lifts, and the whole Creation shakes off its darkness. With the dawning, "all now are stirring, ev'ry field/Ful hymns doth yield." Vaughan offers prayers and personal promises, and in the poem "Praise," he plans to offer all—the spiritual "blossom" sprung from a seed earlier sown and lately reared to its present fulness. As the "infant blossome" from the greater world died and ascended, this microcosmic flower will be prepared for death and offered to the beloved. Humbly, Vaughan rehearses his part:

> If then, dread Lord,
> When to thy board
> Thy wretch comes begging,
> He hath a flowre
> Or (to his pow'r,)
> Some such poor Off'ring;
> ....
> Let him (though poor,)
> Strow at thy door
> That one poor Blossome.
>
> (*Works*, p. 455)

Vaughan begins his next poem, "Dressing," with a verbatim rendering from the Song of Solomon, 2:16–17. Scripture, no longer paraphrased, heightens the level of the poem and of all amorous expectation: "O thou . . . that feedst among the Lillies, 'till the day/Break, and the shadows flee."

Vaughan's achievement of communion is underscored by two analogues from the hermetic writings. First, from the empiricists, Vaughan understands the refining of matter. Lines 5–7 of "Dressing" read:

> Open my desolate rooms; my gloomie Brest
> With thy cleer fire refine, burning to dust
> These dark Confusions. . . .

This alchemical process is itself transformed, immediately, by a quotation from the Anglican Communion Service:

> Thou holy, harmless, undefil'd high-priest!
> The perfect, ful oblation for all sin
> ....
> Give to thy wretched one
> Thy mysticall *Communion*. . . .

Secondly, from the "philosophic" books of Hermes, Vaughan understands that upon reaching the final stage of "enlightenment," the soul should sing hymns appropriate to regeneration.

The initiate, past the last step of purgative refinement, at last understands his relationship to the entire creation by the ubiquity of his enlightened spirit. "O Father, I conceive and understand, not by the sight of mine eyes, but by the Intellectual Operation.... I am in Heaven, in the Earth, in the Water, in the Air, I am in living Creatures, in Plants, in the Womb, every where."[41] The idea of eternity is thus rendered spatially, and it is not hard to see how a Christian concept of divine immanence parallels, a virtual homology, the hermetic hymn. Vaughan prays to extend and overcome himself. He calls upon himself to sing with the stars, saints, creatures, and waters of the world, and he concludes the Easter sequence with an appropriate hymn—a metrical version of Psalm 121, praising an immanent God "Who fils/(Unseen,) both heaven, and earth."

Between these two points lies the heart of Vaughan's argument and assent. The "Bridegroom" who has been followed from his nativity, his baptism and his night-watches to the Passion upon Calvary, is now conceived as flesh restored. On "Easter-day" the Sun's early rays inspire the call

> Awake, awake,
> And in his Resurrection partake,
> Who on this day (that thou might'st rise as he,)
> Rose up....
>
> (*Works*, p. 456)

In response, Vaughan mounts the "narrow way" toward communion with a restatement of the argument he has sustained from the beginning.

The process of his translation, though he wishes it were otherwise, is a natural one. Life beneath the "veil," in the "darkness" of the natural world, must be transformed by an interior magic into whatever final, clarified, resurrected state it has the potential to become. Nature, driven by an innate force, overcomes nature. This must be, since

> ... at first, when things were rude,
> Dark, void, and Crude
> They, by thy Word, their beauty had, and date;
> All were by thee,

> And stil must be,
> Nothing that is, or lives,
> But hath his Quicknings, and reprieves. . . .
> ("The Holy Communion," *Works*, p. 457)

But as flowers require the sun, and as ethical reform requires the guidance of principled rule, so the spiritual betrothal Vaughan is ready to perform needs the medium of ritual for its consummation. Most significantly, the lover needs to know how to enact his love. For his final aim to be achieved, natural models of growth, death, and regeneration must be so translated to create an eternal ring or bond of union from the endlessly repeating cycle of mundane vitality.

Vaughan's soul grows up like a flower, pruned by strictures of rules and lessons and encouraged by intimations of self-transcendence. Finally, invited by sacramental ritual, Vaughan ascends to the altar of his beloved. We overhear the service, in progress—

> Thou doest unto thy self betroth
> Our souls, and bodies both
> In everlasting light.

—and then:

> O rose of *Sharon!* O the Lilly
> Of the valley!
> How art thou now, thy flock to keep,
> Become both *food*, and *Shepehard* to thy sheep.
> (*Works*, p. 458)

This passage literally translates a charge offered to Vaughan at the beginning of his book and recorded in "The Brittish Church." There, the call "O get thee wings! . . . And hast[e] thee so/As a young Roe/Upon the mounts of Spices" was followed by the poet's complaint: "*O Rosa Campi! O lilium Convallium! quomodò nunc facta es pabulum Aprorum!*" Now in Vaughan's native language, the "beasts" are vanquished and the communion is achieved. But this moment of transformation, the second and last in *Silex Scintillans I*, is over almost at once. When the pinnacle is reached, the next step, for the living, must be in descent. The mercurial mists arise, breathed out as this man is "refined," expand to what seems a ubiquity, only to contract and descend once more "as thy hand opes, or shuts."

8

Astrophil's descent from blissful prospect of Stella is tortuously slow. Sensuous kisses, seductive songs, and absence that pretends to be temporary all precede his final grief-filled solitude. Contrarily, and perhaps gratefully, Vaughan is delivered from the blessed ceremonies of Easter with the suddenness of waking from a dream. Following the pledges of "Psalm 121"—"He is alone my help, and hope/That I shall not be moved. ... He is my Pillar, and my Cloud,/Now, and for evermore"—all serenity and stability is shattered. Vaughan begins his "Affliction" in a quiet, self-remonstrant tone that conceals fierce sorrow:

> Peace, peace; It is not so. Thou doest miscall
>   Thy Physick; Pils that change
> Thy sick Accessions into setled health,
> This is the great *Elixir* that turns gall
> To wine, and sweetness; Poverty to wealth,
>   And brings man home, when he doth range.
> Did not he, who ordain'd the day,
>   Ordain night too?
> And in the greater world display
> What in the lesser he would do?
> . . . .
> Beauty consists in colours; and that's best
>   Which is not fixt, but flies, and flowes;
> The settled *Red* is dull, and *whites* that rest
>   Something of sickness would disclose.
> Vicissitude plaies all the game,
>   Nothing that stirrs,
>   Or hath a name,
>   But waits upon this wheel,
> Kingdomes too have their Physick, and for steel,
>   Exchange their peace, and furrs.
> Thus doth God *Key* disorder'd man. . . .
>   (*Works,* pp. 459–60)

Love's vibrant reds and whites, an ancient heraldry of paradox, now become the norm. There will be fire and ice. Indeed, a fixed state is not wholesome—not by nature's example and law. Yet have we not just witnessed a perfect peace and calm? Is noise the way toward harmony? Is disease essential to man's nature, and not alien? Shall we trade peace for violence, and be glad? "And happy I to be so crost,/And cur'd by Crosses," Vaughan announces in "Love and Discipline." He returns to this earlier concern with scant enthusiasm and flagging conviction. The poem is constructed in triplet stanzas that regiment and dispassionately render the argument that a natural flux of joy and tears, dews and frosts, is in itself rewarding.

Cast from the dream and song of an eternal world, Vaughan appears divorced from certainty as well. Principles compete for new priorities. Galenic "cure by contraries" wars with Paracelsus, and through "The Tempest" man plummets to dumb earth.

>   . . . only *Earth*,
> And *Man* (like *Issachar*) in lodes delight,
>   Water's refin'd to *Motion*, Aire to *Light*,
> Fire to all* three, but man hath no such mirth.   *Light
> . . . .   *Motion*
> Thus, groveling in the shade, and darkness, he   *Heat*
>   Sinks to a dead oblivion; and though all
>   He sees, (like *Pyramids*,) shoot from this ball
> And less'ning still grow up invisibly,
>
> Yet hugs he stil his durt. . . .

Beneath the celestial world, and now beneath the "greater world" where nature's process works its vital changes, Vaughan utters in agony the words that began his book:

> Lord! thou didst put a soul here; If I must
>   Be broke again, for flints will give no fire
>   Without a steel, O let thy power cleer
> Thy gift once more, and grind this flint to dust!
>   (*Works*, pp. 461–62)

The pilgrimage must begin again, as it had begun.

The sixteen poems that follow Vaughan's Easter celebration and conclude *Silex Scintillans I* constitute the fulfillment of a cyclical pattern. The end is the beginning. In conclusion, we return to concerns that had been prominent earlier in the book. The haunting, opening lines of "The World"—

> I saw Eternity the other night
> Like a great *Ring* of pure and endless light,
> All calm, as it was bright

—recall with quiet joy the celestial ring of "The Morning-watch," the ring of stars sought through nightly watches, and the bridegroom's ring (Revelation 21:9), a figure designating election that is curiously absent from Vaughan's account of communion and spiritual betrothal. Serene recollection leads Vaughan to scorn a world of mad men—the love poet; the "darksome States-man" moving through illusions of political power "like a thick midnight-fog"; the miser; the "down-right Epicure" who "plac'd heav'n in sense"—but as the poem concludes, he is stunned by the vanity of his own presumed superiority. Who can claim the sanctity of the Ring? In "Misery," a confessional reflection on earlier poems, Vaughan recognizes that "the wind, though gather'd in thy fist,/Yet doth it blow stil where it list" (*Works*, p. 472). Who has the right to certainty in this world? Vaughan rages on, without rest.

> I storm at thee, calling my peace
> A Lethargy, and meere disease,
> Nay, those bright beams shot from thy eys
> To calm me in these mutinies
> I stile mere tempers.

It is not fair to say that Vaughan's amorous and sacred quest ends in despair or disillusionment. He prays to reenter the arena of love, even at the cost of endless paradox and pain. "Lord, bind me up, and let me lye/A Pris'ner to my liberty," he cries. Sick with love, he writes a second poem on the Mount of Olives, recalling past idyls. "The Sap" represents, in shadowy language of the world, a plea for the "rare dew" of the Eucharist. But Vaughan's descent to the world of flesh, blood and mortality is no utter collapse. He recognizes his despair and thus can stand above it. He sees his disillusion from the perspective of the past, and memory permits a degree of stoic control. And the place to which he returns is not exactly the same as that from which he had departed. The heraldry of stones and earth, cryptic hieroglyphics in earlier poems such as "Vanity of Spirit," now reveal clear lessons of an immanent spirit. The Easter hymn of divine ubiquity echoes as more than consolation in Vaughan's last poems.

> Since in a land not barren stil
> (Because thou dost thy grace distil,)
> My lott is faln, Blest be thy will!
>
> (*Works*, p. 463)

Silex Scintillans I begins and ends with a journey. The first is a fantastic vision, filled with strange sights and sounds and cast in the trappings of an enigmatic dream. The last, narrated in the final elegy, "I walkt the other day," is a plainly composed, leisurely amble through a field in winter. The spring, contrasted with a wintery, spiritual deadness in "Regeneration," becomes at last a winter of the outer world that is informed by a new, "inlightened" spring. The sensuous but deceptive vitality of the first poem now yields to an austere portrait of the world's cold body—yet there is life within, as roots maintain their greenness through the winter, preserved by an immanent spirit "in all things, though invisibly." In solemn, yet curious quietude, Vaughan looks for the resurrection of the dead.

In one sense, the structure of *Silex Scintillans I* is linear. The pilgrim's journey must go on, and at the end Vaughan prays to the King of Mercy: "Perfect what thou has begun" ("Begging," *Works*, p. 480). Yet strung upon this vital line are a series of vertical ascents and descents, each attempting to circumscribe Vaughan's journey with a fulfilling form. At the end, a circumscription is indeed accomplished. Vaughan comes back to his beginnings and clarifies his first departures by infusing them with new meaning. The fallen world, cold and dead, becomes the divine creation as Vaughan returns to see, and thus to make it so.

[7]
Silex Scintillans 1655:
"The Life of the World to Come"

> I shall not go to my bed tonight, my love
> is not in it; I shall lie on the gravestone—
> break, if you must, my poor heart.
>
> There is nothing between him and me
> tonight but earth and coffin and shroud;
> I have been further many a time, but never
> with a heavier heart.
> —Welsh *penillion,* from *A Celtic Miscellany*

> Be off, my sorrowing rhymes, to the hard stone
> That hides my dearest treasure in earth;
> There, call her who from Heaven responds,
> Though in a deep, dark place her mortal self be laid.
>
> Tell her how weary of living I am,
> Weary of plying life's horrible waves;
> But, gathering at last these poems together,
> Step by step I follow her path
>
> Saying her, only, dead and alive
> (alive, as she is dead and immortal),
> So that in the world she be known and loved.
>
> May her wish be to watch my journey,
> My passing, near her now; may she meet me,
> Draw me to her, as she is, in Heaven.
> —Petrarch, *Rime* 333

> ... why should not the Creator impose a fresh form on the same common matter, so preserving continuity with the personality in this life, while making its new form appropriate to its environment?
> —Origen, on the resurrection of the body: glossed by Henry Chadwick, *Early Christian Thought*

Whoever sets experience before doctrines gains admission to the tortuous course of passion. It leads, for lovers, to places of death. "Ma 'l cieco Amor et la mia sorda mente/mi traviavan sì ch' andar per viva/forza mi convenia dove Morte era," Petrarch exclaims, summarizing earlier phases of his life: "By the vitality of blind Love and a deaf mind, I had to go where Death was" (*Rime*, 290). The imperative must be admitted; the adjectives need not. Love is not immune to sight. What if the mind, even in seeking to abandon such bondage, participates in and guides love's transformations by imagining, hope, and powers of will, as Divinity is said to move the greater world through a mediating spirit? This is not too hard to conceive, thanks to the analogy, yet it may be too hard to do. But if desire is intelligently and compassionately moved *by another* of whom and of whose ways one can be certain, then individual weaknesses may be compensated. Then changes can be seen to urge an understandable course and dying, locus of this trajectory, can be sighted, studied, and newly defined.

Silex Scintillans I begins with a young man, hurried, desperate, uncertain of himself, yet for whom another certainly exists. Only the other, sensed as a spirit, can confirm the man's existence. Its history can shape his perception of the changes in his life, for the spirit can move in exact and purposeful ways. These have been recorded and seen, seen and recorded. The man, unsure of even a hidden identity but afraid of its denial, is defensive, meandering, and lazy. The night, a time well ordered as the starry sky, is occasion for their meeting. The spirit passes by, attentive yet remote, knocking, turning away. At first it is a tentative presence, like one who approaches a lover with the ambivalence of desire and superiority. Then, perhaps by a kind of sympathy or sublime envy (wanting the man disembodied, like itself), the volatile spirit advances, bends, and strikes. It assumes manifestations or types, and the man catches sight. He shapes desire by the contours of what he perceives. Pursued, he becomes the seeker, the pilgrim, ever more considerate in his actions, until at last, in ritual climax, the symbols of the spirit are taken and consumed. Now, faced only by the invisibility beyond manifest forms, momentarily lost in that white gaze, the man is suddenly rendered all the more concrete. He becomes, or comes to, himself—aware of his own existence, realized in this sense, and alone. Such is the pathos of new life, the loss of its becoming.

In these not-quite fantastic terms the story of *Silex Scintillans I* can be reviewed (if neither contained, nor foretold). By stressing interaction of characters, the summary may help to explain the poignancy that Vaughan's drama gains, in adjournment, when the adored one—the projection and presence toward which the poet moves and by which the sequence is generated—is lost. Gone is the resurrected God, a loss that illuminates a ledger of others. Gone is the nearer "one for whom I mourn": a youth, a child. Gone as well are the man's own youth and childhood, aspects and prospects of a former life lost with the culture that nourished them. The psychological experience appears, in the geometry of retrospect, as a parabola that moves from depth, to height, to depth. Though no further confirmation of the pattern may be needed, one more departure must be recorded. Vaughan's Amoret, his wife Catherine Wise, died in 1653.[1]

Sickness continues as the apparent condition for poet, church, and nation. But the seed of their recovery has been sown, Vaughan knows, surely as a hidden greenness holds to its new life beneath the wintry plains of earth. A metamorphosis is at hand. The man who suffers love to the fullest is marked for something more.

Even Ovid's lovers, according to their special anguish, are transformed to rocks or trees, birds, statues, or stars. A better fate awaits the Christian courtier of sonnet cycles. His loss must be a shadowed kind of grace. *La Vita Nuova* contains the seed of the *Commedia*. The first part of Petrarch's *Rime* is followed by a second: "sometimes a man who departs weeping sees things that gladden his eyes and heart."[2] Sidney may have written "certain sonnets" in relief of Astrophil; Spenser adds an "Epithalamion" to transform courtly agony with the joys and promises of marriage; Drummond adds a "second part" to his *Poems,* and turns his attention from this life to the life of the world to come. Habington, Vaughan's most immediate predecessor in the genre, combines the "marriage solution" of the *Amoretti* with Drummond's intimations of resurrected life to complete the story of *Castara.* Vaughan follows this example in the *Poems* of 1646. Amoret is wed, but mortal union yields to dreams of blissful times shared in a world restored, like Eden.

On March 20, 1655, Henry Crips and Lodowick Lloyd registered *Silex Scintillans: Sacred Poems and private Ejaculations, The second Edition, In two Books*—the last great issue of the Renaissance "sonnet tradition." Book II begins, rejoining the liturgical and typological sequences of the preceding volume, with "Ascension-day." It concludes with the antitype to this event, the Day of Judgment, resurrected life, and the "boundless, Empyrean themes" of the world to come. Vaughan thereby returns to complete comment on subjects introduced in the first series of poems of Book I.

"Ascension-day," forty days after Easter, is an occasion to contain and transcend the sense of insufficiency and loss that shrouds the conclusion of *Silex Scintillans I.* For Vaughan does not view the occasion ("remov'd / So many Ages from me") from the perspective of the present where he sits, reads, and waits. Rather, present conditions and prospects are surveyed from the height of an intense, meditative experience. The initial sensation is of release, liberty and delight. Then, as the last traces of the "Master" fade toward a clouded vanishing point, Vaughan imagines the tears of others, earlier abandoned, and the way their love portends relief.

> With these fair thoughts I move in this fair place,
> And the last steps of my milde Master trace;
> I see him leading out his chosen Train,
> All sad with tears, which like warm Summer-rain
> In silent drops steal from their holy eyes,
> Fix'd lately on the Cross, now on the skies.
> And now (eternal Jesus!) thou dost heave
> Thy blessed hands to bless, these thou dost leave;
> The cloud doth now receive thee.
> ....
> Come then thou faithful witness! come dear Lord
> Upon the Clouds again to judge this world![3]

As if in the eternal present of a dream, the poet "now" participates in these ancient gestures. The experience, reified, relived, frames the promise of a timeless future. Justice, blessed life, and the love sought in the watches and sacramental series of Book I is and will be fulfilled. At the end of Book II Vaughan recounts:

> By this milde art of love at length
> Thou overcam'st my sinful strength.
> ....
> Gladness, and peace, and hope, and love,
> The secret favors of the Dove,
> Her quickning kindness, smiles and kisses,
> Exalted pleasures, crowning blisses,
> Fruition, union, glory, life
> Thou didst lead to.
> ....
> Thy next *Effects* no tongue can tell.
>
> ("To the Holy Bible," *Works,* p. 541)

As far as Vaughan's experience in love is refined and perfected, *Silex Scintillans II* is a continuation and completion of the first volume. But continuation is a misleading term if it suggests further unfolding of a plot. Once the last steps of the Saviour are traced, the search motif and ritualistic drama come to an end. In the place of a narrative sequence is, more simply, systasis—a structure of interrelated hymns and contemplative responses to the theme, *memento mori*. The action contained, as we will see, is of reflection, intercession, and enlightenment. But these interior measures combine to effect a gradual strengthening of the power one needs to endure in this world.

The overall form of *Silex Scintillans I* derives from meditative watches, themselves patterned upon an "empirical idea" of growth and transformation—a natural, chemic, and organic process. By the beginning of *Silex Scintillans II* this process, but for its final restoration and perfection, has been completed. After 1650 Vaughan writes as an alchemist of human emotions whose "experiment" has been stalled in time. His materials have been calcined, their bodies mortified. An essence, vaporized, lingers like mist in a glass vessel. The solution sits and is watched by a man, his vital development halted, who can do nothing to hasten the end. He thinks of Paul's epistle to the

Philippians (4:11)—"I have learned, in whatsoever state I am, *therewith* to be content"—and then exclaims: *"Resolution, Reader, is the Sanctuary of Man, and Saint Pauls content is that famous Elixir, which turnes the rudest mettall into smooth and ductible gold: It is the Philosophers secret fire, that stomack of the Ostrich which digests Iron, and dissolves the hard flint into bloud and Nutriment"* (*Works,* p. 217). This catalytic advice depends upon the magical logic of analogy or correspondence. If the soul and mind achieve content, which is lesser than but *like* "true Comforts" of the world to come, the heart and all contingent matter will be affected, nourished, and drawn toward a sublime repose. This is the idea of maturation. One might recall that the tears of "Ascension-day," like warm summer rain, foster no budding but a maturing capacity for life, superposed upon the miraculous death that started and will end it. Development is no longer marked by outer and sudden signs. It is now internal, gradual, slowly approaching true "tincture." So Vaughan will attain to patience—a willingness to accept the vision of himself he has obtained.

The self-portrait in *Silex Scintillans II* is of a man who has undergone a distinct renewal, and in light of that recognition has seen his losses and limitations all the more clearly. Now he must find a way to sustain and to be sustained by both perceptions. Then translation to a greater joy can come, when it will come, for the process that in time defines and confines his expectations will at the end provide release. Vaughan's thoughts turn upon a deepening conservatism. He withdraws, "leaving the world their day," to sustain a "secret fire," the first effects of which are acceptance and content. Vaughan had lived to die before his death. Now, in a state like death, he muses on the sign of life, a single beam of light glowing in gathering darkness.

> It glows and glitters in my cloudy brest
>   Like stars upon some gloomy grove,
> Or those faint beams in which this hill is drest,
>   After the Sun's remove.
>   ("They are all gone into
>   the world of light!" *Works,*
>   p. 484)

Books I and II of *Silex Scintillans* are therefore related as the beginning and ending of a plot and a process, but at the same time they are quite different in concept and execution.[4] Book I is about death and rebirth in life. Book II is about the life of a man whose soul and mind are engaged in the affairs of death, resurrection, and another world. In it Vaughan moves nowhere. His state is firmly fixed within a final, restorative circle cosmic in proportion. We have tracked the "borders of immortality," Vaughan writes, but now "Death is [the] Crosse, to which many waies leade, some direct, and others winding, but all meet in one Center" (*Works,* p. 300).

1

"Ascension-day," beginning Vaughan's new book, corresponds to the opening poem of the 1650 edition as antitype relates to type. Cryptic hieroglyphics, experienced uncomprehendingly in "Regeneration," are here transformed and clarified. Recall that *Silex Scintillans* begins with a chronicle in eight scenes: a "primros'd" setting; a mountainous path; a pair of scales; a fresh field; a grove of stately height; a fountain; a bank of flowers; and a rushing wind. In "Ascension-day," as Christ's translation and ascent clarify the pattern of mortal life, the old primrosed way once "hung with shade" becomes bright "Primros'd fields" nourished by the tears and spicy ointment of Saint Mary Magdalen. The mountain is the Mount of Olives. Old fields become the fragrant plains of Bethany "which shine / All now as fresh as Eden, and as fine." The scales become the terms of Judgment, and the fountain is now a pure spring, pouring streams like "dissolv'd Pearls." It is "ne'r marr'd with floods, nor anger'd with a showre." The flowers growing upon a bank move now within the garden to merge with the figure of the Virgin who reclines, pure, upon the purest earth. The stately grove, once roofed and confined as branches mixed and twined together, bursts open:

> Heav'n above them shin'd like molten glass,
> While all the Planets did unclouded pass.

As the procession passes, sighs and whispers of angels fill the air.

Vaughan projects a vision of nature as a new Eden populated by saints and angels, and rejoices. Though the effect of "Ascension-day" is not that of spare, systematic typology, Vaughan's "fair thoughts" are engaged in a scheme. Old experience is being transformed and stabilized. By the introduction of New Testament figures, shadowy hieroglyphics become "realized" and in this sense fixed. The terms of "Ascension-day" therefore excite no real speculation or searching out of meaning beyond what is explicit and explicitly portended. This resurrection points to the next. The old Eden, where sin transpired, becomes the new, where redeemed men walk. The old Adam, his "garments" dark and spoiled, becomes new, clean and white. Bone is brought to bone; man is "rebuilt"; clay ascends. So, lacking a motive for the search motif that generates a narrative in *Silex Scintillans I,* we will proceed in this book by variations on a theme marked by emotional changes that invert the parabola of Book I to move from height, to depth, to height.

In the poems following "Ascension-day" Vaughan aims to display and sustain his initial, transcendent vision of events to come. This he accomplishes in "White Sunday" and "The Proffer"[5]—

> Think you these longing eyes,
> Though sick and spent,
> And almost famish'd, ever will consent
> To leave those skies,
> That glass of souls and spirits, where well drest
> They shine in white (like stars) and rest.
>
> (*Works*, p. 487)

—but the first elegy of *Silex Scintillans II* and a series of "readings" from nature's book of hieroglyphics deliver the poet from his dream. In "Cock-crowing" the veil of flesh, of mortal life, intervenes and "shadows thee from me." In "The Starre" Vaughan reluctantly begins to contemplate the life of mundane creatures or "What ever 'tis, whose beauty here below / Attracts thee." "The Palm-tree" is a forthright object lesson in the patience required for enduring life beneath the veil. This poem appears addressed to Vaughan by one who fully understands his plight.

> Dear friend sit down, and bear awhile this shade
> As I have yours long since; This Plant, you see
> So prest and bow'd, before sin did degrade
> Both you and it, had equall liberty
>
> With other trees: but now shut from the breath
> And air of *Eden*, like a male-content
> It thrives no where. This makes these weights (like death
> And sin) hang at him; for the more he's bent
>
> The more he grows. Celestiall natures still
> Aspire for home.
> . . . .
>
> Here is the patience of the Saints: this Tree
> Is water'd by their tears, as flowers are fed
> With dew by night; but One you cannot see
> Sits here and numbers all the tears they shed.
>
> (*Works*, pp. 490–91)

However Vaughan may have intended the kindly, imperative address of his poem, the opening phrase is a literal rendering from George Herbert's "Love Unknown."[6] So it is this "most glorious true *Saint*" who directs Vaughan toward an understanding and acceptance of his fallen state. Trapped in time between one Eden and the next, mortally excluded from either, how is a man to thrive? Strangely, the example illustrates, and with "the patience of the Saints," concludes the voice of the Revelator.

Against the example of the bent and burdened palm Vaughan sets the way of some who know to die before death comes. They "walk to the skie / Even in this life" ("Ascension-Hymn," *Works*, p. 483). Their sustained, detached existence is both incredible and attractive to Vaughan, and the essays he wrote or translated between 1650 and 1655 suggest his devoted, eclectic interest in asceticism. A few examples will serve to indicate the range of his researches. At one extreme, Vaughan documents an eremitic community established by regenerate Egyptian fathers and reportedly seen by Saint Jerome.[7] "They lived dispersed up and down the wildernesse, and separated from one another in several Cells or Cots but knit all together in the perfect bond of Charity." The separate habitations, from which their dwellers seldom strayed, allowed for private "watching." At the other extreme, Vaughan translates from Nieremberg the solution by which Cato "made his way out." The man for whom mortal life has lost all promise may literally achieve a death to it by suicide. "His legs could not carry him off, and therefore hee ran away upon his hands. But it is all one, flye with which he will, it is a plain flight; his busie and searching fear, which in him ... was most Sagacious, shew'd him this postern or backdoor, which he most basely fled out at" (*Works,* p. 239).

Between monastic and literal "death to life" come a variety of ways by which people can pursue an experiential presence and knowledge of death. "The Funeral rite of the *Tebitenses* ... is to turn the inside of their garments outward; they manifest that part which before was hidden, and conceale that part which before was manifest; by which they seeme, in my opinion, to point at the liberty of the soul in the state of death, and the captivity of the body, whose redemption must bee expected in the end of the world. This inversion by death is reparation, and a preparative for that order wherein *all things shall be made new*" (*Works,* p. 287). On a more regular basis, Tibetan *Lamae* summon people to prayer "with the hollow, whispering sounds of certain Pipes made of the bones of dead men." Since they maintain that "a constant commemoration of death [is] as beneficial to the Soul as devotion," the worshippers always carry with them mementoes made of bones, "and they drink constantly out of a Skull" (*Works,* p. 295). The most natural and ubiquitous figure of death in life, as "*Hermes* in his *sacred book* contends," is breathing. "Nature doth every minute commend unto us this memoriall of death ... respiration was given to man, as a sign of that last efflation, in which the Soul parts from the body. Wee should therefore as often as wee breath, remember death, when we shall breath our last, when the Spirit shall returne unto him that gave it. Our whole life is nothing else but a repeated resemblance of our last expiration" (*Works,* p. 296).[8] Reminders of death are found in repeated social, ritual, or natural actions. By repetition we are made aware of form; by form we comprehend constancy, permanence, and the resurrected life.

Mortal effects of the *memento mori,* if one can adduce them from Vaughan's translation "Of Temperance and Patience," are essentially twofold. First, the soul attempts to isolate itself from bodily afflictions by a kind of retirement, involution, or *"Antiperistasis."* In an organic sense, the soul "evacuates" its mundane quarter. Next, however, there comes an awareness of the necessity for natural, virtuous activity—as opposed to "that unnaturall *Vacuity of not being*"—and with it an increased capacity for good works. The life of the soul and that of mortal man are mutually dependent and mutually sustaining, though they are headed, in time, in opposite directions. Nieremberg composes a lengthy and effusive passage on this point.[9] Vaughan says, most simply:

> They are all gone into the world of light!
> And I alone sit lingring here;
> Their very memory is fair and bright,
> And my sad thoughts doth clear.
> <div align="right">(<i>Works,</i> p. 483)</div>

Though his eyes are misted at the end, Vaughan writes the elegy above without tears. Resurrection and ascension, composing and resolving prior meditations on the death of a friend, a youth, a child, a god, are recollected now. Figures of the dead are mnemonically restored within the heart of the living. They glow there like jewels, at once calling the poet to a transcendent life and clarifying, relieving the burden of his mortal state. Their transcendent life, akin to Vaughan's own nocturnal ascents and vicarious experience of Ascension Day, inspires an inner transformation not from sorrow to joy, but from recurrent, unendurable misery to a mean, temperate state that can be sustained. "Of Temperance and Patience" provides a mundane, "peristaltic" analogy, headed by an aphorism from the most wise *"Nazianzen":*

> *Patience digesteth misery.*
> Concoction and Digestion of meats are the daily miracles of the stomach: they make dead things contribute unto life, and by a strange *Metamorphosis* turne Herbes, and almost all living Creatures into the Substance of Man, to preserve his particular *Species:* No otherwise doth Virtue by Patience (which is her stomack,) transform and turne all damages into benefits and blessings, and those blessings into it self. *Lupines,* or bitter Pulse, if steep'd in water, will grow sweet and nourishing: Patience doth macerate miseries, to

fatten it selfe with them. Certaine Divine Raies break out of the Soul
in adversity, like sparks of fire out of the afflicted *flint*.
(*Works*, pp. 248–49)

As we already know, Vaughan shares his author Nieremberg's seemingly innate belief that organic, psychological, and cosmic processes are essentially alike. So, regardless of grotesque alignments, the attainment of virtue by patience and the reception of food by the stomach both have a nourishing, settling effect, like the content after repast. To see how a kind of holy living is thereby encouraged, consider the example of the bird. He "by nature lifts himself above the earth upon his wings, he passeth from hence into the cleare confines and neighbourhood of heaven, where he dwells for a time, and looks with contempt upon this inferior darksome portion of the world: when hee descends towards the earth, he keepeth still above us, he lodgeth in the height and freshnesse of the trees, or pitcheth upon the spires or ridges of our houses, or upon some steepe rock, whose height & inaccessibleness promise him securitie; something that is eminent and high he alwaies affects to rest upon" (*Works*, p. 229). Transcendent, psychic experience, like the flight of a fledged bird, settles the descending man at a higher level of intent and purpose than had been before attained. The descent is natural and inevitable,[10] since "God gave it [his *spiritus* or sustaining breath] not *continual* and *even* . . . but refracted and shifting, to shew us that we are not permanent but transitory" (*Works*, p. 296). This example constitutes a most powerful reminder of death and resurrection, for "descent" is prefigured by the Creation and Christ's first coming, and it foreshadows the second coming, Judgment, and final perfection. As a forerunner of the Last Things, an event that for some may be held an ascetic or mystical failure can become for Vaughan a providential sign and a guide to holy living.

But "descent" is also prefigured by Adam's fall, and in this sense it must be interpreted in light of residual weakness as well as mutability.[11] Although Vaughan would not go as far as to celebrate Transgression's Type as "fortunate," he can, like Milton, see the event within an overall scheme of human experience, natural law, scriptural eschatology, and hence divine will and care. Long after the Fall, and shortly after Vaughan's reminder of it, the rule of temperance and patience is received. With this helpful but insufficient guide, a love-sick man begins his solitary way.

2

Vaughan remembers his beloved in "gleams and fractions." As a distant witness to the spirit's Pentecostal descent, the poet celebrates "White Sunday." In "The Favour" he rededicates both nights and mornings to watching for

> . . . thy bright looks! thy glance of love
> Shown, & but shown me from above!
> Rare looks! that can dispense such joy
> As without wooing wins the coy.
>
> (Works, p. 492)

Such moments—fragmentary, transcendent gleams in an otherwise darkened fabric of mortal life—are leading to effects other than those prepared for in *Silex Scintillans I*. No longer a stairway to mystical communion, these "lights" provide fresh anticipations and impetus for witnessing things nearer at hand. Vaughan contemplates the veil of creation. "Cock-crowing," "The Starre," "The Palm-tree," "Joy," "Psalm 104," "The Bird," and "The Timber," closely juxtaposed, are all readings from nature's book.

Vaughan can find joy in the boundaries imposed upon the created world by drawing upon the words of the Psalmist. His metrical version of Psalm 104 sets the terms and tone for a morning hymn in "The Bird":

> Hither thou com'st: the busie wind all night
> Blew through thy lodging, where thy own warm wing
> Thy pillow was. Many a sullen storm
> (For which course man seems much the fitter born,)
>   Rain'd on thy bed
>   And harmless head.
>
> And now as fresh and chearful as the light
> Thy little heart in early hymns doth sing

The Life of the World to Come 199

> Unto that *Providence,* whose unseen arm
> Curb'd them, and cloath'd thee well and warm.
>   All things that be, praise him; and had
>   Their lesson taught them, when first made.
>
> So hills and valleys into singing break,
> And though poor stones have neither speech nor tongue,
> While active winds and streams both run and speak,
> Yet stones are deep in admiration.
> Thus Praise and Prayer here beneath the Sun
> Make lesser mornings, when the great are done.
>   (*Works,* pp. 496–97)

This poem resolves, however, in unfinished darkness and anticipation of the last and consummately refining "Day-spring." As the bird must weather the storms of night, his head tucked beneath the pillow of his own warm wing, Vaughan understands that he must pass his solitary years with a patience that enlightens and will *"make joy sure."*

In Vaughan's most famous "hieroglyphic," a rooster dreams all night of paradise. Instinctively, he prepares himself for the light. The poet dreams the dreaming bird, wishing to be like it. His inner longing is activated by and recreates bonds of "magnestisme" between creature and Creator. The bonds generate a "Pulse" that "beats still for light" and anticipates, as Vaughan projects, "A love-sick souls exalted flight." This vital activity is entirely confined by the "Veyle . . . the cloke / And cloud which shadows thee from me," just as Vaughan must depend on what can be said of his lowly intercessor. But even so retained, there is a degree of exaltation to be discovered—by the creatures, and in them for the man. This poem concludes with a prayer for company. Stay with me where I must stay, Vaughan pleads.

To further appreciate Vaughan's urgent prayers in the veiled context of nature's ways that he has built around them, let us return to the source for Nieremberg's lesson on patience. Gregory of Nazianzus states, in an intimate, contemplative voice that Vaughan would wholly have admired,

> Perhaps there are other reasons for this [the binding of soul to body] which only God, who bound them together, and those who are instructed by God in such mysteries can know, but as far as I and men like myself can perceive, there are two: one, that it [the

soul] may inherit the glory from above by means of struggle and
wrestling with things below, being tried as gold in the fire by things
here, and gain the objects of our hope as a prize of virtue, and not
merely as the gift of God. This indeed was the will of the supreme
Goodness, to make the good even our own, not only because sown
in our own nature, but because cultivated by our own choice. . . .
The second is that it may draw to itself and raise to heaven the
lower nature, by gradually freeing it from its grossness, in order
that the soul may be to the body what God is to the soul, itself
leading on the matter that ministers to it, and uniting it as its fellow
servant to God.[12]

As God is the active agent in the soul's vital growth, so the soul
comprehends its confinement by actively attending the body,
preserving it against the final resurrection and beatitude. This
is the glory of "good works," which may seem an arduous
struggle, as well as the natural process that the hermeticist who
wrote "Cock-crowing" can both elicit and despair.

Though Vaughan demonstrates his belief in such mundane
spiritual "works," and is soon to embark on a career of ministering to others as a physician, the glory he recalls and still
desires is of another form entirely—as blooms are of another
form from the stalks they depend upon. The soul in this sense
only graces the body's growth and health or glorifies its imminent decline. Vaughan, given to organic analogies, anticipates a
sudden transformation. "Jesus, my life!" he prays:

> . . . how shall I truly love thee?
> O that thy Spirit would so strongly move me,
> That thou wert pleas'd to shed thy grace so farr
> As to make man all pure love, flesh a star!
> A star that would ne'r set, but even rise,
> So rise and run, as to out-run these skies,
> These narrow skies (narrow to me) that barre,
> So barre me in. . . .
> ("Love-sick," *Works,* p. 493)

This poem drifts into concatenation, as if to secure by art what
nature can only expect and work so gradually toward. Vaughan
cries for the explosion, the catharsis that he knows will follow
growth. Just as buds will suddenly bloom, or as medicinal balm
"clarifies" from a mixture of distilled ingredients, flesh that is
healed and refined becomes a star.

3

A kinship between Vaughan and the Alexandrian Patriarchs, or even the Desert Fathers like Paul the Hermit whose *Life* the poet quotes on several occasions, is at times remarkable.[13] If Gregory of Nazianzus's description of the natural world awakening on Easter day,[14] for example, is read beside Vaughan's lyric evocations of Easter dawn, one cannot fail to recognize likenesses in perception and temperament. What such correlations establish is less a case for conscious imitation on Vaughan's part than a broad example of cultural similitude. The early Christians of Alexandria, or those like Gregory who were schooled there, were facing a new theological era from the perspective of what one might call "old science." For them, perceptions of the manifest world and legends about it as well as a young and relatively simple Christian faith must confront and accommodate a new world of the mind and spirit made rigorous by ascetic or so-called gnostic thinking. Vaughan, along with the more scholarly Cambridge Platonists, living in an age increasingly persuaded by the perceptions of a "new science," is looking back to old forms of theology. And while the new Academics seek to make religion reasonable, Vaughan is looking for a way to simplify, combine, and contain the volatile elements of his existence. The Alexandrian *allegoria* appeals to both. So the voices of Philo, Clement, Origen, Gregory, and others sometimes meet Vaughan's in passing, at a nexus between this world and the next that now has become the province of literary history.

Vaughan and the Alexandrians have a number of texts in common—the Holy Scriptures and the *Hermetica,* to name only two—and Vaughan has some fragments from the "Primitive Christians," if only by way of Nieremberg's essays and the text of Saint Basil from which he derived an epigraph for *Silex Scintillans*. So if one can acknowledge considerable sympathy and at least a few moments of actual contact between Vaughan and his Alexandrian forerunners, some exegetic parallels between the poet, Clement, and Philo Judaeus may be instructive in considering the next phase of *Silex Scintillans II*.

In poems following his metrical rendition of Psalm 104, Vaughan transforms an awareness of divine immanence to the status of Providence. The love-sick man, lately abandoned upon earth, needs to feel that he is constantly watched and tended. So convinced, he can attend his own mortal duty—to endure and survive an illness that brings him to despair of life itself. Vaughan searches for signs of the immanent spirit in all conceivable places—in all earthly operations. There is even a secret *"Resentient"* in dead trees, he discovers.[15] Ubiquity is the first test of providence. Vaughan reveals a second through a series of references to the story of Ishmael.

Vaughan identifies himself with Ishmael first by allusion—

> If my way lies through deserts and wilde woods;
> Where all the Land with scorching heat is curst;
> Better, the pools should flow with rain and floods
> To fill my bottle, then I die of thirst.
> ("The Timber," *Works,* p. 498)

—and then by direct reference to the *"weeping Lad"* who was sent with his mother into the desert and would have died of thirst had God not heard his cries (Genesis 21:14–19):

> Why is my God thus slow and cold,
> When I am most, most sick and sad?
> Well fare those blessed days of old
> When thou didst hear the *weeping Lad!*
> ("Begging," *Works,* p. 500)

The desert setting, the aridity of it, represents Vaughan's inner state at this stage of his reflection upon achievement and loss. As the Creator is unresponsive, "slow and cold," so the inner creative spirit appears remote or gone. The Man-child, himself, is arid.

Between these two references, the figure of the outcast child is compounded in "The Jews." Here the Hebrew race becomes the forlorn *"eldest* childe"—as Ishmael was Isaac's elder—and then the "lost Son" of Luke, chapter 15. Vaughan sees himself in both figures and understands that both were redeemed, or "healed." Thus the Jews are drawn into a Christian eschatology. (Will warring sects be so enlightened, and reformed?)

> ... surely he
> Who lov'd the world so, as to give
> His onely Son to make it free,

> Whose spirit too doth mourn and grieve
> To see man lost, will for old love
> From your dark hearts this veil remove.
>
> (*Works*, p. 500)

Vaughan's eschatological vision shapes Old Testament history, as well as present times, into a shadowy lesson of providence, and in anticipation of its end he confesses and prays:

> My sins long since have made thee strange,
> A very stranger unto me;
> No morning-meetings since this change,
> Nor evening-walks have I with thee.
> . . . .
> Dear Lord! restore thy ancient peace,
> Thy quikning friendship, mans bright wealth!
> And if thou wilt not give me ease
> From sicknesse, give my spirit health!
>
> (*Works*, pp. 500–1)[16]

In the poem "Providence" these prayers, as the cries of Ishmael, are heard. Begging tears of the young and the distressed are turned to smiles by a "sacred and secret hand," and just as "poor *Hagar*" was shown "that holy Well" that could save her child, Vaughan comprehends the ever-running, "chaste fountains" of Providence from which mere drops or momentary glimpses had fallen to him before.[17]

We have moved upward from a recognition of immanence, to signs of providential doctrine sung by "poor birds" (*Works*, p. 506), to an understanding of Providence as an unending and ever-effective idea. The transition that Vaughan both subtly and suddenly accomplishes is anticipated in a more systematic allegory on the context of Ishmael's distress, composed by Clement of Alexandria. Clement quotes Philo in order to render a correlation between natural philosophy, which is the province of Hagar and her son Ishmael, "born after the flesh," and the providential "wisdom" represented by Sarah and her "child of promise."[18]

> 'But as the encyclical branches of study contribute to Philosophy, which is their mistress; so also philosophy itself co-operates for the acquisition of wisdom . . .' Wisdom is therefore queen of philosophy, as philosophy is of preparatory culture. For if

philosophy 'professes control of the tongue, and the belly, and the parts below the belly, it is to be chosen on its own account. But it appears more worthy of respect and preeminence, if cultivated for the honour and knowledge of God.' And Scripture will afford a testimony to what has been said in what follows. Sarah was at one time barren, being Abraham's wife. Sarah having no child, assigned her maid, by name Hagar, the Egyptian, to Abraham, in order to get children. Wisdom, therefore, who dwells with the man of faith . . . was still barren and without child in that generation, not having brought forth to Abraham aught allied to virtue. And she, as was proper, thought that he, being now in the time of progress, should have intercourse with secular culture first (by Egyptian the world is designated figuratively); and afterwards should approach her according to divine providence.[19]

Ishmael, the child of earth, represents the generation that brings an end to barrenness and shows the way to Providence. Allegorically, by the mechanism of a nearly overt platonic pedagogy, secular study leads to true wisdom.

Vaughan is thinking in the same direction as Philo and Clement; it may be that he knew their commentaries. But if so, he strays from their platonic script in two important respects. First, he does not shift his attention to the story of Sarah, Isaac, and the "promise" of Abraham's seed. He continues to consider himself in the role of the "regenerate outcast" whose way lies through the desert still. Until he is actually able to feel forgiveness, love, and the sense of "blessing" these emotions may bestow, his is the "seed growing secretly."[20] Secondly, Vaughan's Ishmael is not relieved by God, according to the "ancient way." Rather, by the anachronism that typology allows, his thirst is quenched by the tears of Christ. Two poems titled "Jesus Weeping" (*Works*, pp. 502 and 503) and a beautiful account of the King of Grief passing into Jerusalem on "Palm-Sunday" (*Works*, p. 501) punctuate this sequence to issue the only remedy the new Ishmael can hope for: "O healing tears! the tears of love! / Dew of the dead! which makes dust move / And spring . . . Pity which overflows thy heart!"

Vaughan understands Providence by recognizing its demonstration in times of greatest distress. His own "sicknesse" becomes a mild privilege in light of Jesus' pain and sorrow. So, as the wisdom of Providence is consistent with its example, Vaughan vows to bear "the proverb'd griefs of holy *Job*"[21] that he may secure "but one *green Branch* and a *white robe*" and be dressed as the multitude before the Lamb in Revelation 7:9. From Pliny comes the curiosity that cattle feeding on Pontic wormwood are free from "gall."[22] Vaughan adapts this wonder of homeopathy to his resolve:

> Great King of love and truth!
> Who would'st not hate my froward youth,
> And wilt not leave me, when grown old;
> Gladly will I, like *Pontic* sheep,
> Unto thy wormwood-diet keep
> Since thou hast made thy Arm my fold.
> ("Providence," *Works*, p. 506)

The theme of ecclesiastical and political reform is brought nearer resolution as Vaughan's personal resolve becomes a perspective upon continuing public hostilities. A stern glance is cast toward the enemy, the avaricious and violent—"May his Crown, like his hopes, be clay, / And what he saves, may his foes spend!" (*Works*, p. 506)—but Vaughan's promising recognition comes by questioning the necessity of fear and imprecations. The question is implicit in the poem "Providence." "The Sun doth set," he reflects, and leaves the world in current darkness. But next morning it shines again, fresh and fair, over all below. That symbol of restoration and unity overwhelms fears of mortal plots and power. "None can sequester or let / A state that with the Sun doth set / And comes next morning fresh as he," Vaughan proclaims. Yet how is the analogy to be realized? Its terms contain a feeling, a spirit of hopefulness awaiting release, portrayal beyond words on a page.

No similitude, idea, or edict will change the nature of others or the world. But hope lies in one man's capacity for sustained lament of the human condition that, guided by a vision of original and resurrected life, extends and manifests itself in acts of charity. The bearer of grief, applying the lesson of the symbolic sun, following its course in the motions of his own life, can become the medium of renewed and restorative compassion. His tears, like

> ... silent dew shall breed
> Lillies and Myrrhe, where the curs'd seed
> Did sometimes rule.
> (*Works*, p. 505)

So Vaughan retrieves aspects of the character he so ardently sought, sighted, and lost, but by whose providence "would'st not hate . . . and wilt not leave me."

4

The idea of Providence is sustained in a series of *exempla* drawn from the lives of biblical women. Mary, Rachel, and Mary Magdalen—virtuous all and so hymned in "The Knot," "The Ornament," and contemplated in "St. Mary Magdalen" (*Works,* pp. 506–9)—contrast with the dark example of "The Daughter of *Herodias*," who, once a beheader, now lies beheaded as a lesson in divine justice.[23] Mary, the "Bright Queen of Heaven," becomes a "true Loves-knot" by which man's inferior essence is nourished by God, and "we are his body grown." Rachel, the sheep-keeping Syrian maid of Genesis 29:9, shows the victory of humility and native simplicity over the "latest Modes of pride and lust." Mary Magdalen, the convert, is by far the most engaging of Vaughan's holy women. She has a prominent position in the poem "Ascension-day" where her tears, spices, and ointments are early tidings of an "intercourse and mirth / Of Saints and Angels." Now, responding to the image of Mary in John 12:3 ("Then took Mary a pound of ointment of spikenard, very costly, and anointed the feet of Jesus, and wiped his feet with her hair"), Vaughan sees her as a model for the transformations wrought by love.

Vaughan reads from Luke 7:47: "Her sins, which are many are forgiven, for she loved much." He paraphrases:

> . . . her Art of love,
> Who lov'd much and much more could move.
> . . . .
> Her Art! whose pensive, weeping eyes,
> Were once sins loose and tempting spies,
> But now are fixed stars, whose light
> Helps such dark straglers to their sight.

This hyperbolic, Ovidian metamorphosis from weeping eyes to fixed stars is intended as a figurative lesson that others can draw from the Magdalen's conversion and as a demonstration of the cause and process of Providence. The cause is a reciprocal love;

the effect is a type of resurrection. As Origen once explained, "All of us who have accepted the existence of Providence maintain that the underlying matter is capable of receiving the qualities which the Creator wills to give it."[24] The love of the Saviour reveals a direction for this will, but only those capable of feeling, responding, "loving much" can fully comprehend the new "Covenant" between earth and heaven,[25] the process of change and consummate metamorphosis. Vaughan writes:

> If this worlds friends might see but once
> What some poor man may often feel,
> Glory, and gold, and Crowns and Thrones
> They soon would quit and learn to kneel.
> ("The Seed growing secretly," *Works*, p. 510)

This recognition leads to the most intimate poems of *Silex Scintillans II*, and the next stanza of "The Seed growing secretly" introduces their subject:

> My dew, my dew! my early love,
> My souls bright food, thy absence kills!
> Hover not long, eternal Dove!
> Life without thee is loose and spills.

Set outside the context of this series on holy women, Vaughan's phrase "my early love" should refer to the "author of Providence" whose "eternal, living wells / None stain'd or wither'd shall come near." But in context the reference may be to Amoret—Catherine Wise—whose death (ca. 1653) is the probable occasion for two ensuing elegies, "As time one day by me did pass" and "Fair and yong light!"[26]

The first of these poems is a study in shifting lights. From "mourning light" seen through a dusky glass, thin, even lines of sunbeams show; one "beamy line" of remembered love shines from the *"nightpiece"* of the past. Death's dark mysteries, by this light unveiled, reveal

> A beauty far more bright
> Then the noons cloudless light.
> (*Works*, p. 512)

Framed by ever-changing natural lights, the memory of

Amoret shines evenly and clear. One "line," perhaps recorded on some document or interleaf of a family bible, contains both her life and death. From it Vaughan understands the narrow, direct *"Holy Way"* from earth to heaven. This "Fair and yong light," cast elegiacally, becomes his intercessor and "guide to holy / Grief and soul-curing melancholy."

Vaughan's melancholy is not caused by the lesions of death and absence alone. In the second of these companion elegies the poet confesses an errant and hard heart. He had not loved much, or well.

> Fair and yong light
> ....
> Whom living here I did still shun
> As sullen night-ravens do the Sun,
> And lead by my own foolish fire
> Wandred through darkness, dens and mire.
> How am I now in love with all
> That I term'd then meer bonds and thrall,
> And to thy name, which still I keep,
> Like the surviving turtle, weep!
>
> (*Works*, p. 513)

This is a terrible, sorrowing discovery—a bitter reminder of the heart of stone and lethargic passion lamented and chastened in *Silex Scintillans I*. It provides more than a mere clue to Vaughan's dread sense of isolation and lost contact with the sensations of love. "O do not thou do as I did," he has said. "Do not despise a Love-sick heart!" ("Begging," *Works*, p. 500). His stony heart, at last softened by both actual and scriptural death, now has nowhere to turn its love but back upon itself. A former vain heartlessness, a false freedom pursued without reward, yields the tragic necessity of love's becoming its own barrier to external, temporal fulfillment. Vaughan, yearning, reaches out. Yet his ardor must turn at the borders of eternity to descend, within, and dwell upon images of the heart.

No lesson of old Adam's fall is as compelling as this experience, but no words are more appropriate for Vaughan now than those that Adam had to hear. The Paradise, as early love, is lost. But by the way of Virtue, Patience, Temperance, and Love, "thou ... shalt possess / A Paradise within thee, happier farr."[27] It requires all the prior meditations on Providence, and the healing lessons of Temperance and Patience he really did not want to hear, for Vaughan to feel that he can still be loved, and later say:

> But I am sure, thou dost now come
> Oft to a narrow, homely room,
> Where thou too hast but the least part,
> My God, I mean *my sinful heart.*
> ("The dwelling-place," *Works,* p. 516)

5

Eremitic Christianity deals wholly in the isolating condition just described. So in light of Vaughan's solitude, his sympathetic tie with the "old, white Prophets" of the desert is no wonder. Their physical isolation nurtures an involuted love directed not at the self but at another being (or another form of being) who is literally awaited, yet is at the same time recollected, known, and in this sense inwardly possessed. Self-transcendence is desired as passionate energy transfers from the outer to the inner being. Vaughan approaches a description of such "indwelling" in the poem "Childe-hood." He achieves it in "The Night." But first, by the power of some gracious intercessor, he recovers from a sick desire for violence against others and against himself.

Following the companion elegies to Amoret, Vaughan writes a wildly fanciful poem on Joshua 24:27 called "The Stone." The poet begins with a feverish, suicidal scheme to secrete himself, unmindful or wrongly mindful of any who may have cared about his life. Willful violations of visual symmetry and exegetic form reveal a theme of destruction to body and to mind.

Josh. chap. 24. ver. 27.

[And Joshua said unto all the people, Behold this stone shall be a witness unto us; for it hath heard all the words of the Lord which he spake unto us: it shall be therefore a witness unto you, lest ye deny your God.]

> I have it now:
> But where to act, that none shall know,
> Where I shall have no cause to fear
> An eye or ear,
> What man will show?

> If nights, and shades, and secret rooms
> Silent as tombs,
> Will nor conceal nor assent to
> My dark designs, what shall I do?
> . . . .
> They hear, see, speak,
> And into loud discoveries break,
> As loud as blood.
>
> (*Works,* pp. 514-15)

Vaughan is prevented from his "dark designs" by an interceding awareness. The text he has happened upon, which he would like to escape or deny, is glossed at first with alert caution. All creation is sentient and watching. No secret act will go unwitnessed, Vaughan must remember, for

> . . . I (Alas!)
> Was shown one day in a strange glass
> That busie commerce kept between
> God and his Creatures, though unseen.

These lines, punctuated by a parenthetical sigh while yielding to an evenness of rhyme and meter, point back to the elegy where bonds of love and the arm of Providence are made the same:

> As time one day by me did pass
> Through a large dusky glasse
> He held, I chanc'd to look
> And spyed his curious book. . . .
>
> (*Works,* p. 512)

In the elegy, the "commerce . . . between/God and his Creatures" is rendered and kept by memory of a woman's love. That light, so bright and clear, shames while it informs the man, and now drives him to consider an act conceived in despair of having to live on, despair of ever really being better, or equal to a love he cannot keep from recollecting. But since that bond still affects his life, the life cannot be taken or held valueless. So while intercession comes overtly by way of a spiritual lesson[28]—that one is free to do as he wills but is always observed (even by stones) and will have to account for all acts on Judgment Day—Vaughan would have us remember that he feels the guide and restraint of Providence in the form of a holy woman's sustained devotion. The interceder is, in an experiential sense, she—a patient woman, surely, and one who loved in the face of hostility and neglect. As the embodiment of virtues that *Silex Scintillans II* is primarily about, she leads Vaughan's thoughts from a nadir of self-rejection to a commitment against violence in any form. The once-warlike Silurist, seeing that "thy Saints are not the Conquerors," prays for "patience here. . . . A sweet, revengeless, quiet minde, / And to my greatest haters kinde" ("The Men of War," *Works*, p. 517).

Vaughan's assemblage of poems to the Virgin Mary, Rachel, and Magdalen, and the intimate elegies following them become increasingly significant as the sequence *Silex Scintillans II* approaches a concluding celebration of resurrected life. The poet has sought a substantive, experiential bond between life and death, this life and a next, through hermetic, scriptural, and sacramental means. Now the bond comes glimmering to life as the memory of something lost and lately rediscovered, the one "work" that he intimately and truly knows—an early love that lives on within, imparting a reality to the man / god Vaughan could never know in the flesh, the spirit he reads and dreams about, and the Father standing remotely behind both. Dante, Petrarch, Drummond, and other lovers knew the intercessions of holy women, to which Vaughan has just awakened. The effect brings him, as those before him, to life.

The final joys actually known to the poet of *Silex Scintillans* will come as "The secret favors of the Dove," *her* "quickning kindness." Before these,

> O what high joys
> The Turtles voice
> And songs I hear!
> ("The Feast," *Works*, p. 535)

But for now the radiant character of Vaughan's interceder assumes a lunary form to shine, veiled, through a night not unlike the many nights of watching he has already passed through. It is the time of the body's sleep and the spirit's life, when light to mortal senses is necessarily reflected by an intermediary.

> Through that pure *Virgin-shrine,*
> That sacred vail drawn o'r thy glorious noon
> That men might look and live as Glo-worms shine,
> And face the Moon:
> Wise *Nicodemus* saw such light
> As made him know his God by night.
>
> ("The Night," stanza 1, *Works,* p. 522)

Nicodemus saw the healing wings of God; he spoke with the Son at midnight. That "can never more be done," Vaughan assents, but one can gaze upon the light reflected (as the moon reflects the sun) by Mary, Queen of Heaven and "true Loves-knot."[29] The "*Virgin-shrine* ... drawn o'r thy glorious noon" additionally recalls the calm and sacred grave shrouding "a beauty far more bright/Then the noons cloudless light" that Vaughan has elegized as Amoret's.

The readers of *Silex Scintillans I,* Vaughan's "The Night" is almost familiar. It recalls and elaborates upon a scriptural text central to "Regeneration" (John 3:2–9) and rejoins the longings of night watches, but there is an important difference. In Book I Vaughan's meditative searching moves mainly in worlds exteriorly conceived. His thoughts penetrate the earth and can ascend through the cosmos to the sphere of stars. The body's sleep is there the spirit's *release.* Here, however, the night is "my souls calm retreat." Instead of extending thoughts and aspirations beyond dark solitude, in search of another being, Vaughan now withdraws to the very heart and center of himself. From the darkness of that homely room, remembered voices might be softly calling, as deep within, "Spirits their fair kinred catch."

> Dear night! this worlds defeat;
> The stop to busie fools; cares check and curb;
> The day of Spirits; my souls calm retreat
> Which none disturb!
> *Christs* progress, and his prayer time;
> The hours to which high Heaven doth chime.
>
> Gods silent, searching flight:
> When my Lords head is fill'd with dew, and all
> His locks are wet with the clear drops of night;
> His still, soft call;
> His knocking time; The souls dumb watch,

> When Spirits their fair kinred catch.
> ("The Night," stanzas 5 and 6, *Works*, pp. 522-23)

From dreamlike asyndeton Vaughan descends in two full-sentence stanzas through the waking world to himself, and to the heart of another night. In dark seclusion, the masque of death, Vaughan watches and listens. Memories, reviving loved ones lately gone into a world of light, have earlier cast their beams against this darkness. In the concluding stanza of "The Night," Vaughan prays to sight their Original.

> There is in God (some say)
> A deep, but dazling darkness; As men here
> Say it is late and dusky, because they
> See not all clear;
> O for that night! where I in him
> Might live invisible and dim.

The brilliance, and then stunning power of these lines is such that it seems almost a vanity to ask what Vaughan means. He has here found the language to engage a theme so often elusive or defiant, and we are left in wonder of the transcendence that he utters, "invisible and dim," hovering just within and beyond our perception or grasp. Something is there and not there, with and then without form, transparent, then thinly veiled, endlessly vanishing and reappearing. Is this the way it will end? Is the spirit invisible, and resurrected flesh just dimly seen? The sense of mystery is compelling; we may forget that Vaughan is praying. He is of this world, but remotely. And in this world "where all mix and tyre / Themselves and others, I consent," and run, and err. The calm, redeeming vision, the modest version of an ancient night recreated in Vaughan's magnificent address, allows the triumph of consent. This is the point of *Silex Scintillans II*.

Some may be capable of an ascetic magic, and "walk to the skie/Even in this life":

> Fair, solitary path! Whose blessed shades
> The old, white Prophets planted first and drest:
> Leaving for us (whose goodness quickly fades,)
> A shelter all the way, and bowers to rest.

> Who is the man that walks in thee? who loves
> Heav'ns secret solitude, those fair abodes
> Where turtles build, and carelesse sparrows move
> Without to morrows evils and future loads?
>
> Who hath the upright heart, the single eye,
> The clean, pure hand, which never medled pitch?
> Who sees *Invisibles,* and doth comply
> With hidden treasures that make truly rich?
>
> ("Righteousness," *Works,* p. 524)

But for Vaughan, to whom passionate and chemic bonds between soul and body represent a final truth as well as a present condition, such righteous and lucid sighting of invisibles entails a resurrection at the end of time.

6

Vaughan approaches a vision of Judgment and the resurrected life first by contrasts and then by a gentler counterpoint that suggests harmony and continuity between this life and the next. The contrasts are external. Vaughan casts a final glance upon the world's battleground, a "Sad, purple well" of blood and dying voices calling out, as Abel's blood first called, against injustice and violent death. The men of war fight on.

> What thunders shall those men arraign
> Who cannot count those they have slain,
> Who bath not in a shallow flood,
> But in a deep, wide sea of blood?
> A sea, whose lowd waves cannot sleep,
> But *Deep* still calleth upon *deep:*
> Whose urgent *sound* like unto that
> *Of many waters,* beateth at
> The everlasting doors above,
> Where souls behind the altar move,
> And with one strong, incessant cry
> Inquire *How long?*
>
> ("Abels blood," *Works,* pp. 523–24)

These lines combine material from Genesis 4:10, Psalms 42:7, and Revelation 1:15, within the context of Revelation 7:8–11.

Like the beasts who there watch as seals of the Lamb's book are opened, Vaughan sees times grow worse. "Sin every day commits more waste,/And thy old enemy, which knows/His time is short, more raging grows" (*Works,* p. 531). Compared to the new life, no life appears more distant and wrong than this. Vaughan is astonished (again) that One could cease cries for vengeance, pray "for those that did him kill," and bring relief to the bloody remnants of the world. But having bound himself to this humane type, having prayed that his own character *be* the one who heals and is restored, Vaughan comes to resemble himself more and more. The restoration, in final regard to public themes, is a matter of sheer and cohesive will: to love without violence, to witness violence and maintain love.

The world within, to which Vaughan's thoughts retire, is nearer paradise.

> A heart is that dread place, that awful Cell,
> That secret Ark, where the milde Dove doth dwell
> When the proud waters rage:
> . . . .
> This litle *Goshen,* in the midst of night,
> And Satans seat, in all her Coasts hath light,
> . . . .
> Thus is the solemn temple sunk agen
> Into a Pillar, and conceal'd from men.
> And glory be to his eternal Name!
> Who is contented, that this holy flame
> Shall lodge in such a narrow pit, till he
> With his strong arm turns our captivity.
> ("Jacobs Pillow, and Pillar," *Works,* pp. 527–28)

In the poem above Vaughan returns to *"Jacobs Bed,"* introduced as one of the strange places in "Regeneration," and considers himself in the image of the solitary Jacob, Isaac's son whose seed was blessed but who lived in mournful solitude through times of civil war. Then, Jacob slept on stones—"but cold relief"—and dreamed of a ladder ascending to heaven and blessedness. The rock became a pillar, and the pillar God's temple. Vaughan completes the cycle. The temple sinks to a pillar, to dust; the outer shrine is transformed within, and concealed. But unlike Jacob, who could only dream, "hope for and believe," "we a healing Sun by day and night,/Have our sure Guardian. ... And feel a friend most ready, sure and kinde."

The quality of Vaughan's inner assurance and sense of worth is vastly strengthened. The "sicknesse" is past. His dread of abandonment has vanished, or nearly so.[30] He feels the presence of a friend. Nothing could be more simple, or in this context more profound and exalting. Vaughan's series on Judgment and new life sustains this simplicity and sureness. "The day of Judgement," "Psalm 65," "The Throne," "Death," and "The Feast" (*Works,* pp. 530–36) are neither formidable, doctrinal poems nor terror-ridden prophecies like the "Day of Judgement" in *Silex Scintillans I.* The end comes easily and swift. Dramatic effects needed for the communion poems in Book I here are less apparent. This climax is managed with the effortlessness of firm prediction. Since scriptural passages abound to be quoted, paraphrased, or more loosely glossed, Vaughan's preface to the concluding series—

> So thou, who didst the work begin ...
> Wilt finish it[31]

—literally anticipates his consignment to the book that accounts more than any other for his own. Moreover, a process has been set in motion, the end of which is established at the beginning. Since we know what naturally and typologically must occur, the only problem is one of execution. This is no barrier to one who now knows that love has been renewed and whose "heart is clean & steddy" (*Works,* p. 534).

The dominant figure of Vaughan's climactic series is not Christ the judge, but Christ the gardener and physician. Centuries of providential care, celebrated in the georgic "Psalm 65," have established a familiar pattern: in the end, "The year is with thy goodness crown'd." The end of time, like the end of the agricultural year, will be a "harvesting" of transformations organically wrought. In "The day of Judgement" Vaughan initiates the scheme. As if the subterranean promise, the hidden greenness of the elegy concluding *Silex Scintillans I,* had at last burst through the earth to life, "The dead, like flowers, arise/Youthful and fair to see new skies." In "Death," holy living, dying, and resurrection are portrayed in the figure of "physic's flower":

> As harmless violets, which give
> >   Their virtues here
> For salves and syrups, while they live,
> Do after calmly disappear,
> And neither grieve, repine, nor fear:
>
> > So dye his servants; and as sure
> > >   Shall they revive.

The ceremony of the Eucharist is now "The Feast" at which all the world will sit, eat, and be made new. On ordinary mornings, dew shines on the earth like tears "the sad world wept to be releast." On the last morning dew springs up wine, as an inner magic of communion is realized and enacts a literal, universal metamorphosis.

7

A vast, cosmic circle, momentarily caught in images and dreams during the progress of *Silex Scintillans,* describes a form for the sequence as a whole. The cycle of regeneration circumscribing Book I and the repeating types and antitypes of Book II appear in retrospect as two circles framed at last by a third, concentric with them and containing both. In "The Waterfall," Vaughan's final hieroglyphic, the act inaugurating time that Vaughan reflects upon in Book I conjoins the action of time's end that Book II anticipates. The ultimate and "real" past and future frame the mortal masque of one man's life. That spirit

> Which first upon thy face did move,
> And hatch'd all with his quickning love
>
> > (*Works,* p. 538),

becomes the author of a resurrected estate and glorious liberty. For "what God takes," he will "restore." The proof lies in "The Book" that emerges from the shadows of Eden and at the end seems to dissolve in our very hands, into the imagination of another Eden shining beneath a seventh seal somewhere beyond our time.

> Thou knew'st this *papyr,* when it was

Meer *seed,* and after that but *grass;*
Before 'twas *drest* or *spun,* and when
Made *linen,* who did *wear* it then:
What were their lifes, their thoughts & deeds
Whither good *corn,* or fruitless *weeds.*

   Thou knew'st this *Tree,* when a green *shade*
Cover'd it, since a *Cover* made,
And where it flourish'd, grew and spread,
As if it never should be dead.

   Thou knew'st this harmless *beast,* when he
Did live and feed by thy decree
On each green thing; then slept (well fed)
Cloath'd with this *skin,* which now lies spred
A *Covering* o're this aged book,
Which makes me wisely weep and look
On my own dust; meer dust it is,
But not so dry and clean as this.
Thou knew'st and saw'st them all and though
Now scatter'd thus, dost know them so.

   O knowing, glorious spirit! when
Thou shalt restore trees, beasts, and men,
When thou shalt make all new again,
Destroying onely death and pain,
Give him amongst thy works a place,
Who in them lov'd and sought thy face!

                                             (*Works,* p. 540)

Through all the world's changes Vaughan sees a natural and refining magic move. As a stream's end, as in an ocean of forms, all things resolve to the utter and essential simplicity of themselves. May it be so, Vaughan says, for one who sought the form in the Book of Nature's volatile arriving.

   At the end of a *canzone* one finds an "envoy" sending the song away on whatever missions it may have; Vaughan leaves us with formalities[32] and "L'Envoy." As the poet gratefully and graciously hymns the final joys he knows—

                  . . . and thou cast by
With meek, dumb looks didst woo mine eye,
And oft left open would'st convey
A sudden and most searching ray
Into my soul, with whose quick touch

> Refining still, I strugled much.
> By this milde art of love at length
> Thou overcam'st my sinful strength,
> And having brought me home, didst there
> Shew me that pearl I sought elsewhere.
> Gladness, and peace, and hope, and love,
> The secret favors of the Dove,
> Her quickning kindness, smiles and kisses,
> Exalted pleasures, crowning blisses,
> Fruition, union, glory, life. . . .

—we may be encouraged to return to another, earlier book of *Poems*. There a younger, less seasoned lover imagined the sentient witness of "a fresh Grove in th'Elysian Land." There are he and his beloved, a "most blest paire!"

> . . . As here on Earth
> Thou first didst eye our growth, and birth;
> So there againe, thou'lt see us move
> In our first Innocence, and Love:
> And in thy shades, as now, so then,
> Wee'le kisse, and smile, and walke agen.

The Last Effects are in another language altogether.

> Ζῇ ὁ Θεὸς καὶ ὁ κύριος Ἰησοῦς Χριστὸς
> καὶ τὸ Πνεῦμα τὸ ἅγιον.[33]

> Thus all things long for their first State,
> And gladly to't return, though late.
> Nor is there here to any thing
> A *Course* allow'd, but in a *Ring;*
> Which, where it first *began,* must *end:*
> And to that *Point* directly tend.
> —Boethius, *De Consolatione*,
> Metrum 2, Lib. 3, ll. 43–48,
> trans. Henry Vaughan

Appendix

Silex Scintillans 1655:
The Missing Emblem

Henry Vaughan's "Authoris (de se) Emblema" with its stunning engraving, a heart of flint being transformed to a weeping countenance, is probably the best known example of seventeenth-century emblem poetry. The emblem and poem survive with extant copies of *Silex Scintillans* 1650 and have been reproduced in most modern editions, but Vaughan apparently chose to omit them from the final copy of his book. This omission has perplexed many readers, for the emblem is by no means mere decoration.[1] It presents the subject of spiritual renewal integral to the book and serves to interpret that experience as a sudden and seemingly violent act of "separation." An explanation of the omission is demanded, if it can be shown that the decision to cancel was Vaughan's.

Vaughan was involved, at least indirectly, with the details of publishing his book. Henry's twin brother Thomas negotiated the printing of the 1650 edition with his own publisher, Humphrey Blunden.[2] *Silex Scintillans* was registered on March 28, 1650. The title page, on which the engraving appears, reads "printed by T.W. for H.Blunden." Vaughan published four books prior to the second edition of *Silex Scintillans* in 1655. Blunden was not engaged in these projects.[3] But *Olor Iscanus*, published in 1651 with an ornately illustrated title page, was printed by "T.W."—presumably the same man whose initials appear on the title page of *Silex Scintillans* 1650. T. W.'s probable connection with these two printings, and his absence from any further recorded employment on Vaughan's books, may have something to do with the fact that neither the second edition of *Silex Scintillans,* nor the reissue of *Olor Iscanus* (1679), nor any of Vaughan's other publications contain pictorial designs. This possibility is unlikely, however, for the availability of printer's materials is not a major consideration.

Blunden died late in 1654 or early 1655. His shop and some copyrights were taken over by Henry Crips and Lodowick Lloyd, who registered *Silex Scintillans: Sacred Poems and Private Ejaculations, The second Edition, In two Books* on March 20, 1655. Detailed arrangements were, no doubt, again relayed from the poet to the publisher's shop in London by Thomas Vaughan.[4] Pages of the 1650 edition signed A^1, which had contained "Authoris (de se) Emblema," and A^2 with the engraving and title, are missing from the 1655 copy. In their place are new signatures A^2–B^8: an unadorned title page, a lengthy prose "Preface," and two dedicatory poems, the first of which is a revision and expansion of the 1650 "Dedication."

The strongest evidence to suggest that the emblem and poem were intentionally omitted is the simple fact that the unsold sheets of the 1650 edition are incorporated as "Book I" of the 1655 volume. Since the emblem and Latin poem were printed on pages of an 8° sheet that, beginning with signature A^{4r}, is included in the 1655 text following B^{8v} of Vaughan's new prefatory material, it appears that both were purposefully cut, along with the original "Dedication" on sig. A^3. Though one can imagine some confusion or misunderstanding in the transfer of Blunden's copyrights to Lloyd and Crips, which may have caused the omission, the decision was almost certainly Vaughan's. He clearly chose to omit sig. A^3 in order to revise and expand his "Dedication," and this instruction was regarded by the publisher. Further, Vaughan had signatures B^2 and B^3 of the original canceled in order to revise a poem. It follows that his intention was carried out concerning pages signed A^1 and A^2 as well. The original design may have been lost, or withheld by T. W. It matters little, for there must have been a number of emblems already printed equal to the number of A-signed pages actually reissued.

Why then did Vaughan exclude such a striking and seemingly essential feature from his book? As evidenced by the 1655 prose preface and many of the poems in *Silex Scintillans II*, Vaughan's attitude and tone grow increasingly conservative as his poetic self-representation becomes more and more coherent and purposeful. The interests of a simplified devotional character may have yielded a general and unfavorable reaction against pictorial emblems. But in an age when literature was just developing a capacity for autobiography, and when "correspondences" between visible and invisible worlds were still generally conceded, signets, impresas and personal emblems, "those impressions and Characters which God hath communicated to, and marked all his Creatures with,"[5] were taken quite seriously. Vaughan, like John Donne, understood and accepted such devices as valid and not impious public expressions of inner heritage and character. He used a personal emblem for sealing letters throughout his life, but did not confine himself to a single device. Vaughan's earlier surviving letters—for example, Lambeth MS 1027, f.36B, dated 1662 (see Plate I [b])—bear the signet impression of a heart pierced by an arrow with drops falling downward, and a flower rising up from it on a stalk. Without the flower, this image corresponds to the emblem for *Silex Scintillans* 1650. Vaughan's later letters—for example, National Library of Wales, Wales P2033, dated September 14, 1693 (see Plate I [c])—bear the simple signet impression of a flower, possibly the heliotropion.[6] This information establishes a close tie between Vaughan's authorial "Emblem" and his signet and tells of new emblematic identities that succeed the famous engraving. It is safe to assume that Vaughan considered his emblem for *Silex Scintillans* 1650 as an authentic biographical statement, but not as a limitation or final definition of himself.

By 1655 the emblem of a flinty heart struck by arrows and converted with sudden force into a human countenance was no longer singularly appropriate. A letter dated between 1650 and 1655 bearing the new signet impression would prove this beyond doubt. We have, instead, the evidence of Vaughan's poetry. The supplementary image of a plant in bloom that appears on Vaughan's signet by 1662 develops as an important figure in the poetry of *Silex Scintillans* 1650 and 1655.[7] It is clearly Vaughan's favored image for the regenerate man succeeding from Book I, and in Book II the green and white of stalk and bloom appear frequently, foreshadowing and then representing the "dress" set in Revelation for those who greet the Lamb. The plant and flower themselves represent a vital, coherent, yet mortal and watchful man, the issue of sudden illuminations that have led to genuine spiritual growth, physical recovery, and moral restitution.

I conclude that Vaughan canceled the emblem from *Silex Scintillans* 1655 because it no longer projected an accurate visual concept of himself. The 1650 volume, as it concerns a process of spiritual regeneration, could appropriately begin with an emblem representing that process. But as figures of the regenerate man emerge, the emblem is reconstituted.

> How rich, O Lord! how fresh thy visits are!
> 'Twas but Just now my bleak leaves hopeles hung
>   Sullyed with dust and mud;
> Each snarling blast shot through me, and did share
> Their Youth, and beauty, Cold showres nipt, and wrung
>   Their spiciness, and bloud;
> But since thou didst in one sweet glance survey
> Their sad decays, I flourish. . . .
>
> *(Works,* p. 441)

At the last, Vaughan chose to picture himself in terms he had once used to describe his old friend and mentor Thomas Powell:

> . . . as the *Mary-gold* in Feasts of Dew
> And early Sun-beams, though but thin and few
> Unfolds its self, then from the Earths cold breast
> Heaves gently, and salutes the hopeful *East.*
>
> *(Works,* p. 624)[8]

It is interesting to note that the last writing from Vaughan is a set of marginal annotations to the copy of *Quadripartitum Botanicum* he received in 1682.[9] The book is a compendium of herbs and flowering plants, each listed by their Latin, German, and Danish names. Vaughan provides nearly every botanical reference, until his efforts abruptly cease in the middle of part 3, with common, English plant names: "Liver-wort; Wall-flower; July flowr with round root; wild, yellow Daffodils; Black Hellibor; dandylion; maidenshair; mous-earr." Vaughan occasionally indicates the medicinal value of a plant. "Alysson," for example, is "A foreign plant, or shrub: Whose very sight or touch cures those that have been bitten by mad dogs" (p. 18). "Curiosities" are sometimes noted, too. "Agnus Castus" is the "kind of weed . . . of which the more holy monks & nuns make their girdles" (p. 188).

Vaughan's spiritual character, from 1650 until near his death in 1695, can be traced in three successive visualizations: (1) the weeping penitent being transformed (1650 engraving); (2) the regenerate man issuing from spiritual renewal (1662 signet-emblem); and (3) the regenerate, yet mortal man (1693 signet-emblem). Vaughan chose only the first of these to accompany his "Hymns" of spiritual growth, *Silex Scintillans*. Why a new engraving was not commissioned for the 1655 edition remains a mystery, but one now may surmise what the emblem design could have been. Perhaps a suitable artist was not available. Perhaps Vaughan considered his poetry as fully capable of self-expression. Or perhaps, the poet was simply in too poor health to commission and approve a new engraving. He states in the "Preface" to the 1655 edition, "*I was nigh unto death,* and am still at no great distance from it; which was the necessary reason for that solemn and accomplished *dress,* you will now finde this *impression* in" (*Works,* p. 392).

Vaughan's decision on the question of a new emblem may have been affected by the example of Bishop Paulinus, whose *Life* the poet translated and published in 1654. Vaughan records that Paulinus was petitioned to "suffer his picture to be taken by a limner." He responded, "*What kind of a picture . . . would you have from me, the picture of the earthly, or the Heavenly man? I know you love onely that incorruptible image, which the King of Heaven doth love in you.*" The earthly image could be drawn, but the heavenly man is conveyed by the Word. Vaughan could have derived a similar distinction between symbolic pictures and poetry. Paulinus's next words, however, are an admonishment. "*I am ashamed to picture what I am, and I dare not picture what I am not.*" And how can one picture, except by words addressed to the mind's sight, what one expects at last to be? The unadorned title page of *Silex Scintillans* 1655 may have been Vaughan's response, for the time, to such a question.[10]

But as words aim at works, as Vaughan's medical career

extends the efficacy of his text, the image of the new man is tested and to some extent confirmed. And a new signet-emblem is commissioned. The poet's appreciation of mortal limits, however, remains. His gravestone, still to be seen in the churchyard at Llansantffraed, reads: HENRICUS | VAUGHAN · SILURIS | M · D · OBIIT · AP · 23 · AÑO | SAL · 1695 · AETAT · SUAE · 73 | [Family Coat of Arms] | QUOD IN SEPULCHRUM | VOLUIT | SERVUS INUTILIS: | PECCATOR MAXIMUS | HIC IACEO | + | GLORIA MISERERE. The last part may be translated: "What I wish on my grave—Useless Servant, Greatest Sinner, Here I Lie; Glory [to God on high]; Have Mercy [upon me]."

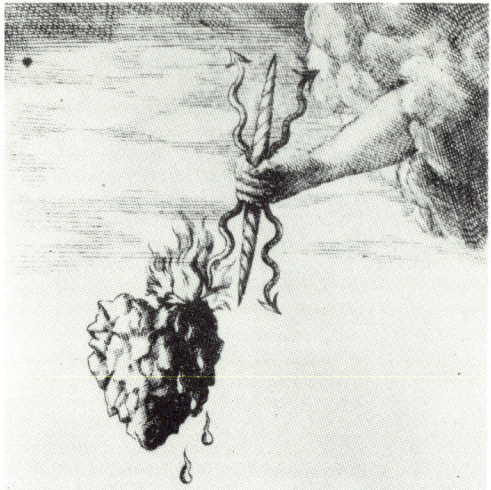

a

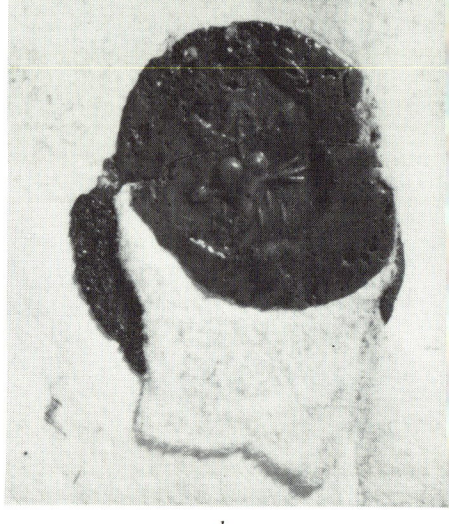

b

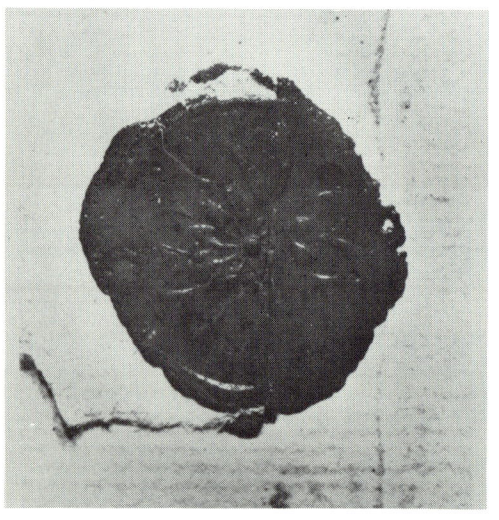

c

(a) The emblem omitted from *Silex scintillans*, 1655, reproduced approximately to the same size as the original from the title-page of the 1650 edition. (b) Impression from a letter endorsed in 1662. This shows a heart pierced by an arrow with drops falling downward and a flower rising up from it on a stalk. Lambeth Palace Library, Sequestered Livings 1650–62, MS 1027, County of Brecon, fol. 36b. The original measures about 15 mm across. (c) Impression from a letter of 14th September, 1693, showing a flower. National Library of Wales, Wales P2033. The original measures about 20 mm across.

Notes

CHAPTER 1: THE LYRIC SEQUENCE: POEMS (1646)

1. *The Works of Henry Vaughan,* ed. L. C. Martin, 2d ed. (Oxford: Clarendon Press, 1957), pp. 1-16. All citations from Vaughan's poetry and prose are, unless otherwise noted, from this edition. Hereafter it is cited in the text as *Works.*
2. William Habington, *Castara,* 3d ed., reprinted by Edward Arber (London: W. C. Bloomsbury, 1870), p. 29.
3. *Le Rime di Francesco Petrarca,* ed. G. Carducci and S. Ferrari (Florence, 1899), p. 7.
4. *Vita Nuova di Dante Alighieri,* ed. L. Pietrobono (Florence: G. C. Sansoni, 1951), p. 115.
5. Ibid., sonnet 41, p. 140.
6. *Le Rime di Francesco Petrarca,* pp. 67-68. The translation of this sonnet, below, is by Samuel L. Borton, University of Delaware.
7. *Petrarch: Sonnets & Songs,* trans. A. M. Armi (New York: Grosset & Dunlap, 1968), p. xxviii. See, also, Ernest H. Wilkins, *The Making of the "Canzoniere", and Other Petrarchan Studies* (Rome, 1951), ch. 9, especially pp. 187-94. And read Thomas P. Roche, Jr., "The Calendrical Structure of Petrarch's *Canzoniere,*" *Studies in Philology* 71 (April 1974): 152-72, to understand a numerological order for the poems in Petrarch's book. The order is based on four major events of the Christian year—Good Friday, Advent, Christmas, and Lent—and is present in the *Rime* not explicitly but symbolically, as the placement and kinds of poems are determined by and secretly represent specific calendar dates.
8. See "To the River *Isca,*" *Works,* p. 39. The opening ten lines constitute an abbreviated catalogue of mythical and real singers, from Apollo and Orpheus to Petrarch, Sidney, and Habington. The reference can be taken as knowledgeable, but Vaughan is more concerned here with rivers by which the poets sang than with their verse.
9. *The Poems of Sir Philip Sidney,* ed. William A. Ringler (Oxford: Clarendon Press, 1962), sonnet 6, pp. 167-68; sonnet 74, p. 204; sonnet 58, p. 194.
10. *The Poetical Works of William Drummond of Hawthornden,* ed. L. E. Kastner (Manchester: At the University Press, 1913), p. 51.
11. *The Works of George Herbert,* ed. F. E. Hutchinson (Oxford: Clarendon Press, 1941), p. 206. This poem was composed in 1609, but, as Herbert surely knew, the sonnet had already been "translated" to sacred status before this time. Indeed, the potential is evident from the beginning. Dante's love sonnets turn to sacred themes at the end of his book. Herbert's perspective would have included Barnabe Barnes's *A Divine Centurie of Spirituall Sonnets,* which appeared in 1595, and Donne's "La Corona" of 1607. Louis Martz considers Robert Southwell as the prime mover in a campaign to "convert the poetry of profane love into poetry of divine love," and Martz's explanation of "The Art of Sacred Parody" is essential to the general topic. See *The Poetry of Meditation* (New Haven, Conn.: Yale University Press, 1962), pp. 184-93. The transition has been considered in many other ways, however. See, for example, L. E. Pearson, *Elizabethan Love Conventions* (New York: Barnes & Noble, 1966), p. 141ff.

12. Habington, *Castara*, p. 54.

13. See F. E. Hutchinson, *Henry Vaughan: A Life and Interpretation* (Oxford: Clarendon Press, 1947), pp. 51–54. Hereafter, this biography will be referred to in the text as *Life*. See also E. L. Marilla's edition of *The Secular Poems of Henry Vaughan* (Uppsala: Lundequistika Bokhandlen, 1958), p. 100: "It is possible to discern a continuity . . . throughout the thirteen poems, from the rejection of the author's initial overtures, through a succession of changes in Amoret's attitude, eventually to marriage, and finally to a peaceful retrospect and reminiscence of courtship."

14. *Thalia Rediviva* (1678) contains a number of early poems and translations that Vaughan was persuaded, finally, to release. Among these are two lyrics to Fida and seven to Etesia. Ordinarily these have been associated with the Amoret poems, and may even have preceded them. See J. D. Simmonds, "Amoret, Etesia, and Catherine Wise," in *The Masques of God: Form and Theme in the Poetry of Henry Vaughan* (Pittsburgh, Pa.: University of Pittsburgh Press, 1972), pp. 204–7.

CHAPTER 2: CRISES IN BRECONSHIRE, 1645–55

1. Vaughan's Latin poems have been translated by French Fogle in his edition of *The Complete Poetry of Henry Vaughan* (New York: Doubleday & Co., 1964). His translation appears here.

2. F. E. Hutchinson, *Henry Vaughan: A Life and Interpretation* (Oxford: Clarendon Press, 1947), p. 49. Hereafter in this chapter this edition will be cited as *Life*.

3. I make this reference unadvisedly, since Freemasons' lodges were not officially chartered until the early eighteenth century, and evidence of their earlier existence and activities is scarce. Sir Edward Mansell, Bart., received an official deputation for South Wales on June 24, 1727, as F. H. Jones reports in his *Freemasonry in Monmouthshire* (Newport, Mon.: R. H. Johns, 1924), pp. 5–6, but "the brethren of Wales" must have been in existence already in order to be thus sanctioned. No evidence supports the existence of the "Silurian" Masons as early as the 1640s, but lodges were being formed at this time. It is well known that Elias Ashmole joined the Masons at Warrington, Lancashire, in 1646. Robert Moray, referred to later in this chapter as Thomas Vaughan's patron, was admitted to the Masons' lodge in Edinburgh on May 20, 1641. See Frances Yates, *The Rosicrucian Enlightenment* (London: Routledge & Kegan Paul, 1972), p. 210.

4. See *Life*, pp. 64–65, and a confirmation by Sir Frederick Rees in "Breconshire During the Civil War," *Brycheiniog* 8 (1962): 4.

5. *The Works of Henry Vaughan*, ed. L. C. Martin, 2d ed. (Oxford: Clarendon Press, 1957), pp. 50–51, lines 50–61. Hereafter in this chapter this edition will be cited as *Works*. The technical language describing "the nimble *Eye*" might be attributable to Thomas Powell's researches on optics. Powell's book, *Elementa Opticae*, was printed in 1651 with a dedicatory poem by Hen. Vaughan *Siluris*. Vaughan's close connection with Powell is discussed later in this chapter.

6. Mrs. Roderick of Newton Farm, Miss Elsie Pritchard of Brecon, and the Reverend Ivor Davies of Hay-on-Wye were interviewed by my student Deborah Chavenson in April 1971. Ivor Davies made this particular point, with which the Reverend J. Jones-Davies—founder of the Brecon Museum, general editor of the "Museum News" and great admirer of Vaughan—substantially agrees. The war occurred, for most citizens of Brecon and vicinity, in the form of various ecclesiastical, political, legal, and economic injunctions. Its threat was to a way of life, more than to life itself. In this sense the civil crisis becomes a strikingly "modern" event. It is no wonder, of course, that this should be the popular twentieth-century interpretation.

7. R. Tudur Jones, "Religion in Post-Restoration Brecknockshire: 1660–1668," *Brycheiniog* 8 (1962): 12. Specific local information in the following paragraphs is, unless otherwise noted, from Jones's study—which covers considerably more ground than its title indicates.

8. This occurred in 1656. See *Life,* p. 199, where Henry Vaughan's letter attempting to solve the matter is printed. The poet's father, a crafty man and very cautious with his money, according to John Aubrey, died only a year after this mishap.

9. For Powell's "crime," see John Walker, *An Attempt towards Recovering an Account of the Numbers and Sufferings of the Clergy of the Church of England, Heads of Colleges, Fellows, Scholars, &c. who were Sequestered, Harrass'd, &c. in the late Times of the Grand Rebellion* (London, 1714), 2:337. The bias, obvious to any reader of Walker's book and advertised by its title, is corrected somewhat by Thomas Richards, who views Powell as a ringleader of the late 1640-early 1650 movement in Brecon to check the power of the Sequestrators and to test Parliamentary policies and authority. See his *A History of the Puritan Movement in Wales, 1639–1653,* and *Religious Developments in Wales, 1654–1662* (London: National Eisteddfod Assn., 1920 and 1923). See also A. G. [Alexander Griffith, vicar of Llyswen], *A True and Perfect Relation* . . . (London, 1654), concerning "The Petition of the Six Counties of South Wales and the County of Monmouth," presented to the House of Commons, 10 March, 1651/2, and supposedly signed by 15,000 people.

Powell's *Quadriga Salutis: The Four General Heads of Christian Religion Surveyed and Explained* was printed in London by Sarah Griffin for Philip Chetwind, in 1657. The quotation is from his dedication to Lady Eleonor Williams, p. A⁴v.

10. See Walker, *An Attempt towards Recovering an Account,* pp. 278–79; Richards, *History,* p. 53, and *Religious Developments,* p. 283. Herbert's arrest appears to have taken place in 1655.

11. Jones, "Religion in Post-Restoration Brecknockshire," p. 13, cites the authority of "oral tradition" for this event, which presumably occurred in 1640. A similar story is related in *The Life and Death of Mr. Vavasor Powell,* ed. E. Bagshaw (n. p., 1671), pp. 126–27.

12. Geoffrey F. Nuttall, *The Welsh Saints: 1640–1660* (Cardiff: University of Wales Press, 1957), pp. 22–23.

13. Ibid., p. 62.

14. See L. C. Martin's note to p. 443, lines 9–18 (*Works,* p. 738).

15. Vaughan praises this order by expanding and embellishing a vision of idyllic spiritual discipline in his translation of Bishop Guevara's "The Praise and Happiness of the Countrie-life":

The Inhabitants of the Country . . . when the *Sabbath day* comes, or other *festivall solemnities* . . . enjoy a more sincere and heavenly comfort, than those that live in *Cities* and *Courts* . . . [for] they never make any difference betwixt *working* and *holy days.* O what a pious and beautifull work it is, when *holy* and *solemne days* are observ'd in the Country, according to the *sacred rules* and *Ordinances of Religion!* The *doore-keepers* of the *house* of *God* set wide open their *beautifull gates,* the *Church-bels* Ring, and every pious Soule is ravish'd with the *Musick,* and is sick of *love* untill he come into the *Courts* of the *Lord.* The *Temples* and *Communion tables* are drest, and the *beauty of holinesse* shines every where. (*Works,* p. 131)

16. Nuttall, *The Welsh Saints,* p. 23.

17. The argument is suggested by H. R. Walley, "The Strange Case of *Olor Iscanus,*" *Review of English Studies* 18 (1942): 27–37.

18. The term is used by Maren-Sofie Røstvig in the introduction to *Mathias Casimire Sarbiewski: The Odes of Casimire, Translated by G. Hils,* Augustan Reprint Society No. 44 (Los Angeles: Clark Memorial Library, University of California, 1953), p. iii. An

applied study of the "garden ecstasy" is provided in Professor Røstvig's revised and expanded essay, "Andrew Marvell's 'The Garden': A Hermetic Poem," in *Andrew Marvell: The Garden*, ed. T. Calhoun and J. Potter, (Columbus, Ohio: Charles E. Merrill Publishing Co., 1970), pp. 75–90.

19. Thomas Vaughan, preface to *The Fraternity of the Rosy Cross*, in *The Works of Thomas Vaughan*, ed. A. E. Waite (New York: University Books, 1968), p. 342.

20. Expressed in the *Life*, variously and throughout. See, for example, p. 182, n. 2, where Hutchinson disqualifies a list of medical metaphors found in Vaughan's poetry and compiled by Edmund Blunden. For Blunden's position on the matter, see *On the Poems of Henry Vaughan: Characteristics and Intimations* (London: Richard Cobden-Sanderson, 1927), p. 11.

21. See A. G. Demus, *The English Paracelsians* (London: Oldbourne Book Co., 1965).

22. See Peter J. French, *John Dee: The World of an Elizabethan Magus* (London: Routledge & Kegan Paul, 1972), p. 40.

23. In *The Rosicrucian Enlightenment*. See her early chapters, and especially ch. 4.

24. Waite's edition of Thomas Vaughan's *Works* gives us Thomas's considerable introduction to the texts, and a short postscript, but not the manifestoes themselves. Yates reprints the manifestoes, as published by Thomas Vaughan, in an appendix to *The Rosicrucian Enlightenment*. For the "agreements" of the Brotherhood, see p. 243.

25. For the connection between Freemasons and Rosicrucians, the former generally precedented by the latter, see *The Rosicrucian Enlightenment*, ch. 15.

26. This possibility is based on the fact that Thomas Vaughan's tract, "The Man-Mouse Taken in a Trap, and tortured to death for Gnawing the Margins of EUGENIUS PHILALETHES" (London, 1650), is dedicated to Matthew Herbert. *Aula Lucis* (London, 1652) is probably dedicated and addressed to Herbert as well. Here the "contemplative" aspects of Thomas's character and research appear to be attributed to his old tutor, now given the Latin "cover-name" Seleucus Abantiades. It seems that Matthew Herbert maintained considerable interest in his pupil's "Rosicrucian" activities. His own active engagement in the movement is rendered doubtful, however, by Vaughan's dedicatory remarks in *Aula Lucis*. See *The Works of Thomas Vaughan*, ed. Waite, pp. ix, 313–14, 489.

27. The collection was discovered by Edwin Wolf of the Library Company of Philadelphia and assessed in *The Book Collector* (1960), 9:275–84. The fourteen books that Wolf found, all signed by Vaughan, are from the library of Dr. William Logan. Wolf conjectures that Logan, a Bristol physician, selected these volumes from Vaughan's library, which may have been sold at auction in Bristol some time after Vaughan's death in 1695. The book on pediatrics is dated 1654.

28. Both of these volumes contain the autograph initials H. V. S[iluris]. The latest date for Vaughan's use of the term *Silurist* with his signature is 1655, as it is printed on the title page of *Silex Scintillans*. After 1650, Vaughan is described as "gentleman" on legal documents and letters (see *Life*, p. 189). After 1671 he began assuming the professional title M.D., though his autograph signatures for 1676 and 1682, as found in dated autographs on two of his medical books, are recorded simply "Vaughan." Though fellow poets like Katherine Philips continued to refer to Vaughan as "the Silurist" (cf. *Works*, p. 617), evidently he stopped using the epithet in 1655. Its appearance in these books therefore suggests that Vaughan obtained them prior to the completion of *Silex Scintillans*.

29. This translation, *The Chymists Key to shut, and to open: or the true doctrine of Corruption and Generation,* was not registered, and the date of its publication is in some doubt. The two copies upon which L. C. Martin bases his edition (*Works*, pp. 593–612) list 1657 as the publication date. Yet Anthony à Wood offers both 1655 and 1656. Wood's report (see *Life*, p. 183) is either wrong, or he had access to an earlier edition, or editions, that did not survive.

30. Henry Vaughan attests Moray's close association with his brother. See "Daphnis: An Elegiac Eclogue," line 116 (*Works*, p. 679), and Martin's note to p. 679 in *Works*, p. 761. Thomas Vaughan's English translations of the *Fama* and *Confessio* correspond most closely to a version in Scots dialect, dated 1633. F. N. Pryce, who introduced an edition of *Eugenius Philalethes' (Thomas Vaughan's) The Fame and Confession* in 1923, thinks that the Scots manuscript and the one Vaughan copied descended from an original, done prior to 1633. Since Moray was Vaughan's Scottish connection, it is possible that this hypothetical original, which must have been held by someone in Scotland, was handed on by him. The *Dictionary of National Biography* contains a detailed sketch of Moray's secretive activities on behalf of King and Country during the later 1640s.

31. This is Robert Boyle's remark, found in *The Works of Robert Boyle* (1744), ed. Thomas Birch, 1:20, and quoted in *The Rosicrucian Enlightenment*, pp. 182–83.

CHAPTER 3: AN INTERREGNUM POETICS

1. *The Works of Henry Vaughan*, ed. L. C. Martin, 2d ed. (Oxford: Clarendon Press, 1957), p. 46. Hereafter in this chapter this edition will be cited as *Works*.

2. *The Works of Thomas Vaughan*, ed. A. E. Waite (New York: University Books), p. 5. This dimension of a hermetic prospectus has much in common with Plato's argument for the descent of the philosopher-king, and with Plotinus. Cf. *Enneads* 4. 8. 6: "The One must not be solely the solitary. If it were, reality would remain buried and shapeless since in The One there is no differentiation of forms. No being would exist if The One remained shut up in itself. More than that, the multiplicity of beings issued from The One would not exist as they do if there did not issue from The One those beings that are in the rank of souls. Likewise, souls must not play the solitaries . . . each thing must unfold, seedlike, from indivisible principle into a visible effect" (trans. E. O'Brien, *The Essential Plotinus* [New York: Mentor Books, 1964], p. 68). See, also, Plato *Timaeus* 41e–42e.

3. *The Works of George Herbert*, ed. F. E. Hutchinson (Oxford: Clarendon Press, 1941), p. 125, as editor L. C. Martin notes (*Works*, p. 745, note for p. 478).

4. *Ibid.*, p. 166, as L. C. Martin again notes. For a discussion of this "borrowing," see E. C. Pettet, *Of Paradise and Light* (Cambridge: At the University Press, 1960), pp. 53–54.

5. E. C. Pettet, *Of Paradise and Light*, pp. 58–70, summarizing the views of many previous critics and adding some remarks of his own, establishes that Vaughan uses the text of George Herbert in the following ways: direct quotation; allusion; reminiscence; and subconscious association. The motives entertained by Pettet include the possibility that Vaughan is "answering" Herbert, that Vaughan believed in Herbert's use of homely imagery and expression, that Vaughan meditated upon Herbert's verse, as he did upon the Bible, and composed poems about this activity, that Vaughan had memorized much of Herbert's verse, and simply that Vaughan was inspired and stimulated by Herbert's example. R. A. Durr, *On the Mystical Poetry of Henry Vaughan* (Cambridge, Mass.: Harvard University Press, 1962), pp. 9–13, provides a list of critical opinions based on comparative analysis. Edward Dowden, with whom I agree most, portrays the language of Herbert's poetry as well as that of the King James Bible as a literary inheritance and working vocabulary for subsequent devotional poetry. Just as conventional diction for English love sonnets was derived from Continental texts in that tradition, so the works of earlier sacred poets and the Bible became the source of language for lovers of the divine. As the secular lover's tribute is extraordinary and his language artificial, so prayer is not a normal, but an acquired speech. Its language must be learned from literary sources of revealed religion and Church practice. See Edward Dowden, *Puritan and Anglican: Studies in Literature* (London: Kegan Paul, Trench, Trubner, & Co., 1900), p. 120. Vaughan's preface to the 1655 edition of *Silex Scintillans*

and his subtitle, "Sacred Poems and Private Ejaculations," quoted verbatim from the title page of Herbert's book, suggest that *Silex Scintillans* is a direct descendent from the former text—a "paraphrase," expansion, or a verbal monument, perhaps, formed from the stones of the Anglican's now ruined "Temple."

6. F. E. Hutchinson, *Henry Vaughan: A Life and Interpretation* (Oxford: Clarendon Press, 1947), p. 22. Hereafter cited as *Life.*

7. John Dryden, *Juvenal,* "Dedication," quoted by Hutchinson, *The Works of George Herbert,* p. 540, note to p. 183.

8. J. R. King suggests part of this comparison by printing passages from "The Retreate" and from Vaughan's translation of *Lib.* 2, *Met.* 5 in double columns. See his *Studies in six 17th century writers* (Columbus, Ohio: Ohio State University Press, 1966), pp. 148–49.

9. Cf. "The Morning-watch," *Works,* pp. 424–25.

10. See J. A. C. Rathmell, ed., *The Psalmes of Sir Philip Sidney and the Countess of Pembroke* (Garden City, N.Y.: Doubleday & Co., 1963), intro., p. xx. Though it was not a popular Psalter, like the Sternhold, Hopkins, and Whittingham *Whole Booke of Psalmes,* the Sidneys' rendition was considered important by major poets such as John Donne ("Upon the translation of the Psalmes by Sir Philip Sidney, and the Countesse of Pembroke his Sister"). See Louis L. Martz, *The Poetry of Meditation* (New Haven, Conn.: Yale University Press, 1962), pp. 273–82, for an assessment of the significance of the Sidney Psalter as compared to Herbert's poetry.

11. Charles Hoole, who taught in a private grammar school near London during the 1640s, writes in his *A New Discovery of the Old Art of Teaching Schools:* "But for gaining a smooth way of versifying, and to be able to express much matter in few words, and very fully to the life, I conceive it very necessary for scholars to be very frequent in perusing and rehearsing *Ovid and Vergil,* and afterwards such kind of Poets, as they are themselves delighted withall, either for more variety of verse, or the wittinesse of conceit sake." He goes on to recommend, specifically, the intralingual "perusing and rehearsing" of Sandys, Ogilby, Herbert and Quarles—a list of contemporary writers that betrays the compiler's generally sound preference. Hoole's text has been edited by E. T. Campagnac (London, 1913), and is quoted by R. L. Sharp, *From Donne to Dryden* (Chapel Hill, N.C.: University of North Carolina Press, 1940), p. 157. The *New Discovery* was published in 1660, but Hoole explains, on the title page of the original edition, that it was "written about twenty three years ago"—about the time Vaughan was "rehearsing" his poetry at Oxford.

12. "On Sir Thomas Bodley's *Library; the Author being then in* Oxford," *Works,* p. 633, lines 5–6.

13. Prologue to Ecclesiasticus, *Apocrypha,* Authorized Version of 1611 (New York: Dial Press, 1924), p. 106.

14. *The First Prayer-Book of Edward VI, Compared With The Successive Revisions of the Book of Common Prayer* (Oxford and London: James Parker & Co., 1877), p. 244. My citations from the Book of Common Prayer will always follow the King James revision, which I assume Vaughan used.

15. Thomas Fuller, "Mr. T. F., His Prayer," in *The Poems and Translations in Verse . . . of Thomas Fuller,* ed. A. B. Grosart (Edinburgh: Crawford & McCabe, 1868), pp. 238–44. The excerpt is from p. 241.

16. See L. C. Martin's note to p. 447, *Works,* p. 739.

17. Thomas Fuller, *The Church History of Britain,* 3d ed., pref. J. Nichols, 3 vols. (London: Thomas Tegg, 1842), 1: 469. The first edition was printed in 1655. Here, Fuller's remark applies specifically to an assessment of Chaucer's language.

18. ———, *The Worthies of England,* ed. J. Freeman (London: George Allent Unwin, 1952), p. 382. The first edition was printed in 1662.

Notes 233

19. *Ibid.*, p. 590.
20. Sir William Davenant, "The Preface to Gondibert . . . With An Answer to the Preface by Mr. Hobbes," *Sir William Davenant's Gondibert*, ed. David F. Gladish (Oxford: Clarendon Press, 1971), p. 18, lines 589–96.
21. "Ode. Of Wit," *The English Writings of Abraham Cowley*, ed. A. R. Waller (Cambridge: At the University Press, 1905), p. 18, stanza 8.

CHAPTER 4: NATURAL MUSIC

1. "Misery," in *The Works of Henry Vaughan*, ed. L. C. Martin, 2d ed. (Oxford: Clarendon Press, 1957), p. 474. Hereafter in this chapter this edition will be cited as *Works*.
2. Henry Reynolds, *Mythomystes*, in *Critical Essays of the Seventeenth Century*, ed. J. E. Spingarn, 3 vols. (Oxford: Clarendon Press, 1908), 1: 163–64.
3. By this term Reynolds basically means "the Generation of the Elements, with their Vertues, and Changes," and "the Courses of the Starres, with their Powers, and Influences." For the text quoted below, see Spingarn, *Critical Essays*, 1: 166.
4. "Resurrection and Immortality" is constructed as a discourse between body and soul. The speaker here is the soul.
5. Cf. Hermes Trismegistus, "A discourse of Mind to Hermes," Lib. 11(2), 19–20a, *Hermetica*, ed. Walter Scott (Oxford: Clarendon Press, 1924), 1:221. The English version of Hermes for Vaughan's time is *The Divine Pymander of Hermes Mercurius Trismegistus . . . translated . . . By that Learned Divine Doctor Everard* (London: Robert White, for T. Brewster & G. Moule, 1650). In this edition, see book 10, pp. 133–35.
6. *The Works of Thomas Vaughan*, ed. A. E. Waite (New York: University Books, 1968), p. 51.
7. This pattern is at work as well in the first two stanzas of "Resurrection and Immortality." S. Robert Shafer, who believes the poem to be a kind of irregular Pindaric ode similar to those popularized by Cowley, uses accented syllables as a standard by which to scan Vaughan's lines. See his *The English Ode to 1660* (Princeton, N.J.: Princeton University Press, 1918), p. 143.
8. Boethius *De institutione musica* 1.1, as glossed by Bruno Meinecke, "Music and Medicine in Classical Antiquity," *Music and Medicine*, ed. D. Schullian and M. Schoen (New York: Schuman, 1948), p. 69.
9. See Frances Yates, *The French Academies of the Sixteenth Century* (London: Warburg Institute; University of London, 1947), especially chs. 3, 4, and 12.
10. See Gretchen Ludke Finney, *Musical Backgrounds for English Literature: 1580–1650* (New Brunswick, N.J.: Rutgers University Press, 1962), chs. 2–6.
11. Boethius *De institutione musica* 1.3, in the text of Gottfried Friedlein, *Source Readings in Music History*, ed. Oliver Strunk (New York: W. W. Norton & Co., 1950), p. 84.
12. *Ibid.*, p. 85.
13. *Ibid.*
14. Yates, *The French Academies*, pp. 56–57: "An important feature of all the French *musique mesurée* is that it is not monodic, but written in four vocal parts. This was a departure from the strict imitation of the antique, for most of the musical humanists believed that ancient music had been monodic. But the academicians deliberately chose not to be strictly 'classical' in this matter because they were of the opinion that the development of harmony and polyphony in the mediaeval and modern period was an advance on classical music, a progressive element. . . . They wished to *restore* the classical emphasis on rhythm, whilst *retaining* the modern development in harmony. . . . In the measured music, the parts are carefully co-ordinated so that each syllable is sung by all

voices at the same time. This 'syllabic homophony' produced what was in effect a new kind of music having a marked *rythme d' ensemble* such as is not found in ordinary polyphony."

15. These equations have been thoroughly documented. See, for example, Armen Carapetyan, "Music and Medicine in the Renaissance," *Music and Medicine*, ed. D. Schullian and M. Schoen, pp. 122–23; John Hollander, *The Untuning of the Sky* (Princeton, N.J.: Princeton University Press, 1961), p. 37 passim; S. K. Heninger, *Touches of Sweet Harmony* (San Marino, Calif.: Huntington Library, 1974), p. 146.

16. Finney, *Musical Backgrounds*, p. 126.

17. Powell's work on "The Art of Musick," which Vaughan surely knew since he collaborated with the author in preparing the book where it appears, contains the spectrum of Boethius's observations, strained through citations from various Renaissance commentators. The study begins: "There is Musick in heaven and Musick on the way thither, in the spheares, as the Pythagoreans affirm: and therefore the soul of man being descended from heaven, & passing through those harmonious spheares, doth naturally delight in Harmony.... Nay, God made the body of man (wherein this musical soul is to sojourn) a kinde of a *living Organ* or Musical instrument.... There is but one pipe to this *Organ*, (to wit) the Weasand; the Lungs are the bellows to make winde, and to inspire this pipe; yet with this one pipe (being variously stopt) we can express a thousand sorts of notes and tunes, and make most ravishing musick; for there is no Harmony that is so delightfull and pleasing to man as *vocal*, or the musick of man's voice." See Thomas Powell, *Humane Industry: or a History of Most Manual Arts* (London: Henry Herringman, 1661), pp. 102–3.

18. Finney, *Musical Backgrounds*, p. 130. The testimony of composers Caccini and Peri is documented, following Miss Finney's own conclusion.

19. Richard Hooker, *Of the Laws of Ecclesiastical Polity*, ed. Ronald Bayne, 2 vols. Everyman's Library (1907), 2: bk. 5, 38, 1, p. 146. Also, see Jerome Mazzaro's interesting "meta-critical" *Transformations in the Renaissance English Lyric* (Ithaca, N.Y.: Cornell University Press, 1970), particularly pp. 94–96.

20. Finney, *Musical Backgrounds*, p. 132.

21. For Vaughan's knowledge and praise of "The Royall Slave," see "Upon the *Poems* and *Playes* of the ever memorable Mr. *William Cartwright*" (*Works*, pp. 55–56), which appeared as a commendatory poem in the 1651 (registered 1648) edition of Cartwright's *Comedies, Tragi-Comedies, with other Poems*. The standard text today is found in *The Plays and Poems of William Cartwright*, ed. G. Blakemore Evans (Madison, Wis.: University of Wisconsin Press, 1951). The play contains a variety of musical forms: solo/chorus songs, an "operatic" drinking song, masque songs and dances, solo airs, a dance done while chanting (I gather) Latin verse. An example of the "expressive" lyric style is the boy's song (Evans, ed., *Plays and Poems of William Cartwright*, p. 212):

> *Come my sweet, whiles every strayne*
> *Calls our Soules into the Eare;*
> *Where they greedy listning fayne*
> *Would turne into the sound they heare;*
> *Lest in desire*
> *To fill the Quire*
> *Themselves they tye*
> *To Harmony,*
> *Let's kisse and call them backe againe.*

22. Frances Yates uses Pontus de Tyard, *Discours philosophiques*, to explain this point. See *The French Academies*, pp. 38–39. The advocate of *furor poëticus* could shift emphasis completely from musical "method" to verbal expression.

23. Such fountains and other machines designed to create musical water-cadences were constructed for the castle and grounds at Heidelberg, geographic center of the Rosicrucian movement. These may have inspired Inigo Jones's designs for use in masques. See Frances Yates, *The Rosicrucian Enlightenment* (London: Routledge & Kegan Paul, 1972), p. 12. Examples appear in Thomas Powell's *Humane Industry* (pp. 37, 38, 40–42, 109), a book to which Vaughan contributed a number of Latin translations (see *Works,* p. 682). The most notorious mid-century accounting of this comparison is, of course, John Denham's "Cooper's Hill." Georges Poulet has some instructive remarks on baroque "water-music" and other such conceptions. See his *The Metamorphoses of the Circle* (Baltimore, Md.: Johns Hopkins Press, 1966), p. 16.

24. Jean Ogier de Gombauld, *L'Endymion* (Paris, 1634), translated by Richard Hurst into the English copy from which Vaughan read in 1639.

25. There is no exact prototype for the line and rhyme pattern of "The Morning-watch," but analogues exist with some frequency in metrical psalm literature. See, for example, the following metrical renderings from the Sidney Psalter: "Psalm 23: Dominus Regit Me"; "Psalm 67: Deus Misereatur"; "Psalm 88: Domine Deus"; "Psalm 103: Benedic, Anima" (J.A.C. Rathmell, *The Psalmes of Sir Philip Sidney and the Countess of Pembroke* (Garden City, N.Y.: Doubleday & Co., 1963), pp. 49, 152, 208, and 238. Since Vaughan insists on the term "hymn," the possible influence of the Pindaric ode, or of the kind of dispersed rhyme one finds, say, in Petrarch, may be dismissed—though the latter clearly affected Sidney's sense of the possibilities in rhyme schemes.

26. Sir Thomas Browne, *Religio Medici,* part 2, in *The Works of Sir Thomas Browne,* ed. Geoffrey Keynes (Chicago: University of Chicago Press, 1964), 1:84. Browne's manuscripts and the 1642 (unauthorized) printing add a statement on the effects of "natural music": "it unties the ligaments of my frame, takes me to pieces, dilates me out of myself, and by degrees, mee thinkes, resolves me into Heaven."

27. Mary Ellen Rickey argues this point in "Vaughan, *The Temple,* and Poetic Form," *Studies in Philology* 59 (1962): 162–70. She maintains that the unrhymed lines of Herbert's "Deniall," which dramatize "the disorder of his [Herbert's] thoughts . . . due to unsuccessful devotions," serve as a model for Vaughan's "Disorder and Frailty." This may be so, but the argument is difficult to sustain in light of the fact that Herbert's stanzas are rhymed, simply, *abab(x)* while Vaughan's are shattered *abab(x)ddeeffd(x)*. Vaughan may have begun with Herbert's scheme in mind, but he proceeds according to some other, stranger music. Generally speaking, I disagree with Miss Rickey's contention that the devices and form of a Herbert poem often determine the shape of an entire poem by Vaughan. "Trinity Sunday," a poem in triplets, is an exception. But even here Vaughan is compelled to carry his syntax over line endings and through the division of the second and third stanzas. Concatenation—a popular device for love poems whereby the word or phrase ending one line is used to begin the next—is loosely incorporated in "The Wreath" but submerged by variations in the ten-syllable couplet lines of "Love-sick." Vaughan creates stanzas from sonnet forms, mutations rhymed *ababccddeffgge* and *abccabdeffegg,* in "The Passion" and "The Mutinie." Mutinous, indeed.

28. See P. Crossley-Holland, "The Growth of Music in Wales," *Music in Wales* (London: R. Stockwell, 1948), p. 16. An example of *hiraeth* is provided in a transcription from the *Robert ap Huw* manuscript, "written in Charles the First's time." The notation, bars from a traditional harp exercise like those used for penillion singing, reads:

Crossley-Holland comments as follows: "Some features . . . appear curious to us. In bar A above, for instance, the "d" . . . is apparently foreign to the harmony. The schoolmen would pronounce this faulty writing, but here it serves to emphasize that sense of passionate yearning which pervades the piece. This *hiraeth,* as the Welshman calls it, . . . this note of emotion echoes and re-echoes in the poetry and music of Wales."

If one follows Crossley-Holland in assuming a basic harmonic structure for each bar, dischordal or disjunctive elements can be heard in measures B and C as well. Note especially the bass "a" in the first bar of C. Given this limited example, it appears that the music is a kind of cross-breed, combining harmonic and modal features. Without an absolute standard, it is difficult to know which notes "belong" and which do not. *Hiraeth* could, conceivably, result from such ambiguity.

If, for the execution of penillion, a singer is added to the rendition of this air, additional disjunctions are in order, for the form is competitive. The singer's melody is slightly different from that of the harp, and the harpist can "challenge" the singer by changing from one traditional air to another without notice. For an assessment of the popularity of poetry resembling or based upon harp stanzas and the pervasiveness of such forms in the seventeenth century, see Thomas Parry, *A History of Welsh Literature,* trans. H. Idris Bell (Oxford; Clarendon Press, 1955), pp. 234–37.

29. Vaughan's letter to John Aubrey, dated July 7, 1673, lists manuscripts written by Thomas Powell "left in my Custodie, & not yet printed." The third of these is titled "Fragmenta de rebus Brittannicis: A short account of the lives, manners & religion of the Brittish Druids and the Bards &c." (*Works,* p. 690). A later letter to Aubrey, Oct. 9, 1694, refers to Bardic "rules & orders . . . & several sorts of measures & a kind of Lyric poetrie" as this information is set down in Dr. John David Rhees's Welsh grammar (*Works,* p. 696).

CHAPTER 5: NATURAL MAGIC

1. "L'Envoy" in *The Works of Henry Vaughan,* ed. L. C. Martin, 2d ed. (Oxford: Clarendon Press, 1957), pp. 542–43. Hereafter in this chapter this edition will be cited as *Works.*

2. For an interesting but all too brief account of the "alchemy" of ejaculatory prayer, see Titus Burckhardt's *Alchemy,* trans. W. Stoddart (London: Stuart & Watkins, 1967), pp. 157–60.

3. Critics have traced Vaughan's poetic structures to a variety of plausible sources. Rosemond Tuve considers the schemes of traditional logic, rhetoric, and Ramist versions of these as determinants for poetic style. Her theory, based on the way poets were educated in the sixteenth and seventeenth centuries, is applied to Vaughan in *Elizabethan and Metaphysical Imagery* (Chicago: University of Chicago Press, 1947), see pp. 148–49; 218–20. A theory of sacred rhetoric derived from Jesuit meditation is offered by Louis Martz in *The Poetry of Meditation* (New Haven, Conn: Yale University Press, 1962). The schematic structure prescribed by Ignatius—memory, analysis, colloquy—applies best to a group of poems with accompanying scriptural texts in *Silex Scintillans,* book 2 (1655). E. C. Pettet (*Of Paradise and Light* [Cambridge: At the University Press, 1960], p. 32) presents a tentative list of Vaughan's "formal meditations." Martz also advances a loose, meditative scheme suggested by St. Augustine as the

formative principle for some of Vaughan's poems. See the chapter on Vaughan in *The Paradise Within* (New Haven, Conn.: Yale University Press, 1964). A theoretical basis for devotional poetry derived from emblem literature is described and applied to Vaughan by Rosemary Freeman—*English Emblem Books* (London: Chatto and Windus, 1948), pp. 149–53. A number of other critics have applied versions of these three analytic methods to select poems from *Silex Scintillans*. A mode of allegorical exegesis is very handsomely applied to "The Waterfall" by Michael Murrin in *The Veil of Allegory* (Chicago: University of Chicago Press, 1969), pp. 135–41. J. D. Simmonds argues for a conservative, Jonsonian structure in *Masques of God* (Pittsburgh, Pa.: University of Pittsburgh Press, 1972). The relative success of a number of prescriptive schemes, each applied to only selected poems, suggests (at least) a shifting methodology on Vaughan's part. As will be seen in chapter 6, some formal variation is required by the narrative and thematic progress of his book. The account offered here is supported in principle by Alan Rudrum, "The Influence of Alchemy in the Poems of Henry Vaughan," *Philological Quarterly* 49 (1970): 469–80.

4. Richard Hooker, *Of the Laws of Ecclesiastical Polity*, intro. R. Bayne, Everyman's Library (1970), 1: 268. Citations from this volume immediately following are from pp. 361, 277, and 268.

5. *Works*, p. 692: a letter to John Aubrey dated June 28, 1680. The letter contains a very candid account of Vaughan's mature attitude toward ties between astrology and medicine. Of astrology: "for my owne part (though I could never ascend higher,) I had butt litle affection to the skirts & lower parts of learning; where every hand is graspinge & so litle to be had."

6. Giambattista della Porta, *Natural Magick*, (1658; reprinted ed., New York: Basic Books, 1957), p. 2. The first edition of Porta's very popular *Magia Naturalis* was printed in 1558. Thomas Powell frequently refers to the book and may have modeled his *Humane Industry: or a History of Most Manual Arts* (London, 1661) upon it.

7. Porta, *Natural Magick*. The exerpts from the text immediately following are on pp. 6–10.

8. Clement of Alexandria, *Stromatum* 6, 4; Migne, *Patrologiae Graecae* (Paris, 1890), 9: col. 253–4.

9. Herodotus, *The Persian Wars*, trans. G. Rawlinson, Modern Library (1942), p. 155.

10. See Henry E. Sigerist, "Empirico-rational Medicine," *A History of Medicine* (New York: Oxford University Press, 1951),1: 314–15. Sigerist denies the plausibility of this identification, but the idea tantalizes Jürgen Thorwald who structures his book on the categories offered by Clement. "For many years," states Thorwald, "this assertion of Clemen[t]'s was regarded as a fable. But was it?" See his *Science and Secrets of Early Medicine*, trans. Richard and Clara Winston (New York: Harcourt, Brace, & World, 1963), p. 47.

11. R. Stern and J. Saunders, *Ancient Egyptian and Cnidian Medicine* (Berkeley, Calif.: University of California Press, 1959), p. 2.

12. Paul Ghalioungui, *Magic and Medical Science in Ancient Egypt* (New York: Barnes & Noble, 1965), pp. 18–37. The passage quoted is from p. 19.

13. Stern and Saunders, *Ancient Egyptian and Cnidian Medicine,* p. 4.

14. This identification, and ensuing associations of Hermeticism with medicine and other arcane interests, has given no little pain to scholars trying to assess the hermetic tradition rationally and systematically. Walter Scott, whose four-volume *Hermetica* (Oxford: Clarendon Press, 1924) stands as the authoritative English translation, announces in the voice of an irritated humanist, in vol. 1, p. 1:

> The Hermetica dealt with in this book [seventeen Greek books which Ficino had collectively called the *Pimander,* a Latin version of a Greek dialogue called 'Asclepius,'

and passages collected by Joannes Stobaeus] may be described as "those Greek and Latin writings which contain religious or philosophic teachings ascribed to Hermes Trismegistus." . . . There is, besides these, another class of documents, the contents of which are also ascribed to Hermes Trismegistus; namely, writings concerning astrology, magic, alchemy, and kindred forms of pseudo-science. But in the character of their contents these latter differ fundamentally from the former. The two classes of writers . . . had little or nothing to do with one another; they were of very different mental calibre. . . . We are therefore justified in treating the "religious" or "philosophic" *Hermetica* as a class apart, and, for our present purpose, ignoring the masses of rubbish which fall under the other head.

Renaissance "Hermeticism" and the collection segregated above have not been comfortable correlated by recent scholars and translators, except for Frances Yates. See her *Giodano Bruno and the Hermetic Tradition* (New York: Vintage Books, 1969), especially ch. 2. The French version of the *Corpus Hermeticum* that supersedes Scott's in scholarly circles—edited by A. D. Nock and translated by A. J. Festugière, 4 vols. (Paris: Société d'Edition "Les Belles Lettres," 1945–54)—maintains Scott's distinction, as does A. J. Festugière's *La Révélation d'Hermès Trismégiste*, 4 vols. (Paris: Librarie Lecoffre, 1949–54) and the commentary by Shumaker. Ross Garner's discussion of Vaughan's Hermeticism in *Henry Vaughan: Experience and Tradition* considers only the standard philosophic *Corpus*. On the other hand, translators and commentators of the seventeenth century tend toward synthesis of the two bodies of hermetic literature. In Dr. Everard's translation of 1650, for example, comment from the hermetic iatrochemist Henry Nolle (along with Paracelsus and others) is prefatorily applied to the "philosophical" books. For Everard, natural philosophy and theology are to be considered in the same light. Vaughan was familiar with both sides of the hermetic coin, and makes no apparent effort to disjoin them.

The Greek *Hermetica* are a curious mixture of Platonic, rational colloquy, dualist precept, and acknowledgment of "the light of nature" as the proper source of knowledge. "God is in all things," but by a ritualistic procedure, evil, corporeal existence is abandoned and *gnosis* achieved. The books were presumably composed by late third-century Hellenized Egyptians, and may exhibit opposing cultural predispositions on the value of natural philosophy. Early Greek alchemical texts appear at about the same time (ca. 300), and there is definite interrelation between these and the philosophical books. See Scott, *Hermetica,* 1: 29, and Jack Lindsay, *The Origins of Alchemy in Graeco-Roman Egypt* (New York: Barnes & Noble, 1970), ch. 8, "Hermes Trismegistos." A nucleus for the varied literature may be forthcoming as earlier Egyptian documents are translated and compared with the Greek texts. If so, the Renaissance syncretists and Clement of Alexandria will be vindicated.

15. Cf. Ficino, as quoted by Wayne Shumaker, *The Occult Sciences in the Renaissance* (Berkeley, Calif.: University of California Press, 1972), p. 202.

16. For a remarkably succinct testimony on Paracelsus's philosophical resources, see Lester S. King, *The Growth of Medical Thought* (Chicago: University of Chicago Press, 1963), pp. 92–111. A more thorough account, as well as a masterful assessment of Paracelsus's texts in a sixteenth-century setting, appears in Walter Pagel's *Paracelsus: An Introduction to Philosophical Medicine in the Era of the Renaissance* (Basel & New York: S. Karger, 1958).

17. Charles Singer, *A Short History of Scientific Ideas* (Oxford: Clarendon Press, 1959), p. 200.

18. As quoted from A. Berthelot's collection, *Alchimistes Grecs*, by Lindsay, *Origins of Alchemy,* p. 177. Festugière, *Révélation,* 1: 74, casts some doubt on the certainty of Zosimos's text.

19. These points are extracted and accorded special significance in King, *The Growth*

of Medical Thought, p. 128, and A. G. Demus, *The English Paracelsians* (London: Oldbourne Book Co., 1965), pp. 30, 34, 38.

20. From *The Hermetic and Alchemical Writings of Paracelsus,* ed. L. W. deLaurence, trans. A. E. Waite, 2 vols. (Chicago: deLaurence, Scott, & Co., 1910), 2: 108–10:

> Seeing that certain medicines are discovered which preserve the human body for a second and subsequent periods of life, which also protect it altogether from diseases, corruptions, superfluities, and other diminutions of its powers; nay, even when these infirmities and corruptions have broken in upon it, take them away, every physician must carefully study these medicines, and learn them from the very foundations.... No fixed limit has been laid down for us, so that on some predetermined day we must die; nor is this left in our own power. [But] we have medicine from Him who has made us, by means of which we can keep the body in that state of soundness wherein it was created, and expell from it all diseases whatsoever.
>
> It is more certain than certainty itself that the restoration and renovation of the body [will] take place, and that by these processes the whole frame can be transmuted to something better. In like manner, we see with our eyes that all metals are in their bodies purged so that they are protected from rust, and that even wood and the dead bodies of corpses are embalmed so that they suffer no further decay. If, therefore, such things as these are possible to Nature, why should any one shrink from our writings, supported, as they are, by examples ... or stand aloof from them because we draw a comparison between the bodies of metals and those of men? We do not suppose them to be one in the same. We know that they are altogether different; but in both we see the same method of conservation, and this is just what would have been inferred from experience, for if a dead body, by means of embalming, can be conserved, by how much more can a living one be kept from decay? Since we have such a means of attaining long life and driving away disease and death, how comes it that so many princes, emperors, kings, and other great persons die premature deaths? Why do they suffer from infirmities?... We have never read or heard of a prince or king who used these remedies with the single exception of Hermes Trismegistus.

The final line of the quotation either considers Hermes in his legendary role as "the greatest king," or means "We have never read or heard of a prince or king who used these remedies *except from* Hermes Trismegistus."

The transmission of hermetic learning from Egyptian and Arabian resources to Europe, through Paracelsus and thence to Albion's shores, is crucial to the Rosicrucian "fable." According to the *Fama,* brother "C.R." traveled to Egypt to take "better notice there of the plants and creatures"—this, after "learning his physic" in Damascus (at the mere age of sixteen), learning Arabic, and translating "the book M. into good Latin, which he afterwards brought with him.... Theophrastus (Paracelsus) ... although he was none of our Fraternity, yet nevertheless hath he diligently read over the book M: whereby his sharp *ingenium* was exalted." See Thomas Vaughan's translation in Frances Yates, *The Rosicrucian Enlightenment* (London: Routledge & Kegan Paul, 1972), pp. 239 and 241.

21. Paracelsus, "The Philosophy Addressed to the Athenians," *Hermetic and Alchemical Writings of Paracelsus,* 2: 252.
22. Paracelsus, "Concerning the Nature of Things," *Ibid.,* 1: 151.
23. *Ibid.,* 2: 124–36.
24. *Ibid.,* 2: 139.
25. A fine example of Paracelsus's ranging, associative style has been rendered from *Das Buch Paragranum* by R. F. C. Hull and R. T. Llewellyn. It appears in Hull's translation of C. G. Jung's "Paracelsus" (1934), *The Collected Works of C. G. Jung,* Bollingen Series XX, Vol. 15, Copyright © 1966 by the Princeton University Press, p. 17.

What then is the physician's art? He should know what is useful and what harmful to intangible things, to the *beluis marinis,* to the fishes, what is pleasant and unpleasant, healthy and unhealthy to the beasts: these are the arts relating to natural things. What more? The wound-blessings and their powers, why and for what cause they do what they do: What *Melosina* is, and what *Syrena,* what *permutatio, transplantatio* and *transmutatio* are, and how they may be fully understood: What is above nature, what is above species, what is above life, what the visible is and the invisible, what produces sweetness and bitterness, what taste is, what death is, what is useful to fishermen, what a currier, a tanner, a dyer, a blacksmith, and a carpenter should know, what belongs in the kitchen, in the cellar, in the garden, what belongs to time, what a hunter knows, what a mountaineer knows, what befits a traveller, what befits a sedentary man, what warfare requires, what makes peace, what makes clerics and laymen, what every calling does, what every calling is, what God is, what Satan, what poison, and what antidote to poison is, what there is in women, what in men, what distinguishes women from maidens, yellow from white, white from black, and red from fallow, in all things, why one colour here, another there, why short, why long, why success, why failure: and wherein this knowledge applies to all things.

26. Don Cameron Allen, *Mysteriously Meant* (Baltimore, Md.: Johns Hopkins Press, 1970), ch. 5.

27. Sir Thomas Browne, *Religio Medici,* bk. 1, sect. 12, *The Works of Sir Thomas Browne,* ed. Geoffrey Keynes (Chicago: University of Chicago Press, 1964), 1:21.

28. *Ibid.,* bk. 1, sect. I, 10 (1:19 in Keynes).

29. Jacob Boehme, *Von der Geburt und Bezeichnung aller Wesen,* 10: 10ff., as translated and quoted by J. J. Stoudt, *Jacob Boehme* (New York: Seabury Press, 1968), p. 101. It should be noted that Humphrey Blunden, publisher for both Henry and Thomas Vaughan and thus in active sympathy with the Rosicrucian cause, was at the same time engaged in publishing English translations of Boehme's works.

30. Rebirth can be seen as the *explicit* message of some Paracelsian texts. Stoudt (Jacob Boehme, p. 95.) refers to *De Secretis Creationis,* the third part of an edition of Paracelsus's works put together by two of Boehme's friends, for the "suggestive" connection between alchemical mercury, sulphur, and salt and the mystical states of purgation, illumination, and union.

31. Cf. Demus, *The English Paracelsians,* pp. 87–105, on Duchesne. Demus pays only slight attention to Croll's *Basilica Chymica* (1609), and Nolle is not mentioned at all.

32. Quercetanus, *The Practice of Chymicall and Hermeticall Physick,* trans. Thomas Tymme, from the preface to his translation, sig. A^3. This text, STC no. 7276, may be found in University Microfilms, *English Books to 1640* (Ann Arbor, Mich.), reel 988.

33. Croll's book combines formulae for the preparation and use of various medicines with admonitions, prayers, and thanksgivings. For an outraged comment on his devotional/scientific style, see Lynn Thorndike, *A History of Magic and Experimental Science,* 8 vols., (New York: Columbia University Press, 1923–58), 5: 649. Interestingly, the "Admonitoria," which comprise nearly half of the Latin text, are omitted from the English translation *Bazilica Chymica & Praxis Chymiatricae, a Royal and Practical Chymistry* (London: for John Starkey and Thomas Passinger, 1670). By 1670, it appears, the effort to synthesize theology and medicine has ceased.

34. *Works,* p. 459. Vaughan's translation of Eucherius's "The World Contemned" states:

> Much Physicall curiosity, much care and many strict observations are bestowed upon the body; much pain it undergoes in hope of health; and deserves the Soule no Medicine? If it be but fit and necessary, that diverse helps and means of healing are sought for the body ... is it not unjust that the Soul should be excluded, and be suffered to languish and putrifie with deadly and spirituall diseases? Shall the Soul

onely be a stranger to those proper and pretious remedies ordained for it by the great Physitian? Yea rather, if so many things are provided for the body, let the provision for the Soul be far more abundant: for if it was truly said by some, that this *fleshly frame is the servant, and the Soul the Mistris*, then will it be very undecent and injurious, if we shall preferre and place the servant before the Mistris."

(*Works*, p. 315)

CHAPTER 6: *Silex Scintillans* 1650: "THE RESURRECTION OF THE DEAD"

1. Frances Yates, *The Art of Memory* (Harmondsworth, Middlesex: Penguin Books, 1969), p. 109; p. 303.

2. I am indebted to Jerome Mazzaro, *Transformations in the Renaissance English Lyric* (Ithaca: Cornell University Press, 1970), for some of the terms used here to describe the lyric sequence.

3. *Philosophy Reformed and Improved . . . Oswald Croll, Discovering the Great & Deep Mysteries of Nature; Paracelsus . . . Philosophy to the Athenians, . . . Englished by H. Pinnell* (London: M. S. for Lodowick Lloyd, 1657), A4^v. Pinnell here refers to Croll's *Royal Chemistry*.

4. Edward Thomas, *The Tenth Muse* (London: Martin Secker, 1917), pp. 47–48.

5. Dante, *rime petrose* #2, lines 9–12. Text from "Appendix," *Petrarch's Lyric Poems*, ed. and trans. R. M. Durling (Cambridge, Mass.: Harvard University Press, 1976), p. 617.

6. Cf. E. C. Pettet, *Of Paradise and Light* (Cambridge: At the University Press, 1960), p. 71.

7. Paracelsus, in *Philosophy Reformed and Improved*, second title page: *Three Books of Philosophy Written to the Athenians* (collected separately), pp. 4–6.

8. *The Works of Henry Vaughan*, ed. L. C. Martin, 2d ed. (Oxford: Clarendon Press, 1957), p. 394. Hereafter in this chapter this edition will be cited as *Works*.

9. See John Milton, *Christian Doctrine*, bk. 1, ch. 17, in the *Complete Works of John Milton*, ed. Maurice Kelley, trans. John Carey (New Haven, Conn.: Yale University Press, 1973), 6:453. Milton's progressive and systematic account of Redemption, Renovation (natural and supernatural), Regeneration, Repentance and Faith, Ingrafting in Christ, Justification, Adoption, and Union and Communion with Christ and His Members (*Christian Doctrine*, 1, ch. 15–24) offers a scheme obliquely applicable to *Silex Scintillans* 1650. Regeneration and growth are made possible by redemption, but Christ's act may not be recognized, at first, as a cause. "Natural Renovation" involves a knowledge of God through evidence of the creation. As Arthur E. Barker explains: ". . . their responsive faith in God is made possible by the redeeming Christ they know not. . . . 'Regeneration' is the effect of the 'supernatural renovation' which follows a willing and believing response to calling with the repentance that this must induce; it extends the process of natural renovation . . . What supernatural renovation restores, in men who exercise their responsibility, their naturally renovated and their new powers thus to obtain salvation, is the divine image." See "Structural and Doctrinal Pattern in Milton's Later Poems," *Essays . . . Presented to A. S. P. Woodhouse*, ed. M. MacLure and F. W. Watt (Toronto: University of Toronto Press, 1964), p. 171. Vaughan's sensitive awakening is likewise followed by a "responsive faith" in the divinity of the creation, an acceptance of moral responsibility and reform, repentance, an ingrafting of the "seed" of divine nature, and union with Christ. Milton's term *Adoption*, a form of election built upon the Father/Son relationship, is not stressed in *Silex Scintillans I*. Neither is the "peace and true tranquillity of mind" to which it leads a part of Vaughan's sustained experience in book 1. Book 2, however, approaches an

awareness of assured salvation, glorification, and transcendent peace—conditions that Milton describes in *Christian Doctrine*, 1, ch. 25.

10. St. Augustine, *The City of God*, trans. H. Bettenson, intro. D. Knowles (Harmondsworth, Middlesex: Penguin Books, 1972), Book 20, ch. 6, pp. 903–6.

11. Pettet, *Of Paradise and Light*, pp. 197, 204–6. On p. 197, n. 4, Pettet cautiously suggests that the poems in *Silex Scintillans* are printed in the order of their original composition. But there is insufficient evidence to prove that the book is a kind of poetic diary. Most general criticism of Vaughan's book includes some recognition of its continuity. The observation appears first in Edmund Blunden's *On the Poems of Henry Vaughan: Characteristics and Intimations* (London: Richard Cobden-Sanderson, 1927), p. 24: "There are many threads and clues which connect the poems of Vaughan and make it more fruitful to read his work as a whole than in separate examples." Louis Martz strongly suspects that "the volume of 1650 is a whole, like Herbert's *Temple*" (*The Paradise Within* [New Haven, Conn.: Yale University Press, 1964], p. 4). R. A. Durr, while not concerned with the order of the poems, collates archetypal motifs by classifying metaphors from various poems. His first order of images includes those bearing on the secret growth of a seed; the next set deals with the dark journey of the soul, and last comes the spiritual espousal. See *On the Mystical Poetry of Henry Vaughan* (Cambridge, Mass.: Harvard University Press, 1962), pp. 29–78. John R. Mulder states, "Many of Vaughan's poems form sequences through correspondence or contrast, imagery, and diction.... Moreover, the theme of one poem leads logically to that of the next." See *The Temple of the Mind* (New York: Pegasus, 1969), p. 147. Stanley Stewart identifies *Silex Scintillans* as an extended devotional work in *The Expanded Voice* (San Marino, Calif.: Huntington Library, 1970), p. 75. Since the completion of these final chapters, A. J. Smith has argued that *Silex Scintillans* is a single poem made of separate lyrics—"Henry Vaughan's Ceremony of Innocence," *Essays and Studies* N.S. 26 (1973): 35–52—as has Kenneth Friedenreich, *Henry Vaughan* (Boston: Twayne Publishers, 1978), p. 120.

12. Thomas à Kempis, *The Imitation of Christ*, trans. Leo Sherley-Price (Harmondsworth, Middlesex: Penguin Books, 1952), p. 27.

13. Frank Kermode, M. M. Mahood, and Ross Garner all agree that the settings of Vaughan's poem are based on engravings from emblem books. There is some contention, however, as to which books are closest to Vaughan's descriptions. Quarles and Wither are primary contenders. Kermode, in "The Private Imagery of Henry Vaughan," *Review of English Studies* N.S. 1 (1950): 215, n. 7, suggests Quarles as he illustrates ten parallels between *Emblemes* and poems in *Silex Scintillans*. Garner, in *Henry Vaughan, Experience and Tradition* (Chicago: University of Chicago Press, 1959), p. 54, prefers Wither's *Emblems* (1635), especially the engraved frontispiece. M. M. Mahood, *Poetry and Humanism* (London: Jonathan Cape, 1950), p. 257 and n.p. 325, sees the poem as a string of conventional emblems, especially typical of engravings for Jesuit emblem books. The common aim of these opinions is to dispel the mystery of the poem. I would contend that since Vaughan does explain his emblematic descriptions in other places (i.e., "The Lampe"), his aim in "Regeneration" is to represent a sense of mystery and awe.

14. The awesome grove of "Regeneration," described as a forest cathedral, is used as a figure to represent the pages of the Old Testament in "Religion." The fountain and bank of flowers from "Regeneration" are now located as the *hortus conclusus* of Canticles 4.12—"My sister, my spouse is as a garden enclosed, as a Spring shut up, and a fountain sealed up."

15. Vaughan's familiarity with this passage from Hermes is well known and has drawn frequent comment. See, for example, L. C. Martin, "Henry Vaughan and 'Hermes Trismegistus'," *Review of English Studies* 18 (July 1942): 302–4. In her article,

"Casimire Sarbiewski and the English Ode" (*Studies in Philology* 51 [July 1954]: 433–60), Maren-Sofie Røstvig traces the hermetic pattern in Sarbiewski's ode "E Rebus Humanis Excessus" and attempts—with limited success, I think—to discover the scheme in Vaughan's poem "The World." Both Martin and Røstvig note Vaughan's translation (or paraphrase from a translation) of the eight-part ascent in his poem "The importunate Fortune, written to Doctor Powel of Cantre" (*Works,* pp. 634–37).

The hermetic eight-fold ascent may derive from Mithraic accounts of heaven. After death, yet prior to the last day when all will live as children of light, the righteous abide in heaven: "It is figured as a staircase with seven portals. These are the seven heavens, the abode of the six great Emanations and of Mithra [the *Sol Invictus*]. Through these the soul ascends, protected by its guardian angel, into the eighth, where it rests in the presence of Ormuzd." From Charles Bigg, *The Christian Platonists of Alexandria* (Oxford: Clarendon Press, 1913), pp. 285–86. This scheme has much in common with the last stages of a system authorized by the Valentinian Theodotus, the remnants of which are accessible in extracts probably made by Clement of Alexandria. Bigg (pp. 57–59) summarizes the *Excerpta ex Theodoto:*

> Christ came, he taught, not for our redemption alone, but to heal the disorders of the whole universe. . . . But for man's sake Christ became Man, taking upon Him our threefold nature, body, soul, and spirit, though his body was spiritual, not gross as ours. Yet He is not the Saviour of all, but of those only who can receive Him, and in so far as they can receive Him. Some there are who cannot know Him. . . . Some again, the spiritual, are predestined to life eternal. They are akin to the light; knowledge once given leads them on inevitably to perfection, annihilating all their earthly passions. Between these hover "the psychic," the feminine souls, to whom faith is granted, but not knowledge. Before the coming of Christ, these were creatures of destiny. . . . But the Incarnation and Baptism of our Lord broke their bonds, and by faith and discipline they become capable of eternal life. In that future existence the soul needs no body, for it is itself a body, as the Stoics taught. It is immortal and for ever blessed. But there are degrees of felicity. The spiritual soar up at once through the seven planetary orbits to the Ogdoad, the region of the fixed stars, where is no more labour nor change. There they await the consummation, when Christ, the great High Priest, shall lay aside His soul, and enter through the Cross—that is the upper Firmament—into the Holy of Holies, taking with Him His children.

In diction, doctrine and aspiration, the system of Theodotus comes very close to the scheme of *Silex Scintillans.* Christ as a healer of the world, the distinction between saintly and "psychic" persons (Vaughan fears that he is among the latter, and wishes to conceive of himself otherwise), the ascent, the starry dwelling place, and the final consummation of Saviour and children are all represented in the poetry, though Vaughan maintains a stoic distinction between "body" and "spiritual body" only within the framework of Christian eschatology: at the last day the body will be refined and purified, and made one with the soul. If it could be proved that Vaughan actually read the *Excerpta,* that he found these ideas there rather than in hermetic or Pauline (Bigg, p. 61) echoes, this footnote would necessarily become an important part of the text it now comments upon.

16. *The Divine Pymander of Hermes Mercurius Trismegistus* . . . , trans. Dr. Everard (London: Robert White for T. Brewster & G. Moule, 1650), p. 33.

17. Ibid., pp. 28–30.

18. Ibid., pp. 80–98. My quotation is from p. 84.

19. The quotation from Stobaeus is from Walter Scott's edition, *Hermetica* (Oxford: Clarendon Press, 1924), 1:392. The passage may be literally translated as "So it is necessary, my child, to leave behind the body before the end, and to prevail against the

active life, and having thus conquered, ascend." Everard took his text from the Latin translation of Patrizzi, who made his own textual alterations and whose sources are not always clear. See Scott, *Hermetica,* 1:37–40 and p. 43 for a general description of the Patrizzi and Everard translations.

20. *The Works of Thomas Vaughan,* ed. A. E. Waite (New York: University Books, 1968), pp. 15–16. See Everard, *The Divine Pymander,* bk. 2, p. 16 for Pymander's statement.

21. Martin (*Works,* p. 728) cites Thomas's "Lumine de Lumine" as a possible source for his brother's poem "Regeneration." This poem, so enigmatic as it stands, seems to be drawn from nearly everywhere. For additional ideas, see Pettet, *Of Paradise and Light,* pp. 101–17, and Durr, *On the Mystical Poetry of Henry Vaughan,* pp. 79–99.

22. *The Works of Thomas Vaughan,* ed. Waite, pp. 298–99. The last line is a gloss on Genesis 2:5 concerning the generations of God, who created every plant before it was in earth, and "every herb of the field before it grew." Then, these "seeds" of plants and herbs were treated with light and water, and they grew. Regeneration is in imitation of the Creation.

23. Ibid., "Euphrates," p. 428.

24. *Works,* p. 305: "*Paracelsus* writes, that the watching of the body is the sleep of the Soul, and that the day was made for Corporeall Actions, but the night is the working-time of Spirits. Contrary natures run contrary courses: Bodies having no inherent light of their own, make use of this outward light, but Spirits need it not. Sunbeams cannot stumble, nor go out of their way. Death frees them from this dark Lantern of flesh."

25. Paul Ghalioungui, *Magic and Medical Science in Ancient Egypt* (New York: Barnes & Noble, 1965), p. 43. Ghalioungui's reference is to S. Sauneron, *Les songes et leur interpretation, Sources Orientales: Egypte Ancienne* (Paris: Les Ed. du Seuil, 1959).

26. A phrase from "Sure, there's a tye of Bodyes!" *Works,* p. 429. See the Appendix on the personal significance Vaughan attached to this figure.

27. See F. E. Hutchinson, *Henry Vaughan: A Life and Interpretation* (Oxford: Clarendon Press, 1947), p. 24. The Welsh cromlech, a structure of stone monoliths covered with hieroglyphics, was traditionally regarded as a tomb.

28. The elegies are generally thought to have been written for Henry's brother William, who died in 1648. It is becoming apparent, however, that the figure of the slain Christ informs these poems as an archetype, and that the poet reflects on his own "death" in the mirror of the compound image.

29. Once removed from his Father's bosom, Christ's life portrays two kinds of "generation," literal and allegorical. Literal generation is defined by the nativity in the Gospels of Matthew and Luke. Allegorical or spiritual generation, the manifestation of divine nature and the revealing of this nature to others, is defined by rites of baptism in the Gospels of Mark and John.

30. The pattern occurs three other times in *Silex Scintillans* 1650—"Regeneration", "Son-dayes", and "Admission"—and once in the 1655 supplement, "The Throne."

31. This concept originates with the Pythagoreans, who considered numbers as things. Eight is the first cube, the cube is the form of the earth, and Poseidon is the γαιηόκος, or earth-upholder. Thus, eight is associated with the earth and its indwelling god. Poseidon, steadfast preserver, is honored on the eighth day of the month, as Plutarch reports at the end of his life of Theseus. Medieval scholastics such as Macrobius see a cosmic interpretation. Eight, the octave, represents the harmony of the spheres, the final perfection of the created universe, succeeding the mutability of the seven moving spheres with the eternal permanence of the eighth. "Then, since regeneration was the putting on of eternal life, this meaning, too, accrued to eight," Alastair Fowler, *Spenser and the Numbers of Time* (New York: Barnes & Noble, 1964), p. 53. Likewise for Hermes, rebirth is achieved after seven stages of purification, figura-

tively upon the eighth sphere. Fowler continues, "There were confirmatory associations with the resurrection (on the eighth day after the beginning of Holy Week), with circumcision (on the eighth day after birth); even—among the more speculative arithmologists—with the number of souls on the Ark. In accordance with this symbolism, baptismal fonts were often octagonal in form." V. F. Hopper (*Medieval Number Symbolism* [New York: Columbia University Press, 1938], p. 12) also associates the number eight with bodily resurrection on the Day of Judgment, the eighth "cosmic period" following the "seven ages of the world."

32. Those who identify William Vaughan by lines 25–28 of "Silence, and stealth of dayes"—

> ... but souls must
> Track one the other,
> And now the spirit, not the dust
> Must be thy brother.
>
> (*Works*, p. 426)

—might be cautioned that the term "brother" is used in a general sense in the Collect concluding the Anglican burial service. "We meekly beseech thee (O Father) to raise us from the death of sin unto the life of righteousness, that when we shall depart this life, we may rest in him, as our hope is this our brother doth. . . ." *The First Prayer-Book of Edward VI: Compared with the Successive Revisions of the Book of Common Prayer* (London: James Parker and Co., 1877), p. 386.

33. *The First Prayer Book of Edward VI* lists "psalms with other suffrages" to be said either before or after the burial of the corpse. Psalms 116, 146, and 139 are recorded. But the 1604 revision of the Book of Common Prayer, which I assume Vaughan used, omits these specific citations.

34. William Harvey, *Anatomical exercitations concerning the generation of living creatures* . . . (London: J. Young, for O. Pulleyn, 1653), p. 458.

35. See Durr, *On the Mystical Poetry of Henry Vaughan*, n. 43, p. 165. The "Center" may be read as the lowest point of the created universe, or it may be the "central station" man supposedly holds between animals and angels.

36. *Works*, p. 140. Vaughan is not true to his promise, for *Solitary Devotions* is scarcely void of Christian rules and "ethics." For example: "When you have received the Sacred Elements, you should not presently after spit, nor eate and drink, but refraine untill they are perfectly digested and resolved" (*Works*, p. 164).

37. See Louis Martz, *The Paradise Within*, pp. 12–13 for an interesting comparison between Vaughan, the churchman without a church, and Herbert, the churchman.

38. Thomas Powell, *Quadriga Salutis, or The Four General Heads* . . . (London: by Sarah Griffin, for Philip Chetwind, 1657), sign. B^{1v}–B^{2r}. Powell notes that his "chatechism" has been "undermyning" for a while. Vaughan was most likely familiar with the work, as he and Powell were in frequent contact.

39. Ibid., p. 27.

40. *Works*, p. 739, note to p. 448.

41. *The Divine Pymander*, trans. Everard, bk. 7, p. 89.

CHAPTER 7: *Silex Scintillans* 1655:
"THE LIFE OF THE WORLD TO COME"

1. See F. E. Hutchinson, *Henry Vaughan: A Life and Interpretation* (Oxford: Clarendon Press, 1947) pp. 195–97 and 107–8; hereafter cited as *Life*.

2. ". . . com'uom talor che piange et parte / vede cosa che li occhi e'l cor alletta," Petrarch *Rime* 325.

3. *The Works of Henry Vaughan*, ed. L. C. Martin, 2d ed. (Oxford: Clarendon Press, 1957), p. 482. Hereafter in this chapter this edition will be cited as *Works*.

4. E. C. Pettet, for other reasons, comes to a similar conclusion: "Part II is both a continuation from Part I and distinct from it, though we must not exaggerate the differences" (*Of Paradise and Light* [Cambridge: At the University Press, 1960], p. 207).

5. This poem appears to derive from a passage in Nieremberg's essay "Of Temperance and Patience" that Vaughan translated between 1650 and 1653. The "proffer" of sinful ways, represented by "black Parasites" who are transformed into Commonwealth politicians and then into the flies of hell, is met with an attitude of angry contempt, righteous impatience, which Vaughan modifies in later poems. As Nieremberg relates: "Patience in this Case must elevate it selfe, and passe into a virtuous anger and contempt of sinfull prosperity: We must be piously impatient of all their proffers and poisonous allurements; Impatient, I say, that we may patiently overcome them" (*Works*, p. 255).

6. As L. C. Martin, among others, has noted. See *Works*, p. 747. For Vaughan's reference to Herbert's saintly life, see "Man in Darkness," *Works*, p. 186.

7. *Works*, pp. 181–82. Vaughan's remarks are derived from *Prologus sancti Hieronymi . . . in libros Vitaspatrum*, which, as Martin notes, is wrongly attributed to Jerome. Vaughan may have been concerned about the question of authorship. As he says in the poem "The day of Judgement":

> When shall those first white Pilgrims rise,
> Whose holy, happy Histories
> (Because they sleep so long) some men
> Count but the blots of a vain pen?
>
> (*Works*, p. 531)

The place described in Vaughan's essay is probably Cellia, or "the community of the Cells," founded before 350 A.D. by St. Amon in the Wâdî 'n-Natrûn valley between Alexandria and Cairo. For a description, see F. A. Meinardus, *Christian Egypt Ancient and Modern* (Cairo: Cahiers d'Histoire Égyptienne, 1965), pp. 146–49; *The Paradise of the Holy Fathers*, trans. E. A. W. Budge (reprint ed., New York: Burt Franklin, 1972), 1: xlvi.

8. Vaughan is consistently attracted by hermetic *exempla*. This one he renders in "White Sunday" as:

> For, though we hourly breath decays,
> And our best *note* and highest *ease*
> Is but meer changing of the *keys*,
> And a *Consumption* that doth please. . . .
>
> (*Works*, p. 486)

9. See *Works*, pp. 249–51.

10. Vaughan appears to contradict this notion only in a fanciful extrapolation upon the natural powers of "The Eagle" (*Works*, p. 626–27). In this poem sustained and transcendent experience, "our souls bold *Heights*," is expressed in the "material dress" of the eagle's flight from earth to the moon, the sun, and finally the stars.

> Here doth he plume and dress himself, the Beams
> Rushing upon him, like so many Streams;
> While with direct looks he doth entertain
> The thronging flames, and shoots them back again.
> And thus from star to star he doth repaire

> And wantons in that pure and peaceful air.
> ....
> Then with the *Orbe* it self he moves, to see
> Which is more swift th'*Intelligence* or *He*.

These lines, interestingly comparable with the "ascent" stanzas of Andrew Marvell's "The Garden," contain the visionary hope but contradict the experiential pattern of *Silex Scintillans*. The overt transcendence of "The Eagle," as well as the unqualified seclusion advocated in "The Bee" (*Works*, p. 672), appear to have been purposefully withheld from the "unfeigned verse" published in 1655, even though eagles and bees figure significantly in some of the poems of *Silex Scintillans II*. Both of these "hieroglyphics" appear as "*Pas-Times* and *Diversions* of a *Countrey Muse*" in Vaughan's last book, *Thalia Rediviva* (1678).

11. Cf. "Ascension-Hymn," stanzas 3-5, *Works*, p. 483.

12. Gregory *Oration* 2. 17 (Migne *Patrologiae Graecae* 35. 425 C), as translated and quoted by Rosemary R. Ruether, *Gregory of Nazianzus* (Oxford: Clarendon Press, 1969), pp. 153–54.

13. *Works*, pp. 141 and 183. See also pp. 181, 339, 342, 354, and 356 for general allusions. Jerome's life of Hilarion is also quoted (*Works*, p. 173), as is the life of Antonius (*Works*, p. 184), which appears in the stories of Paul and Hilarion.

14. *Oration* 44. 10–12 (Migne *Patrologiae Graecae* 36. 617 C–620 A, B; 621 A) is translated and quoted by Ruether, *Gregory of Nazianzus*, pp. 100–1.

15. In "The Timber," *Works*, pp. 497–99. A tree, once flourishing, now lies

> ... beneath the sad and heavy *Line*
> Of death, dost waste all senseless, cold and dark;
> Where not so much as dreams of light may shine,
> Nor any thoughts of greenness, leaf or bark.

But Vaughan, dealing in legends of natural philosophy, understands that the tree can "resent" storms before they arrive, and show by certain signs how far away the storm is. A parallel case is cited:

> So murthered man, when lovely life is done,
> And his blood freez'd, keeps in the Center still
> Some secret sense, which makes the dead blood run
> At his approach, that did the body kill.

Vaughan apparently believes these legends. He clearly *wants* to believe them as proof that the dead are preserved against their resurrection, and for this explicit argument he quotes an even more fantastic "experiment" from Agrippa:

> A great *Philosopher* and *Secretary* to *nature* discoursing of the *resurrection* of the *dead*, tells us, *that he oftentimes lighted upon some of those creatures in that dark state of dormition, and did dissect some of them, and cut off the limbs of others, and yet* (saith he) *could I perceive no signe of life at all in them, their arteries and flesh being as hard and as dry as a stick, but casting them into a pot of seething water, they would soften by degrees, and shortly after stir about, and those very parts which were dissected, would give very clear and satisfactory Indications of life.* This is so strong a *Symbol* of the resurrection, that I think it needlesse to make any application. (*Works*, p. 176)

16. The "change" and "sicknesse" referred to in this poem, "Begging," may allude to a severe illness that Vaughan suffered between 1652 and 1653. See Hutchinson, *Life*, pp. 106–7. The poem dates prior to September 15, 1653, when *Flores Solitudinis* . . .

Collected in his Sicknesse and Retirement was registered, since it appears as part of the prefatory material to this collection of translations.

17. See the last stanza of "The Timber," Works, p. 499.

18. Ross Garner, who comments on Vaughan's identification with Ishmael, notes that The Book of Common Prayer characterizes Ishmael and Isaac in these terms. See *Henry Vaughan: Experience and the Tradition* (Chicago: University of Chicago Press, 1959), p. 21.

19. Clement of Alexandria, "Miscellanies" 1. ch. 5 as translated by W. Wilson, in the *Ante-Nicene Christian Library*, ed. A. Roberts and J. Donaldson (Edinburgh: Clark, 1870–1903), 4: 368.

20. In the poem so titled (Works, p. 510), Vaughan refers to Ishmael in stanza 4:

> O spred thy sacred wings and shake
> One living drop! one drop life keeps!
> If pious griefs Heavens joys awake,
> O fill his bottle! thy childe weeps!

21. "Palm-Sunday," line 44, Works, p. 502. Vaughan understands the story of Job as a scriptural analogue to his own trials. On the unadorned title page to the 1655 edition of *Silex Scintillans*, he quotes Job 35:10–11: "*Where is God my Maker, who giveth Songs in / the night? / Who teacheth us more then the beasts of the / earth, and maketh us wiser then the fowls / of heaven?*"

22. See Martin, notes to page 506, Works, p. 749.

23. Vaughan notes that after Salome had John the Baptist beheaded, "*in passing over a frozen river, the ice broke under her, and chopt off her head*" (Works, p. 503). See Don Cameron Allen, "Henry Vaughan's 'Salome on Ice'," *Philological Quarterly* 23 (1944): 84–85, for sources of the legend.

24. Origen, *Contra Celsum* 4. 57, trans. Henry Chadwick (Cambridge: At the University Press, 1953) p. 231. The passage continues:

> And by God's will a quality of one kind is imposed upon this particular matter, but afterwards it will have a quality of another kind, one, let us say, which is better and superior. Moreover, as from the beginning to the end of the world changes in bodies occur according to ways that have been appointed, possibly a new and different way may succeed after the destruction of the world, which our writings call the consummation;—so it is not remarkable if at the present time, *as the popular opinion has it, a snake is formed out of a dead man, originating from the marrow of the spine, and a bee from an ox, and a wasp from a horse, and a beetle from an ass, and in general worms from most animals.*

Natural "metamorphoses" are thus desultory signs of providential potential. The Incarnation establishes, however, the direction of "consummate" metamorphosis. But the recognition and belief of "a divine spirit . . . in a body" is a matter of individual perspective and inclination. Origen cedes this point to the academic Celsus, and then argues it against him. Some are prepared to see Form and Beauty; others are not. ". . . his body differed in accordance with the capacity of those who saw it, and on this account appeared in such form as was beneficial for the needs of each individual's vision. . . . For he did not appear in the same way both to the multitude and to those able to follow him up the high mountain. . . . To those who are still down below and are not yet prepared to ascend, the Logos 'has not form nor beauty'. . . . However, to those who by following him have received power to go after him even as he is ascending the high mountain, he has a more divine form . . . so glorious and striking and wonderful that the three apostles who went up with Jesus and saw the exquisite beauty fell on their faces" (*Contra Celsum* 6. 77; Chadwick, pp. 390–91). Varying the sense of this distinction only a little, Vaughan is about to argue that only those who "love much" are capable of receiving the "form" of Providence.

25. The old "Covenant 'twixt *All* and *One*," Genesis 9:8–16, established that no further floods would come to destroy the world. The rainbow, sign of this agreement and forerunner of the new "Covenant" of fire and judgment, is the subject of Vaughan's "The Rainbow" (*Works*, p. 509).

26. See ch. 7, note 1. Unlike those published by Vaughan in other books, none of the elegies in *Silex Scintillans* appear with any specific, historical data. Though veiled references such as those found in these "sacred" elegies are typical of the sonnet tradition, I believe that the poet intends an ambiguity between his implied "real" subjects and the Christ figure whose death and subsequent absence is documented explicitly. A brother, a child, and now a wife may thus become "one with his body."

27. John Milton, *Paradise Lost,* 12: lines 575–87. Cf. I Corinthians 13:13; II Peter, 1:5–9.

28. Vaughan augments his initial text with asterisk references to John 5:30, 45, 47, and 48.

29. Christ's body, the "sacred vail" of flesh (Hebrews 10:20), is afforded humanity by Mary, the "*Virgin*-shrine." In medieval thought, Mary, Queen of Heaven, subsumed the ancient place of Cynthia, the moon. See R. A. Durr, *On the Mystical Poetry of Henry Vaughan* (Cambridge, Mass: Harvard University Press, 1962), p. 115.

30. See the opening stanza of "The Agreement" (*Works*, p. 528) for the only moment of doubt from this point until the last of *Silex Scintillans*. In these concluding poems, Vaughan at last writes of himself as a "worthy" man. All further considerations he leaves to other judgment: *"Thy will be done."* There is no visionary testimony of his special blessedness. Election, which may be an issue in *Silex Scintillans I* (i.e., in "The World") is simply not an issue here.

31. "The Agreement," concluding stanza (*Works*, p. 530). These lines echo and fulfill the plea, "Perfect what thou hast begun," that concludes *Silex Scintillans I.*

32. "The Wreath," an artful concatenation, is a final version of the "ring" displayed naturalistically in "The Waterfall." "The Queer" is a riddle; "The Book," "To the Holy Bible," and "L'Envoy" are formal "farewells."

33. Vaughan concludes his poem "To the Holy Bible" by saying "Thy next *Effects* no tongue can tell . . ." He concludes his book by moving further and further away from the known and native tongue in which his poems have been written. First, there is the Latin heading "*S. Clemens apud Basil*" (Basil translates St. Clement) and then the epigraph, in Greek. The phrase is plain: "God, and the lord Jesus Christ, and the holy spirit, live." Vaughan's text for St. Basil has not been confirmed. It could have been an anthology, but six editions containing the Περὶ τοῦ Ἁγίον Πνεύματος (*De Spiritu Sancto:* "On the Holy Spirit") from which the epigraph is taken were printed between 1499 and 1638. Vaughan's reference to Basil, friend of Gregory Nazianzen, follower of Clement and Origen, provides another though final clue to the poet's interest in Alexandrian asceticism and the "Primitive Fathers." His interest, at the end, centers explicitly upon the post-Nicene victory of Trinitarianism: "three persons; one substance." There is a "substantial" bond and continuity between this life and the next.

APPENDIX

1. Cf. Ross Garner, *Henry Vaughan: Experience and the Tradition* (Chicago: University of Chicago Press, 1959), pp. 163–64: "The problem which remains the most vexing for me . . . is why Vaughan omitted from the second, and doubly enlarged, edition of *Silex Scintillans* (1655) the emblem and the Latin poem accompanying it of the first edition (1650)."

2. See W. R. Parker, "Henry Vaughan and his Publishers," *The Library,* 4th ser. 20 (1940): 401–6.

3. Parker cites Plomer's *Dictionary of Booksellers:* "Nothing more is heard of him [Blunden] after 1652." His shop appears to have been inactive until 1654, when two final publications are recorded.

4. E. L. Marilla, "Henry and Thomas Vaughan," *Modern Language Review* 39 (1944): 180–83. Marilla accepts Parker's conclusions about *Silex Scintillans* 1650, and argues, reasonably, that Thomas arranged for the publication of *The Mount of Olives* and *Silex Scintillans* 1655 as well.

5. *The Works of Henry Vaughan,* ed. L. C. Martin (Oxford: Clarendon Press, 1957, p. 583. Hereafter in the appendix this edition will be cited as *Works.*

6. The letters referred to are printed in *Works,* pp. 697 and 698. The documents, with impressions, are housed in the Lambeth Palace Library and the National Library of Wales, respectively. E. M. Williamson, late Bishop of Swansea and Brecon, is responsible for calling this information to our attention. See his lecture-broadcast in the Welsh Home Service, January 8, 1953, published as *Henry Vaughan,* pp. 9–10.

7. R. A. Durr traces the development of this image as "The growth of the Lily." See *On the Mystical Poetry of Henry Vaughan* (Cambridge, Mass.: Harvard University Press, 1962), pp. 31–60.

8. Powell died in 1660. Though this poem was not published until 1678, Vaughan most likely wrote it while Powell was still alive.

9. The annotated *Quadripartitum Botanicum,* Simonis Paulii (Strasbourg, 1667–68), is in the collection of Vaughan's books held by the Library Company of Philadelphia. The half-titled flyleaf is signed "Vaughan: 1682," and the title is inscribed "Vaughan–82, pretium 12s."

10. For Vaughan's record of the Paulinus anecdote, see *Works,* pp. 364–65. Vaughan did have a new personal emblem engraved for his signet, and Paulinus finally yielded to the request for a picture. Two poems accompany it. In the first, Paulinus describes himself as a weeping, repentant sinner. In the second, relating to a baptismal font near which the picture was to be placed, are the lines: ". . . A new birth doth proceede/From the bright streames by an immortall seed." The figure for Vaughan's 1662 signet, coincidentally at least, is perceivable in these two verses.

Bibliography

PRIMARY SOURCES

Bettany, W. A. Lewis, ed. *Silex Scintillans.* London, 1905.

Chambers, E. K., ed. *The Poems of Henry Vaughan, Silurist.* Introduction by H. C. Beeching. 2 vols. London and New York, 1896.

Fogle, French, ed. *The Complete Poetry of Henry Vaughan.* New York: Doubleday & Co., 1964.

Grosart, A. B., ed. *The Works in Verse and Prose of Henry Vaughan, Silurist.* St. George's, Blackburn, Lancashire, 1871.

Lewalski, Barbara K., and Sabol, Edward J., eds. *Silex Scintillans.* In *Major Poets of the Earlier Seventeenth Century.* New York: Odyssey Press, 1973.

Lyte, H. F., ed. *Sacred Poems and Private Ejaculations of Henry Vaughan.* London, 1847.

Marilla, E. L., ed. *The Secular Poems of Henry Vaughan.* Uppsala: Lundequistika Bokhandlen, 1958.

Martin, L. C., ed. *The Works of Henry Vaughan.* 2d ed. Oxford; Clarendon Press, 1957. This is the standard edition from which my citations, unless otherwise noted, are taken.

BIBLIOGRAPHIES

A Comprehensive Bibliography of Henry Vaughan, compiled and annotated by E. L. Marilla, (Tuscaloosa, Ala.: University of Alabama Press, 1948), "includes all editions and reprints of Vaughan and all noteworthy recognition of him up through 1945." *A Bibliographical Supplement* by Marilla and J. D. Simmonds (Tuscaloosa, Ala.: University of Alabama Press, 1963) continues the listings through 1960. For criticism since 1960, there is Robert E. Bourdette's "Recent Studies in Henry Vaughan," *English Literary Review* 4 (1974): 299–310, and the selective "Bibliography: Criticism and Commentary" in Kenneth Friedenreich's *Henry Vaughan* (Boston: Twayne, 1978).

WORKS CITED AND REFERENCES

Note: The student of Vaughan's poetry should have a copy of the Bible and the Apocrypha, in the authorized version of 1611. *The First Prayer-Book of Edward VI, Compared with Successive Revisions of the Book of Common Prayer* (Oxford and London: James Parker and Co., 1877) is also useful.

Alighieri, Dante. *Vita Nuova*. Edited by L. Pietrobono. Florence: G. C. Sansoni, 1951.

Allen, Don Cameron. "Henry Vaughan's 'Salome on Ice'." *Philological Quarterly* 23 (1944): 84–85.

———. *Mysteriously Meant*. Baltimore, Md.: Johns Hopkins Press, 1970.

Aubrey, John. *Brief Lives and Other Selected Writings*. Edited by Anthony Powell. London, 1944.

Augustine, Saint. *The City of God*. Translated by H. Bettenson. Harmondsworth, Middlesex: Penguin Books, 1972.

Bachelard, Gaston. *On Poetic Imagination and Reverie*. Translated by C. Gaudin. New York: Bobbs-Merrill, 1971.

Bagshaw, E., ed. *The Life and Death of Mr. Vavasor Powell*. N.p., 1671.

Barker, Arthur E. "Structural and Doctrinal Pattern in Milton's Later Poems." In *Essays . . . Presented to A. S. P. Woodhouse*. Edited by M. MacLure and F. W. Watt. Toronto: University of Toronto Press, 1964.

Barnes, Barnabe. *A Divine Centurie of Spirituall Sonnets*. London, 1595.

Bigg, Charles. *The Christian Platonists of Alexandria*. Oxford: Clarendon Press, 1913.

Blunden, Edmund. *On the Poems of Henry Vaughan: Characteristics and Intimations*. London: Richard Cobden-Sanderson, 1927.

Boethius. *De institutione musica*. In *Source Readings in Music History*, edited by Oliver Strunk. New York: W. W. Norton & Co., 1950.

Browne, Sir Thomas. *The Works of Sir Thomas Browne*. Edited by Geoffrey Keynes. Chicago: University of Chicago Press, 1964.

Burckhardt, Titus. *Alchemy*. Translated by W. Stoddart. London: Stuart & Watkins, 1967.

Bush, Douglas. *English Literature in the Earlier Seventeenth Century*. Rev. ed. Oxford: Clarendon Press, 1962.

Carapetyan, Armen. "Music and Medicine in the Renaissance." In *Music and Medicine*, edited by D. Schullian and M. Schoen. New York: Schuman, 1948.

Cartwright, William. *The Plays and Poems of William Cartwright*. Edited by G. Blakemore Evans. Madison, Wis.: University of Wisconsin Press, 1951.

Clement of Alexandria. *Stromatum*. In Migne *Patrologiae Graecae*, Vol. 9. Paris, 1890.

———. *Miscellanies*, trans. W. Wilson, in *Ante-Nicene Christian Library*. Vol. 4. Edited by A. Roberts and J. Donaldson. Edinburgh: Clark, 1870–1903.

Cowley, Abraham. *The English Writings of Abraham Cowley.* Edited by A. R. Waller. Cambridge: At the University Press, 1905.

Croll, Oswald. *Basilica Chymica.* Frankfurt, 1609. *Bazilica Chymica & Praxis Chymiatricae.* Revised and augmented by John Hartmann in *Practice of Chemistry.* London: John Starkey and Thomas Passinger, 1670.

———. *Discovering the Great & Deep Mysteries of Nature.* Translated by H. Pinnell. London: M. S. for Lodowick Lloyd, 1657.

Crossley-Holland, P. *Music in Wales.* London: R. Stockwell, 1948.

Davenant, Sir William. *Sir William Davenant's Gondibert.* Edited by D. F. Gladish. Oxford: Clarendon Press, 1971.

Demus, A. G. *The English Paracelsians.* London, Oldbourne Book Co., 1965.

Dowden, Edward. *Puritan and Anglican: Studies in Literature.* London: Kegan Paul, Trench, Trubner, & Co., 1900.

Drummond, William. *The Poetical Works of William Drummond of Hawthornden.* Edited by L. E. Kastner. Manchester: At the University Press, 1913.

Duchesne, Joseph (Quercetanus). *The Practice of Chymicall and Hermeticall Physick.* Translated by Thomas Tymme. London, 1605.

Durr, R. A. *On the Mystical Poetry of Henry Vaughan.* Cambridge, Mass.: Harvard University Press, 1962.

Everard, (Dr.), trans. *The Divine Pymander of Hermes Mercurius Trismegistus . . . translated . . . By that Learned Divine Doctor Everard.* London: Robert White, for T. Brewster & G. Moule, 1650.

Festugière, A. J., trans., and Nock, A. D., ed. *Corpus Hermeticum.* 4 vols. Paris: Société d'Edition "Les Belles Lettres," 1945–54.

Finney, Gretchen Ludke. *Musical Backgrounds for English Literature: 1580–1650.* New Brunswick, N.J.: Rutgers University Press, 1962.

Fowler, Alastair. *Spenser and the Numbers of Time.* New York: Barnes & Noble, 1964.

———. *Triumphal forms: Structural patterns in Elizabethan poetry.* Cambridge: At the University Press, 1970.

Freeman, Rosemary. *English Emblem Books.* London: Chatto and Windus, 1948.

French, Peter J. *John Dee: The World of an Elizabethan Magus.* London: Routledge & Kegan Paul, 1972.

Friedenreich, Kenneth. *Henry Vaughan.* Boston: Twayne Publishers, 1978.

Fuller, Thomas. *The Church History of Britain.* 3d. ed. 3 vols. London: Thomas Tegg, 1842.

———. *The Poems and Translations in Verse . . . of Thomas Fuller*. Edited by A. B. Grosart. Edinburgh: Crawford & McCabe, 1868.

———. *The Worthies of England*. Edited by J. Freeman. London: George Allent Unwin, 1952.

Garner, Ross. *Henry Vaughan: Experience and Tradition*. Chicago; University of Chicago Press, 1959.

Ghalioungui, Paul. *Magic and Medical Science in Ancient Egypt*. New York: Barnes & Noble, 1965.

de Gombauld, Jean Ogier. *L'Endymion*. Translated by Richard Hurst. London, 1639.

Grierson, H. J. C. *Cross Currents in English Literature of the Seventeenth Century*. Harmondsworth, Middlesex: Penguin Books, 1966.

Griffith, Alexander. *A True and Perfect Relation*. . . . London, 1654.

Habington, William. *Castara*. 3d ed. Reprint. London: Edward Arber, 1870.

Harvey, William. *Anatomical exercitations concerning the generation of living creatures*. . . . London: J. Young, for O. Pulleyn, 1653.

Heninger, S. K. *Touches of Sweet Harmony*. San Marino, Calif.: Huntington Library, 1974.

Herbert, George. *The Works of George Herbert*. Edited by F. E. Hutchinson. Oxford: Clarendon Press, 1941.

Herodotus. *The Persian Wars*. Translated by G. Rawlinson. Modern Library, 1942.

Hill, J. E. Christopher. *Change and Continuity in Seventeenth Century England*. London: Weidenfeld and Nicolson, 1974.

———. *The Century of Revolution*. Edinburgh: T. Nelson, 1961.

Hollander, John. *The Untuning of the Sky*. Princeton, N.J.: Princeton University Press, 1961.

Hooker, Richard. *Of the Laws of Ecclesiastical Polity*. Edited by Ronald Bayne. 2 vols. Everyman's Library, 1907.

Hopper, V. F. *Medieval Number Symbolism*. New York: Columbia University Press, 1938.

Huntley, Frank L. *Sir Thomas Browne*. Ann Arbor, Mich.: University of Michigan Press, 1962.

Hutchinson, F. E. *Henry Vaughan: A Life and Interpretation*. Oxford: Clarendon Press, 1947.

Saint Jerome (attributed to). *The Paradise of the Holy Fathers*. Translated by E. A. W. Budge. Reprint. New York: Burt Franklin, 1972.

Jones, F. H. *Freemasonry in Monmouthshire*. Newport, Mon.: R. H. Johns, 1924.

Jones, R. Tudur. "Religion in Post-Restoration Brecknockshire: 1660–1668." *Brycheiniog* 7 (1962): 12.

Jung, C. G. "Paracelsus." In *The Collected Works of C. G. Jung,* edited and translated by R. F. C. Hull and R. T. Llewellyn. New York: Bollingen Foundation, 1966.

Kempis, Thomas à. *The Imitation of Christ.* Translated by Leo Sherley-Price. Harmondsworth, Middlesex: Penguin Books, 1952.

Kermode, Frank. "The Private Imagery of Henry Vaughan," *Review of English Studies* N.S. 1 (1950): 215.

King, J. R. *Studies in Six Seventeenth Century Writers.* Columbus, Ohio: Ohio State University Press, 1966.

King, Lester S. *The Growth of Medical Thought.* Chicago: University of Chicago Press, 1963.

Leishman, J. B. *The Metaphysical Poets.* Oxford: Clarendon Press, 1934.

Lewis, C. S. *The Allegory of Love.* London: Oxford University Press, 1936.

Lindsay, Jack. *The Origins of Alchemy in Graeco-Roman Egypt.* New York: Barnes & Noble, 1970.

Mahood, M. M. *Poetry and Humanism.* London: Jonathan Cape, 1950.

Marilla, E. L., "Henry and Thomas Vaughan." *Modern Language Review* 39 (1944): 180–83.

Martin, L. C. "Henry Vaughan and 'Hermes Trismegistus'." *Review of English Studies* 18 (July 1942): 302–4.

Martz, Louis. *The Paradise Within.* New Haven, Conn.: Yale University Press, 1964.

———. *The Poetry of Meditation.* New Haven, Conn.: Yale University Press, 1962.

Mazzaro, Jerome. *Transformations in the Renaissance English Lyric.* Ithaca, N.Y.: Cornell University Press, 1970.

Meinardus, F. A. *Christian Egypt Ancient and Modern.* Cairo: Cahiers d'Histoire Egyptienne, 1965.

Meinecke, Bruno. "Music and Medicine in Classical Antiquity." In *Music and Medicine,* edited by D. Schullian and M. Schoen. New York: Schuman, 1948.

Milton, John. *Christian Doctrine. The Complete Works of John Milton,* edited by Maurice Kelley and translated by John Carey, vol. 6. New Haven, Conn.: Yale University Press, 1973.

Miner, Earl. *The Metaphysical Mode from Donne to Cowley.* Princeton, N.J.: Princeton University Press, 1969.

Mulder, John R. *The Temple of the Mind.* New York: Pegasus, 1969.

Murrin, Michael. *The Veil of Allegory.* Chicago: University of Chicago Press, 1969.

Nicolson, Marjorie Hope. *The Breaking of the Circle.* Rev. ed. New York: Columbia University Press, 1960.

Nuttall, Geoffrey F. *The Welsh Saints: 1640–1660.* Cardiff: University of Wales Press, 1957.

Origen. *Contra Celsum.* Translated by Henry Chadwick. Cambridge: At the University Press, 1953.

Pagel, Walter. *Paracelsus: An Introduction to Philosophical Medicine in the Era of the Renaissance.* Basel and New York: S. Karger, 1958.

Paracelsus. *The Hermetic and Alchemical Writings of Paracelsus.* Translated by A. E. Waite and edited by L. W. deLaurence. 2 vols. Chicago: deLaurence, Scott, & Co., 1910.

———. *Philosophy to the Athenians.* Translated by H. Pinnell. London, 1657.

Parker, W. R. "Henry Vaughan and his Publishers." *The Library* 4th series, 20 (1940): 401–6.

Parry, Thomas. *A History of Welsh Literature.* Translated by H. Idris Bell. Oxford: Clarendon Press, 1955.

Paulii, Simonis. *Quadripartitum Botanicum.* Strasbourg, 1667–68.

Pearson. L. E. *Elizabethan Love Conventions.* New York: Barnes & Noble, 1966.

Petrarch, Francesco. *Lyric Poems.* Translated by R. M. Durling. Cambridge, Mass.: Harvard University Press, 1976.

———. *Le Rime di Francesco Petrarca.* Edited by G. Carducci and S. Ferrari. Florence, 1899.

———. *Sonnets and Songs.* Introduction by T. Mommsen, translated by A. M. Armi. New York: Grosset & Dunlap, 1968.

Pettet, E. C. *Of Paradise and Light.* Cambridge: At the University Press, 1960.

Plato. *Timaeus.* Translated by B. Jowett. In *The Collected Dialogues,* edited by E. Hamilton and H. Cairns. New York: Bollingen Foundation, 1963.

Plotinus. *The Essential Plotinus.* Translated by E. O'Brien. New York: Mentor Books, 1964.

Porta, Giambattista della. *Natural Magick.* 1658. Reprint. New York: Basic Books, 1957.

Poulet, Georges. *The Metamorphoses of the Circle.* Baltimore, Md.: Johns Hopkins Press, 1966.

Powell, Thomas. *Elementa Opticae.* London, 1651.

———. *Humane Industry: or a History of Most Manual Arts.* London: Henry Herringman, 1661.

———. *Quadriga Salutis, or The Four General Heads of Christian Religion Surveyed & Explained.* London: by Sarah Griffin for Philip Chetwind, 1657.

Rees, Sir Frederick. "Breconshire During the Civil War." *Brycheiniog* 8 (1962).

Richards, Thomas. *A History of the Puritan Movement in Wales, 1639–1653.* London: National Eisteddfod Assn., 1920.

———. *Religious Developments in Wales, 1654–1662.* London: National Eisteddfod Assn., 1923.

Richmond, H. M. *The School of Love: The Evolution of the Stuart Love Lyric.* Princeton, N.J.: Princeton University Press, 1964.

Rickey, Mary Ellen. "Vaughan, *The Temple,* and Poetic Form," *Studies in Philology* 59 (1962): 162–70.

Roche, Thomas P. "The Calendrical Structure of Petrarch's *Canzoniere.*" *Studies in Philology* 71 (1974): 152–72.

Røstvig, Maren-Sofie. "Andrew Marvell's 'The Garden': A Hermetic Poem." Revised essay, in *Andrew Marvell: The Garden,* edited by T. Calhoun and J. Potter. Columbus, Ohio: Charles E. Merrill Publishing Co., 1970.

———. "Casimire Sarbiewski and the English Ode," *Studies in Philology* 51 (July 1954): 443–60.

Rudrum, Alan. "The Influence of Alchemy in the Poems of Henry Vaughan," *Philological Quarterly* 49 (1970): 469–80.

Ruether, Rosemary R. *Gregory of Nazianzus.* Oxford: Clarendon Press, 1969.

Sarbiewski, Mathias Casimire. *The Odes.* Translated by G. Hils. Augustan Reprint Society, Los Angeles, Calif.: Clark Memorial Library, University of California, no. 44. 1953.

Sarbiewski, Mathias Casimire. *The Odes.* Translated by G. Hils. Augustan Reprint Society, no. 44. Los Angeles, Calif.: Clark Memorial Library, University of California, 1953.

Scott, Walter, ed. and trans. *Hermetica.* Oxford: Clarendon Press, 1924.

Shafer, S. Robert. *The English Ode to 1660.* Princeton, N.J.: Princeton University Press, 1918.

Sharp. R. L. *From Donne to Dryden.* Chapel Hill, N.C.: University of North Carolina Press, 1940.

Shumaker, Wayne. *The Occult Sciences in the Renaissance.* Berkeley, Calif.: University of California Press, 1972.

Sidney, Sir Philip. *The Poems of Sir Philip Sidney.* Edited by W. A. Ringler. Oxford: Clarendon Press, 1962.

———. *The Psalmes of Sir Philip Sidney and the Countess of Pembroke.* Edited by J.A.C. Rathmell. New York: Doubleday & Co., 1963.

Sigerist, Henry E. *A History of Medicine.* Vol. 1. New York: Oxford University Press, 1951.

Simmonds, J. D. *Masques of God: Form and Theme in the Poetry of Henry Vaughan.* Pittsburgh, Pa.: University of Pittsburgh Press, 1972.

Singer, Charles. *A Short History of Scientific Ideas.* Oxford: Clarendon Press, 1959.

Smith, A. J. "Henry Vaughan's Ceremony of Innocence," *Essays and Studies* N.S. 26 (1973): 35–52.

Smith, James. "On Metaphysical Poetry." In *Determinations,* edited by F. R. Leavis. London, 1934.

Southwell, Robert. *The Poems of Robert Southwell.* Edited by J. H. McDonald and N. P. Brown. Oxford: Clarendon Press, 1967.

Spingarn, J. E., ed. *Critical Essays of the Seventeenth Century.* 3 vols. Oxford: Clarendon Press, 1908.

Stern, R. and Saunders, J. *Ancient Egyptian and Cnidian Medicine.* Berkeley, Calif.: University of California Press, 1959.

Stevens, John. *Music and Poetry in the Early Tudor Court.* London: Methuen, 1961.

Stewart, Stanley. *The Expanded Voice.* San Marino, Calif.: Huntington Library, 1970.

Stoudt, J. J. *Jacob Boehme.* New York: Seabury Press, 1968.

Thomas, Edward. *The Tenth Muse.* London: Martin Secker, 1917.

Thorndike, Lynn. *A History of Magic and Experimental Science.* New York: Columbia University Press, 1923–58.

Thorwald, Jürgen. *Science and Secrets of Early Medicine.* Translated by Richard and Clara Winston. New York: Harcourt, Brace, & World, 1963.

Tuve, Rosemond. *Elizabethan and Metaphysical Imagery.* Chicago: University of Chicago Press, 1947.

Vaughan, Thomas. *Eugenius Philalethes' (Thomas Vaughan's) The Fame and Confession.* Edited by F. N. Pryce. N.p., 1923.

———. *The Works of Thomas Vaughan.* Reprint. Edited by A. E. Waite. New York: University Books, 1968.

Walker, D. P. *Spiritual and Demonic Magic from Ficino to Campanella.* London: Warburg Institute, University of London, 1958.

Walker, John. *An Attempt towards Recovering . . . the Numbers and Sufferings of the Clergy. . . .* Vol. 2. London, 1714.

Wallerstein, Ruth. *Studies in the Seventeenth-Century Poetic.* Madison, Wis.: University of Wisconsin Press, 1950.

Walley, H. R. "The Strange Case of *Olor Iscanus.*" *Review of English Studies* 18 (1942): 27–37.

Warnke, Frank J. *European Metaphysical Poetry.* New Haven, Conn.: Yale University Press, 1961.

Warren, Austin. *Rage for Order.* Chicago: University of Chicago Press, 1948.

―――. *Richard Crashaw: A Study in Baroque Sensibility.* Baton Rouge, La.: Louisiana State University Press, 1939.

White, Helen C. *The Metaphysical Poets: A Study in Religious Experience.* New York: Macmillan Co., 1936.

Wilkins, Ernest H. *The Making of the "Canzoniere" and Other Petrarchan Studies.* Rome, 1951.

Williamson, E. M. *Henry Vaughan.* London: Welsh Home Service, 1953.

Wolf, Edwin. "Some Books of Early English Provenance in the Library Company of Philadelphia." *The Book Collector* 9 (1960): 275–84.

Yates, Frances. *The Art of Memory.* Harmondsworth, Middlesex: Penguin Books, 1969.

―――. "The Emblematic Conceit in Giordano Bruno's *De Gli Eroici Furori* and in the Elizabethan Sonnet Sequences." In *England and the Mediterranean Tradition.* Edited by Warburg/Courtauld Institute. Oxford, 1945.

―――. *The French Academies of the Sixteenth Century.* London: Warburg Institute, University of London, Routledge & Kegan Paul, 1947.

―――. *Giordano Bruno and the Hermetic Tradition.* New York: Vintage Books, 1969.

―――. *The Rosicrucian Enlightenment.* London: Routledge & Kegan Paul, 1972.

Index

Agrippa, Cornelius, 85, 115, 247
Alchemy, language of, 34–35, 110, 118–20, 124, 126, 128–30, 239–40
Alexandrian Patriarchs, 201, 243, 249
Allen, Don Cameron, 121, 248
Andrewes, Lancelot, 46
Anselm, Saint, 51
Aristotle, 121
Augustine, Saint, 140

Bacon, Francis, 53
Barker, Arthur E., 241
Barnes, Barnabe, 227
Baroque, 76–77, 79
Basil, Saint, 201, 219, 249
Berry, James, 47
Bettany, W. A. Lewis, 67
Bigg, Charles, 243
Blunden, Edmund, 230, 242
Blunden, Humphrey, 220–21, 240, 250
Bobart, Jacob, 39
Boehme, Jacob, 53, 122–23, 240
Boethius, 48, 67; "Felix nimium prior aetas...," 68–69; on music, 88–91
Book of Common Prayer, 74, 164, 173, 179–80, 245; outlawed by Parliament, 46
Boyle, Robert, 55
Breconshire (Powys), 38, 42–44, 47, 54, 59–60, 102; Brecon Cathedral, 38; Priory Grove, 38
Browne, Sir Thomas, 76, 96, 121–22, 235
Burckhardt, Titus, 236

Cambridge Platonists, 201
Camerata, the, 91, 94
Cartwright, William, 91, 234
Celsus, 248–49
Chadwick, Henry, 248

Charles I, King, 39
Civil War, 39, 40, 42, 58–60, 147; battle of Rowton Heath, 40–41, 43; Parliamentary edicts, 44, 46–47
Clement, of Alexandria, 113–14, 201, 203–4, 238, 243, 249
Cowley, Abraham, 78, 233
Cradock, Walter, 44, 46, 171
Crashaw, Richard, 71, 76
Crips, Henry, 189, 221
Croll, Oswald, 53, 123, 126, 136, 240
Crossley-Holland, P., 235–36

Dante, *La Vita Nuova*, 19–22, 135, 154, 162, 188, 211; *rime petrose*, 138; *Commedia*, 188
Davenant, Sir William, 77–78, 83, 92
Dee, John, 53
Demus, A. G., 240
Denham, John, 235
Descartes, 62, 77
Desert Fathers, 201, 209, 246
Dionysius the Areopagite, 51
Donne, John, 79, 110, 222, 232; *Poems* (1633), 29; Sermons, 46
Dowden, Edward, 231
Drummond, William, *Poems*, 29–31, 162, 188, 211
Dryden, John, 69
Duchesne, Joseph (Quercetanus), 53, 123, 125
Durr, R. A., 231, 242, 244, 245, 249, 250

Ebers, Georg, 114
Ecclesiasticus, 73
Egyptian medicine, 114–15, 118, 121
Emblem literature, 108, 121, 139, 237, 242
Empiricism, 62–63, 66
Eucherius, Bishop, 51

261

Everard, (Doctor), 150, 238

Ficino, Marsilio, 115–16, 148
Finney, Gretchen L., 91, 234
Fludd, Robert, 53
Fogle, French, 228
Fowler, Alastair, 244–45
Fox, George, 44–45, 46, 84, 171
Freeman, Rosemary, 237
Freemasons, 40, 54, 228, 230
French academies, 88, 90
Friedenreich, Kenneth, 242
Fulke Greville, Lord Brooke, 110
Fuller, Thomas, 74–75, 77, 83, 232

Galen, 54, 113, 115, 116, 121, 125, 183
Garner, Ross, 242, 248, 249
Ghalioungui, Paul, 151
Griffith, John, 43
Griffiths, John, 43
Guevara, Don Antonio de (Bishop), 51

Habington, William, *Castara*, 31–33, 34, 162, 189; "Upon a dimple in Castara's Cheeke," 20, 32, 162
Harvey, William, 167
Herbert, George, *The Temple*, 29, 30, 71–72, 98, 110, 138, 168, 175–76, 235; "Affliction (5)," 99; "The Altar," 138; "The Church-porch," 140, 168; "The Flower," 66–67; "The H. Communion," 74; "Love Unknown," 194; "A Parodie," 69; "Peace," 66–67; "Prayer," 75; "The Sacrifice," 138; "The Starre," 74; "Sunday," 75
Herbert, Matthew, 42, 44, 54, 67, 230
Hermes Trismegistus, 113–15, 117, 195; hermetic medicine, 51, 112–21, 165; *Hermetica*, 201, 237–38; *The Pymander*, 148–50, 180; Stobaeus, 150. *See also*, Night watch
Herodotus, 114
Hippocrates, 113, 121, 125
Hobbes, Thomas, 79
Hooker, Richard, 91, 108–9, 122
Hoole, Charles, 232
Hopper, V. F., 245
Horace, 69
Hutchinson, F. E., 41, 52, 68

Jerome, Saint, 246, 247

Jonson, Ben, 32, 36, 77, 79, 177
Jones, Inigo, 91
Jones, R. Tudor, 229

Kempis, Thomas à, 141
Kermode, Frank, 242
King, Lester S., 238

Lawes, Henry, 91
Llansantffraed, parish and church, 40, 225
Lloyd, Lodowick, 189, 221
Lloyd, Marmaduke, 40
Llwyd, Morgan, 44
Logan, Doctor William, 230
Luther, Martin, 122
Lyric sequence, 133–37; form of, 18, 63, 104; secular and sacred, 19, 28; and sonnet sequence, 32, 38. *See also:* Dante; Drummond; Habington; Petrarch; Sidney; *Silex Scintillans;* Spenser; Vaughan, Henry, *Poems* (1646)

Mahood, M. M., 242
Maier, Michael, 53
Marilla, E. L., 228, 250
Martin, L. C., 67, 170, 242–43, 246
Martyrology, 41
Martz, Louis, 227, 232, 236, 242, 245
Marvell, Andrew, 69, 76, 247
Mazzaro, Jerome, 241
Metrical psalms, 70–71, 90, 96–97, 102, 107
Milton, John, 76, 139–40, 197, 208, 241–42
Mommsen, Theodor, 24
Montaigne, Michel de, 56, 122
Moray, Robert, 55, 228, 231
Mulder, John R., 242
Murrin, Michael, 237

Nazianzus, Gregory of, 196–97, 199–200, 201, 249
Newton Farm, 40, 43, 80, 103
Nichols, Giles, 45
Night watch, 143–52, 158, 163, 190, 211; hermetic versions, 148–51, 159, 166, 175, 176, 178; scriptural precedents, 143–46; therapeutic dream, 151–52
Nolle, Heinrich, 54, 113, 123–27, 238
Number symbolism, 134, 162, 244–45

Origen, 248–49
Ovid, 48, 67, 134, 188, 206
Oxford, 53, 54; Jesus College, 39; physic garden, 39

Pagel, Walter, 238
Paracelsus, 53, 54, 77, 113–14, 115–21, 136, 149, 183, 238, 239–40, 244; *Book . . . to the Athenians*, 138–39; Paracelsian revival, 53, 54–55, 121–28, 133
Parker, W. R., 250
Parry, Thomas, 236
Paulii, Simonis, *Quadripartitum Botanicum*, 223–24, 250
Paulinus, Bishop of Nola, 51, 224
Pearson, L. E. 227
Pembroke, Mary Sidney, Countess of, 28, 71, 232, 235
Perrott, John, 43
Petrarch, *Rime*, 22–25, 134–35, 137, 138, 154, 162, 175, 187, 188, 211, 218; "Quando io movo," 20; "L'oro e le perle," 22–23; on memory, 134
Pettet, E. C., 140, 231, 236–37, 242, 244, 246
Philips, Katherine (Orinda), 56, 88
Philo Judaeus, 201, 203–4
Pinnell, H., 136, 139
Plato, 77, 116; *Timaeus*, 116
Plotinus, 117, 231
Porta, Giambattista della, 111–12
Poulet, Georges, 235
Powell, Thomas, 42, 43, 56, 90, 102, 111, 250; *Elementa Opticae*, 228; *Humane Industry*, 234, 235, 237; *Quadriga Salutis*, 43, 171, 229, 245
Powell, Vavasor, 44, 46, 84, 171
Price, Herbert, 40
Prytherch, Samuel, 43

Quarles, Francis, 71, 242

Reynolds, Henry, *Mythomystes*, 82–83, 233
Richards, Thomas, 229
Rickey, Mary Ellen, 235
Roche, Thomas P. Jr., 227
Rosicrucians, 53, 55, 70, 133; *The Fame and Confession*, 53; social aims, 103–4
Røstvig, Maren-Sofie, 242–43
Royal Society, 53, 55
Rudrum, Alan, 237
Ruether, Rosemary R., 247

Sandys, George, 71
Sarbiewski, Casimire, 48–50, 67
Scaliger, 54
Scott, Walter, 237–38, 243–44
Shafer, S. Robert, 233
Shakespeare, William, 77
Shumaker, Wayne, 238
Sidney, Sir Philip, *Astrophil and Stella*, 25–28, 34, 110, 162, 175, 182, 188; poetics, 77–78
Sigerist, Henry E., 237
Simmonds, J. D., 228, 237
Smith, A. J., 242
Southwell, Robert, 227
Spenser, Edmund, *Amoretti*, 28, 188–89
Stewart, Stanley, 242
Stoudt, J. J., 240
Surrey, Henry Howard, Earl of, 25, 29

Theodotus, 243
Thomas, Edward, 137
Thorndike, Lynn, 240
Thorwald, Jürgen, 237
Tretower, 43
Tuve, Rosemond, 236
Tymme, Thomas, 123–24

Vaughan, Henry; Silurist, 40, 42, 103, 211, 230; medical library of, 54, 103, 105, 136, 230; *Silex Scintillans*, and sonnet sequences, 25, 28, 35–36, 61, 104, 134–35; *Silex Scintillans*, and hermeticism, 52, 105–6, 109–10, 128–30, 133, 136. See also, Hermes; *Silex Scintillans*, order and form of, 87, 132–37, 140, 157, 185, 187–88, 217, 242. See also, Lyric sequence
Vaughan, Henry, *Works cited*, POETRY: *Poems* (1646), 32–36, 38, 188–89, 219; "To my Ingenuous Friend, R. W.," 33; "Les Amours," 33, 34; "To Amoret. The Sigh," 20; "To Amoret, Walking in a Starry Evening," 34; "To Amoret gone from him," 35; "An Elegy," 33; "A Rhapsodie," 33; "To Amoret, *of the difference 'twixt him, and other Lovers, and what true Love is*," 35; "To Amoret Weeping," 33; "Upon the Priorie Grove. . . ," 35, 219; *Olor Iscanus*, 47–51,

57, 61, 220–21; "*Ad Posteros*," 38–39, 42, 67; "To the River *Isca*," 227; "To his retired friend, an Invitation to Brecknock," 59–61; "*Monsieur Gombauld*," 92–93; "An Elegy on the death of Mr. R. W....," 40–41, 59, 110; "Upon the *Poems* and *Plays* of ... William Cartwright," 91, 234; "To ... Mrs. K. *Philips*," 88; "To Sir William D'avenant....," 92; "The Praise of a Religious life by *Mathias Casimirus*," 48–50, 143; *Silex Scintillans I*, title, 108; subtitle, 106; motto, 132, 143, 157; engraving, 137–40, 220–25; "*Authoris (de se) Emblema*," 137, 220–21; "The Dedication," 137, 139, 221; "Regeneration," 140, 141–45, 146, 155, 159, 161–62, 185, 192–93, 212, 215, 242; "Death," 140, 142, 145–46; "Resurrection and Immortality," 84–90, 95, 97, 140, 145–46; "Day of Judgement," 87, 140, 216; "Religion," 146–47, 242; "The Search," 142–43, 147, 148, 161; "*Isaacs Marriage*," 147–48; "The Brittish Church," 147, 155, 181–82; "The Lampe," 53, 242; "Mans fall, and Recovery," 153–54; "The Showre," 155; "Distraction," 154–55; "The Pursuite," 156; "Mount of Olives," 155; "The Incarnation, and Passion," 130, 155; "The Call," 155; "Thou that know'st for whom I mourne," 156–57; "Vanity of Spirit," 157, 159, 185; "The Retreate," 69, 159; "Come, come, what doe I here?," 159–60, 161; "Midnight," 160, 161; "Content," 161; "Joy of my life!" 160–61; "The Storm," 161; "The Morning-watch," 95–98, 140, 151, 158, 160–63, 166, 167, 184; "The Evening-watch," 158, 162–63; "Silence, and stealth of dayes!" 163–64; "Church-Service," 165–66; "Buriall," 164–65; "Chearfulness," 165–66; "Sure, there's a tye of Bodyes!" 154, 166–67; "Peace," 166; "The Passion," 165–66, 172–73, 235; "And do they so?" 106, 165–66, 167; "The Relapse," 167–68; "The Resolve," 167–68; "The Match," 71–72, 167–68; "Rules *and* Lessons," 80, 167–69, 170; "Corruption," 169; "H. Scriptures," 169–70; "Unprofitablenes," 127, 223; "Christs Nativity," 97–98, 174;

"The Check," 107, 174–75; "Disorder and frailty," 174–75, 235; "Idle Verse," 168; "Son-dayes," 75–76, 174; "Repentance," 173–74, 175–76; "The Burial of an Infant," 177–78; "Faith," 176–77; "The Dawning," 178; "Admission," 178; "Praise," 178–79; "Dressing," 73–74, 170, 179; "Easter-day," 140, 180; "The Holy Communion," 140, 181–82; "Psalm 121," 70, 180, 182; "Affliction," 128, 182–83; "The Tempest," 129, 183–84; "Love, and Discipline," 183; "The Law, and the Gospel," 170–71; "The World," 94–95, 97, 184, 249; "The Mutinie," 235; "The Constellation," 110–11; "Misery," 79–82, 184; "The Sap," 185; "Mount of Olives," 184; "I walkt the other day....," 63–67, 185; "Begging," 139, 185; *Silex Scintillans II*, Preface to, 51–52, 170, 221, 224; "Ascension-day," 189–90, 191, 192–93, 206; "Ascension-Hymn," 194; "They are all gone into the world of light!" 191, 196; "White Sunday," 193, 198, 246; "The Proffer," 107, 193; "Cock-crowing," 110–11, 193, 198–200; "The Starre," 193, 198; "The Palm-tree," 193–94, 198; "Joy," 98–100, 198; "The Favour," 198; "Love-sick," 200, 235; "Trinity-Sunday," 235; "Psalm 104," 70–71, 198, 201; "The Bird," 128, 198–99; "The Timber," 198, 202, 247; "The Jews," 202–3; "Begging," 200, 208, 247; "Palm-Sunday," 204; "Jesus Weeping" (I & II), 204, 205; "The Daughter of *Herodias*," 206; "Providence," 203–5; "The Knot," 206; "The Ornament," 206; "St. Mary Magdalen," 206; "The Rain-bow," 249; "The Seed growing secretly," 207, 248; "As time one day by me did pass," 207–8, 210; "Fair and yong light!" 207–8; "The Stone," 209–10; "The dwelling-place," 209; "The Men of War," 211; "Childe-hood," 209; "The Night," 76, 209, 211–13; "Abels blood," 106, 214–15; "Righteousness," 213–14; "Jacobs Pillow, and Pillar," 215–16; "The Agreement," 216, 249; "The day of Judgement," 189, 215, 216; "Psalm 65," 70, 216; "The Throne," 216; "Death,"

216–17; "The Feast," 211, 216–17; "The Water-fall," 128, 217, 249; "Quickness," 94; "The Wreath," 235, 249; "The Queer," 249; "The Book," 217–18, 249; "To the Holy Bible," 190, 211, 218–19, 249; "L'Envoy," 103–4, 107–8, 218–19, 249; epitaph, 219, 249; *Thalia Rediviva*, "To . . . Thomas Powel," 223; "The Eagle," 246–47; "To Mr. M. L. *upon his reduction of the* Psalms *into Method*," 70; "*On Sir* Thomas Bodley's *Library*. . . ," 72; "The importunate fortune. . . ," 243; "The Bee," 247;

Vaughan, Henry, *Works cited,* PROSE: *Olor Iscanus*, "Of the Benefit we may get by our Enemies" (Plutarch), 51; "Of the Diseases of the Mind and the Body" (Plutarch), 51; "Of the Diseases of the Mind and the Body" (Maximus of Tyre), 51; "The Praise and Happinesse of the Country-Life" (Guevara), 229; *The Mount of Olives, or Solitary Devotions*, 45–47, 87, 140–41, 144, 151, 170–71, 245; "Man in Darkness," 47, 127–28, 194–95, 247; *Flores Solitudines*, "To the Reader," 191; "To the onely true and glorious God. . . ," 247–48; "Of Temperance and Patience" (Nieremberg), 118, 195–97, 246; "Of Life and Death" (Nieremberg), 41–42, 143–44, 151, 192, 195, 197; "The World Contemned" (Eucherius), 240–41; "Primitive Holiness . . . the Life of blessed Paulinus," 72–73, 224, 250; *Hermetical Physick* (Nolle), 51, 104–5, 125–26, 128; *The Chymists KEY* (Nolle), 124–25; Letters, 109, 222, 236, 237, 250. *See also Silex Scintillans II;* "Begging"

Vaughan, Thomas, 39, 42–43, 45, 53, 54, 55, 59, 79, 124, 220–21, 250; on Agrippa, 85; and Paracelsus, 121; address to the "Brethren R. C.," 62; *Anthroposophia Theomagica*, 150; *Lumine de Lumine*, 150–51; translation of Rosicrucian manifestoes, 239

Vaughan, William, 41, 163–64, 244, 245

Walker, John, 229
Watkyns, Rowland, 42
Welsh bards, 98, 235–36
Wilkins, Ernest H., 227
Wilkins, John, 55
Williams, David, 43
Williams, Matthew, 42
Williams, Richard, 43
Williamson, E. M., Bishop, 250
Wise, Catherine (Amoret), 137, 188–89, 207, 209, 210–12
Wither, George, 242
Wolf, Edwin, 230
Wyatt, Sir Thomas, 25, 29

Yates, Frances, 53, 90, 134, 233–34, 235, 238

Zosimos, 117